SELF-MANAGEMENT

SELF-MANAGEMENT ON TRIAL

Milojko Drulović

SPOKESMAN BOOKS

First published in Paris in 1973 by Librairie Fayard
Revised and extended edition first published in Great Britain in 1978
by Spokesman, Bertrand Russell House,
Gamble Street, Nottingham, NG7 4ET
for the Bertrand Russell Peace Foundation.

ISBN 0 85124 231 6 Cloth
ISBN 0 85124 232 4 Paper

Printed in Great Britain by Bristol Typesetting Co. Ltd,
Barton Manor, Bristol

Contents

CONTENTS

List of Tables and Diagrams

LIST OF TABLES AND DIAGRAMS

Foreword

Milojko Drulović has written a major socialist textbook which should be read by everyone who is concerned to develop democracy and socialism together, each as part of the other. He has described and discussed the experience of Yugoslavia which has charted that very course for itself and is working to establish genuinely democratic institutions within a country that came to socialism through revolution and war, and has not yet adopted political pluralism.

Every nation draws heavily upon its own national history and communal experience when seeking answers to contemporary problems and Yugoslavia is no exception. The unification of a State containing 'six republics, five nations, four religions, three languages and two alphabets' was a formidable achievement in itself. There were only two possible ways of governing such a country: by central dictatorship or by painfully constructing a pattern of consent on the basis of an evolving democracy that could reconcile the many differing strands and interests into one. World interest in Yugoslavia derives from the fact that she has set herself the task of attempting to transform a classic communist dictatorship of the proletariat into a real socialist democracy.

The partisans under Tito's leadership liberated their own country from the Axis powers which gave them a self-confidence not available to other Eastern European communist regimes brought into being by the advance of Soviet troops. But until the break with Stalin in 1948, the heavy hand of the Comintern and Moscow played a large part in sustaining administrative socialism run from the centre.

Though the aspirations for self-management began much earlier than 1948, they only began to emerge when the split with Russia forced self-reliance on them. This new-style socialism was developed in a series of constitutional innovations extending from the re-organisation of industrial enterprises, through the communes, the regions and republics up to the highest organs of the Federal State.

Milojko Drulović describes all these new forms of government—industrial, local and national—in great detail and with a wealth of statistics. It is greatly to his credit that he does not conceal the difficulties, the conflicts and the failures as well as the successes. It is indeed as a candid critique that his analysis acquires its credibility. All those who dislike the centralised communist dictatorships of the East; and who are not satisfied by the tendencies towards technocratic monopoly control of society which are emerging in the capitalist west, are bound to be interested in a developing country that is seeking to democratise its socialism and is ready to be self-critical.

'One of the most acute needs of contemporary socialism' writes Drulović, 'is to link socialism and democracy'. Later he adds, 'No state with the best administration and police can be a substitute for the enthusiasm of the individual who knows the future of the community is in his own hands.' Writing of Yugoslavia's contribution to this debate, he argues that 'self-management is a way of solving problems related to the social position and interests of every individual. Government or management in a socialist society cannot be the privilege of politicians and the intelligentsia. Self-management is an effort to eliminate coercion as far as possible from social relations, to replace simple execution, of orders by direct participation in decision making, conflicts by discussion, political and other fights by reasoned argument, domination and force by elections.'

To sum it all up he asserts that 'man in socialism should not be a mere cog but the hub of the universe, the goal to which everything is directed.'

With those words, Milojko Drulović concludes his book. I commend it to all those who are engaged in the same search for democracy and socialism.

Tony Benn
London, August 12, 1978.

Preface
(For English Edition)

The book *Self-Management on Trial* was originally written for the Fayard Publishing House of Paris in 1973. Since then, it has appeared in a number of other languages (Portuguese, Italian, Romanian, Slovakian, Turkish, German) and in a second French edition, while a Spanish edition is currently being prepared. Following its first appearance in French, the book was also issued in the author's own language, Serbo-Croatian.

The wide interest aroused by this publication surprised both publishers and author. It serves to indicate that in the world of today self-management is a topic worthy of discussion. The French Revolution of 1789, and other bourgeois revolutions, eliminated the antagonism between the aristocracy and commons, but themselves became entangled in an antagonism they failed to comprehend—that between rich and poor, between capital and labour. The socialist revolutions of the present century have aimed at eliminating the social antagonisms between capital and labour, but many failed to perceive the antagonisms that arise when bureaucracy and technocracy gain control over man's work. Having learned a lesson from such histories, and above all from its own experience, socialist Yugoslavia turned to self-management in the wish, among other things, to avoid these dangers.

Since the first edition of this book, numerous changes have occurred in the Yugoslav system (the adoption of the new Constitution in 1974, and of an original law of fundamental importance which elaborated the system of self-management relations from the base to the summit of society in 1976).

For later editions, the author has not essentially changed the book, but appended a short additional text, the afterword. The book has been augmented twice, for the German edition of 1976, and the second French edition in 1977. The present English version has further additions and has been statistically updated.

What's New?

In the meantime, several vital questions relating to self-management have been engaging Yugoslavs' attention: How to ensure that the society as a whole functions on self-management principles? How to organise not only the enterprise but the entire community, from the base to the summit, in conformity with these principles? Warned by undesirable tendencies that appeared in practice, we were aware that if self-management were restricted to factories, while the system remained unchanged in the communes, republics, autonomous provinces and the Federation, the weed of bureaucracy would soon strangle the young plant.

The problem was how to strengthen the self-management power of the producers at the base, to counter technocracy and the centres of economic power (banks and large enterprises), how to ensure that the producers controlled the movement of social accumulation (capital) at all levels—from the base to the Federation.

It became essential to organise the social activities (education, science, culture, social welfare services) more in keeping with the spirit of self-management, and establish a natural democratic relationship between the people employed in these activities and those directly engaged in material production in the factories. These vital social services, on which Yugoslavia spends almost one third of its national income, were for a long time outside the mainstream of self-management, being dependent on state budget financing and the administration. The process of changing this is not yet completed, and is by no means rapid and easy.

On the basis of nearly three decades of experience, solutions to these problems were devised and incorporated in the 1974 Constitution and the 1976 Law on Associated Labour.

Real-life situations made other demands, one after another: self-management had to be capable of waging a permanent struggle against bureaucratic tendencies; the people had to be kept fully informed so as to be able to take decisions and exercise their self-management rights; narrow, short-sighted and local interests had to be discouraged and integration fostered; major decisions concerning the development of the Yugoslav community had to be taken on the basis of democratic concensus among the republics, and not imposed from one centre.

Self-management is not simply a form of political democracy but also an economic relationship between workers. It follows that economic decision-making cannot be alienated from the workers and usurped by the technocracy. It may be said that in Yugoslavia both the State and technocracy have been deprived of power. On the other hand, the worker does not expect the government to give him his wages. A worker's earnings depend both on the success of his enterprise as a whole and on his personal work. He has the right to oblige the executive personnel to carry out a particular policy.

The results in the economic sphere have been good: Yugoslavia ranks among the countries with a very high rate of economic growth. Indeed, it is the only country which has managed in this period to reduce the gap in development level separating it from the industrially advanced states.

But it would be onesided to dwell only on the favourable aspects. As President Tito recently pointed out when addressing the Eleventh Congress of the League of Communists, the level of productivity is still considerably below that in the highly developed countries, a fact which makes it difficult for Yugoslav goods to compete on foreign markets. The level of technical equipment, personnel and the actual self-management system offer opportunities for greater progress than has been made in recent years. He likewise noted the appearance of isolationism and autarchy both at enterprise level and in the large and small sociopolitical communities. He criticised unjustified duplication of industrial capacities, and uneconomic investments, which were often the result of ignoring the workers' views. President Tito also pointed to the need for better utilisation of working time, and criticised the excessive tax burden borne by the economy as well as cases where the bureaucracy and executive personnel still exert too great an influence on management.

Unemployment is another serious economic, social and

B

political problem in Yugoslavia which can be resolved within the country. About 80,000 persons are now returning annually from temporary work abroad. Their employment in Yugoslavia will enable the country to benefit by the knowledge and experience they gained working in modern factories abroad. The difference between the developed and underdeveloped parts of the country has still not been appreciably reduced. This is a sensitive issue politically as well as economically, in view of Yugoslavia's multi-national structure.

Undesirable features, however, cannot be removed overnight. The full implementation of self-management is almost a task for a whole epoch, not a brief span of time.

Workers have not always enough understanding of economic affairs to take complex decisions in the domain of production, marketing, integration and technology, and therefore need highly-trained experts, executives and specialised services. To help them correct information must be presented to them in an accessible fashion as a precondition for decision-making. Under self-management, the worker controls not only his executive-manager, but also the politicians—up to the very highest level of organised associated labour.

Will the Workers 'Eat Up Everything'?

At the last elections, held in the spring of 1978, about three million working people were elected to workers' councils and delegations. In fact, all working people and other citizens can express their views through a variety of forms (referendums, meetings of the working people, and so on).

The efficiency of the self-management system depends both on the amount of experience gained and on the educational level of the workers. In less than three decades since the introduction of the initial forms of self-management (worker management in factories), copious experience has been acquired and the workers' educational level raised. Now three-fifths of employed persons in Yugoslavia have at least secondary schooling, or an intermediate level of vocational training.

Fears were expressed that the workers would 'eat up everything', in other words, that immediate personal considerations and the 'consumer mentality' would prevail when it came to making decisions. In practice this has rarely proved the case:

the workers are concerned to ensure a steady year-to-year increase in their earnings and are prepared to approve long-term investments. The worker delegates, however, complain that over the past two years the amount of financial resources left to the enterprises has decreased, in relative terms, and that the State (i.e. administration) still takes a large share of their income in the form of various fiscal obligations, a situation which is not conducive to the long-term development of enterprises.[1]

National Regions—A Feeling of Independence

Yugoslavia must take into account the fact that it is a multinational country and that the national regions (republics and autonomous provinces) have attained varying degrees of development. For more than a thousand years, the nations which now form Yugoslavia have had different histories. This accounts for their highly pronounced feelings of independence. Any attempt to impose a centralised system of government under such conditions would inevitably be courting disaster. Stalin accused us of being excessively nationalistic. His great mistake was that he failed to understand Yugoslavia's national diversity, arising from its past history. Still today, people in various quarters are speculating about Yugoslavia's future as a state, in view of its multi-national structure. Naturally enough, all the nations do not see eye to eye on all questions: for instance, whether priority in investment should be given to farming, mining, tourism or power production. But no nation is shortsighted and narrowminded enough to jeopardise, for the sake of a few million dollars, its true national interests, which depend on the unity and strength of the Yugoslav community as a whole.

It is not enough to provide the legal basis and machinery and expect self-management to function automatically. It calls for a continuous process of consultation, countless activities in which the consciousness and responsibility of the individual and the collective come to the fore. In such a social situation, the political organisations (League of Communists, Socialist

---

1. This criticism was voiced by worker delegates at the Eleventh Congress of the League of Communists of Yugoslavia (held June 20–23, 1978, in Belgrade).

Alliance, Trade Unions and others) cannot forcibly impose their authority but must exert their influence by means of persuasive argument.

The epithet 'socialist' by itself does not automatically bestow an aura of historical progressiveness. The same applies to the names of political parties, in this case the League of Communists of Yugoslavia. The League can fulfil its role as the ideological and political vanguard of the working class only if it is democratically linked with all socialist and democratic forces in the country. Without such a policy, Yugoslavia would not have been able to play its well-known role in the Second World War, or become what it is today. The League of Communists is not a communist party of the classical type or the dominant element of a one-party system. The Socialist Alliance of Working People, the largest political organisation, contains certain elements of traditional political pluralism that inevitably still survive, but taken as a whole, there is no political pluralism of the type found in bourgeois societies.

As distinct from a multi-party democracy, here we have pluralism of self-management interests. In day-to-day social relations numerous interests of different kinds find expression though not through the formation of different parties. This is a process whereby pluralism as a monopoly of political parties is replaced by true self-management political pluralism. Our society is not and cannot be either monolithic or amorphous. The working class itself has several strata, so that its interests cannot be reduced to one political formula. These varying interests confront one another and come to the forefront in associated labour, in all its forms and interconnections; they are likewise apparent in the domain of social activities, in local communities and self-managing communes; these interests also appear in relation to the self-managing autonomy of the republics and provinces; they find expression in democratic relations in the Federal system; citizens' ideological and political interests find an outlet for expression in the many socio-political and other organisations. The League of Communists can act only in close co-operation with all democratic political forces, and not by creating a political monopoly for itself. Yugoslav experience in this respect is quite specific. In essence, the Yugoslav system is not a one-party system, but neither does it provide for the multi-party pluralism of bourgeois society. Self-management does not allow any political monopoly by any forces outside self-management. Although the parliamentary system of the capitalist era ensured the citizen wide freedom and gave the working class and progressive forces a chance to strive for greater social influence, there is no reason to consider this system the ideal of democracy for all times and in all conditions.

The Ideal of Industrial Democracy and Self-Management

I have followed with great interest the initiatives undertaken by the trade unions and Labour Party of Great Britain towards the introduction of certain forms of industrial democracy. Aware of the inevitability of change, the younger generations are questioning the existing institutions and the traditional relationship between capital and labour which those institutions reflect, re-examining the economic and social goals and seeking new solutions. They do so without aggressiveness, but with an impressive firmness of purpose. What concerns them are vital issues such as industrial democracy, worker control, devolution, local self-government, employment, protection of the environment, and others. The progressive forces of British society, above all the younger generations, are preoccupied with how to change the educational system, which tends to deepen the existing class distinctions.

In Great Britain (as in Yugoslavia), young people protest over the growth of bureaucracy, when the quality of urban life declines, if local government representatives devote insufficient time and energy to public affairs. Whether it is a question of housing construction, the use of solar energy or the banning of nuclear weapons, they are adopting an increasingly mature and responsible attitude, realising that these are issues that affect the future as well as the present. They are not satisfied by cautious reform and even less by an uncritical acceptance of the existing establishment as something eternal and unalterable.

The greater the degree of class distinction and bureaucratic control, the stronger the dissatisfaction of the young. British society came through the economic upheavals of the thirties. The war and loss of empire, though it shook this society, did not seriously undermine it, or cause any really far-reaching transformation of its institutions. It is still regarded as one of the most stable societies among the developed Western countries. Clearly the workers are one of the cornerstones of the 'British way of life'. During the period of economic prosperity that followed the era of postwar austerity, there was relatively little unrest among them. However, the depression of recent years has aroused doubts and serves as a serious warning.

The trade unions have long been trying to obtain worker participation in the management of factories and companies. Conservative elements do not look with favour even on the part played by the unions in public and political life at present, and certainly disapprove strongly of the union and Labour Party demands regarding industrial democracy. Most probably, the majority of them are convinced that the 'British way of life' needs to be defended. But it can no longer be defended by the oratorical skill of young men sharpened in debating clubs and party political duels. It can be defended only by changing, by adapting to the demands of the times and the realities of life.

This has given rise to numerous proposals on how to improve the existing establishment. The idea of devolution is based on the belief that government is too centralised and that Parliament has too much power, to the detriment of the individuality of the traditional national entities and the specific character of the regions in which they live. Hence the demand for regional parliaments.

The supporters of the idea of industrial democracy put forward logical arguments in its favour: the economy is moving from one crisis into another; it is becoming increasingly evident that technocratic management is not good at solving socio-economic problems; the employment structure has changed; general education has attained a higher level; the role of the trade unions is growing stronger; the workers are not content to be robots simply for the sake of having employment. Trade unions in Britain are calling for greater powers for the workers and more influence over their working conditions. Democracy does not stop at the factory gate, they say.

More and more people are accepting the need for a radical expansion of industrial democracy by way of worker representation on boards of directors, coupled with a major role for trade-union organisations. The employers' protests and the fierce resistance of the opposition indicate that this progress by the workers, which is coming ever closer, is not to be underestimated. Workers' control, that is, their representation in management, can be a transitional phase which starts when the workers begin to speak out against selfishly motivated and irresponsible management. But under such conditions, worker control will not be able to take over responsibility for all management decisions. It can gradually ensure, however, that these decisions serve the workers' interests to the greatest possible extent.

We must respect the fact that one of the pillars of the British system is private property. But the curbing of the interests of ownership for the benefit of the workers, the participation of workers in decision-making and income distribution, can be one of the ways towards the ultimate disappearance of large-scale private ownership.

In the final analysis, representative democracy offers relatively limited possibilities for those concerned to influence the process of decision-making. The chances of changing the system by means of this type of democracy are also limited. Under such conditions, worker participation in the management of factories and companies would usher in gradual changes in production relations, that is to say, the democratisation of working conditions. If radical solutions are impossible within the framework of the traditional system, at least gradual changes for the better can be achieved.

When comparing Yugoslav experience in self-management and British ideas for reforming the establishment, one must not forget the differences that are the outcome of centuries of history. These differences are political, class, cultural, social, professional, and in level of development. Though the historical and social conditions have nothing in common, there is surprising similarity in the ideas behind worker participation in management in both countries.

William Straker, leader of the British miners in the twenties, once stated: 'The workers first of all thought they would be satisfied if they gained higher wages and better living conditions. Wages and living conditions improved, but the dissatisfaction did not vanish . . .'. Straker went on to speak of the worker's need to share in management, to believe that he was working for society, for himself, and not simply for private ownership.[2]

Straker's idea was very similar to that of Marx: 'Society will not find its balance until it revolves around the Sun of labour'.

These ideas have always constituted the basic motive of socialist self-management.

It is indeed true that a society will have difficulty in achieving balance and stability unless the real creators of its goods and future—the producers—have their say in the management of industry and public affairs.

'Welfare State'

The higher educational level of the working class in West European countries, the steadily rising living standard, and greater political involvement have all helped increase awareness of the need to overcome the alienation which is a feature of the living and working conditions of the vast majority of working people. The 'Welfare State' has been unable to resolve the social and working status of these people. The problem now is how to move forward from highly developed parliamentary capitalism to a new and developed socialist society, while retaining those good features that have been achieved. And these are certainly not inconsiderable. Above all, there are the socialist-inspired measures of state policy such as the nationalisation of certain key sectors of industry, the highly developed and humane social welfare programme, and so on.

Over the past thirty years, the capitalist world economy has been able to attain a relatively powerful growth rate and relatively high level of employment. Much of the population in capitalist countries believed they were living in a society that would provide lasting prosperity. But the seventies brought the worst recession since the Second World War, giving rise to large-scale unemployment once again. Galloping inflation and balance of payments difficulties are typical features of the present period. Those same countries have entered a phase of

2. The quotation is taken from the address by Ken Coates at the Symposium on The Socialist System held in Cavtat (Croatia) in 1977.

slower growth and higher unemployment than at any time in the foregoing three decades. The question of a democratic path to socialism, regarded from the perspective of a developed capitalist society, is one of the key issues of our day. The ideal of worker participation in direct management of their own economic and political interests has gained such strong support that fewer and fewer people are willing to express open opposition to it. The readiness of capital (including American) to accept a degree of worker participation is prompted by the need to ensure discipline and a steady rise in output and labour productivity. A typical example of this is West Germany.

Yugoslavs are very proud of their self-management experience, dating back almost thirty years. But there is no 'royal road', no 'architect of the future', no 'last prophet', no political theology and eternal models applicable to all.

One lesson has been learned from experience, though: only a policy which mobilises the masses to participate in decision-making can become a true driving force. The weakness of workers' parties today often lies in the fact that they are primarily, if not exclusively, preoccupied with how to gain power. Government power is only the first step in the building of socialism, even when power has been seized by armed revolution. The building of a socialist society, the attainment of a new quality of life for both society and the individual, call for bold changes in social life and institutions, with the direct participation, above all, of those whose labour provides the basis for the whole of society—the direct producers.

Milojko Drulović
Belgrade, June 25, 1978.

Introduction

After a lecture I gave some years ago in the Jacobin Club in Paris, probably on the basis of press comments, I was approached by the publisher *Fayard* with the suggestion that I should 'edit' this lecture for publication in book form.

I accepted this proposal, since I have directly followed and participated in self-management over the past twenty years, either as a 'producer', as a member of the Federal Assembly, secretary of the League of Communists in Belgrade or as director of the *Politika* publishing house.

This task of 'editing' was an arduous one, for it entailed, among other things writing two hundred pages instead of the fifteen needed for the lecture.

The almost thirty-year evolution of self-management in Yugoslavia is still often regarded abroad as an experiment. And sometimes in Yugoslavia too. At best as a noble Utopia, but still a Utopia.

Yugoslavia is regarded as a country of paradoxes, the principles of a free market are coupled with the fundamental principles of a Marxist economy—with planning; the workers meet 'to set their own wages' for the coming year; they decide on matters concerning resources, modernisation programmes and investments in factories; the League of Communists of Yugoslavia has renounced part of its powers —direct executive government—in favour of those employed in factories and institutions; the trade unions represent the workers, including those elected to the bodies of worker management.

All this has happened in a country which ended the war with an agrarian population forming 76 per cent of the total, and a *per capita* national income of 200 US dollars, of which only 20 came from industry; in a country which in this period has just acquired its first generation of modern industrial workers, its first generation of car-drivers.

Such a description of Yugoslavia is an over-simplification.

Who would be able to engage a whole society of twenty millions for twenty years in laboratory experiments? Unfortunately, Yugoslavia was deprived by unlucky circumstances of the peace needed even for work on subjects of a truly experimental character.

In socialist countries, Yugoslav self-management is officially termed revisionism, anarcho-syndicalism, pseudo-liberalism and who knows what other 'ism'. In the West, some take us as a model of the first phase of industrial revolution, which most of Europe passed through two hundred years ago.

Under pressure from left and right, Yugoslavs are inclined, when foreigners talk of their experiences, to make an apologetic defence of self-management, with the feeling that they are defending it from attack. Not because of criticism as such, but because of the one-sided ideological dimension of that criticism.

On the other hand, in socialist countries—Cuba, the Soviet Union, Hungary, China—noticeably more respect is now being paid to market laws in a socialist economy, on both the economic and ideological plane. The more developed industrial states of Western Europe, for their part, seek more effective planning methods, a higher degree of regionalisation and decentralisation, various forms of worker participation and joint decision-making.

If the purpose of self-management is to allow the greatest possible participation of the individual in management and direct democracy, and if the term 'management' covers not only the actual guiding of the production process but also distribution of the surplus product (profits), then everyone will want to know whether this original model in Yugoslavia has led to a high level of growth. In other words, does self-management socialism merely achieve a more equitable division of the available goods, or does it meet the scientific requirements for growth? Is it capable of holding the community together, does it really allow the development of the essential freedoms and economic initiative? Finally, are we able to tell the real truth about self-management and not simply describe it as it should be, according to our conceptions and laws?

At the present moment, self-management in Yugoslavia is exposed to the most effective possible control of dynamic and independent factors such as modern technological progress and the international market. The degree to which Yugoslavia can meet these two challenges is the surest test of the capacity of the system and method the country has chosen to promote its development and its own concept of socialism.

In these twenty years, self-management has assumed the character of a democratic and techno-economic revolution. The national liberation struggle and armed revolution in Yugoslavia were its 'ten days that shook the world', but the revolution really begins on the eleventh day, when the questions of man and his freedom, and relations between people are on the agenda.

The purpose here is to present at least some of the rich experience and modest results which have furthered the democratic and economic progress of Yugoslavia—but also the numerous weaknesses and inconsistencies that have accompanied our development. Good intentions are not enough. One must become familiar with a multitude of facts to gain an insight into the complex Yugoslav economic and social situation. I shall endeavour to provide, in the first place, information about our experiences.

Something must also be said of the long and varied histories of the kindred peoples who were united in a single state only fifty years ago.

There are four clues, if they may be so-called, which help to unravel the Yugoslav puzzle: the varied and troubled history of its regions, its multi-national composition, the wide differences in levels of development, and its specific path of revolutionary struggle in recent decades.

I shall be satisfied if I answer at least one question: is self-management a fiction or reality? I believe that this 'fiction' became a reality even before this was realistically expected.

Despite the numerous weaknesses, it is felt in Yugoslavia that self-management has called forth and reinforced a profound social, moral, anthropological and even techno-economic revolution in our society.

But we do not believe in miracles or the gods who created

man, nor have we faith in those mighty rulers of society who
rely on technology and force, and not on social consciousness
and a democratic structure.

I believe that my task is, before all else, to provide system-
atic information on experiences that may be of many-sided
interest to the reader—from the social as well as the economic
aspect.

Someone may perhaps find some sources of inspiring ideas
in this experience. And even those who wish to challenge
self-management should first get acquainted with it.

Chapter One

Historical Background

Six republics in one

'Six republics, five nations, four religions, three languages, two alphabets—one state!' exclaimed the Indian politician and philosopher, Radakrishnan, after his first visit to Yugoslavia in the fifties.

This neat summary is no longer quite accurate, however, for at the last census, in March 1971, a sixth nationality—Moslem—was recognised.

Yugoslavia, with 21,718,000 inhabitants, consists of the republics of Serbia (with the autonomous provinces: Vojvodina and Kosovo), Croatia, Bosnia-Herzegovina, Slovenia, Macedonia and Montenegro.[1]

In addition to the six nations, Yugoslavia has nine sizeable national minorities: Albanians, Hungarians, Turks, Slovaks, Romanians, Bulgarians, Italians, Czechs, Gypsies, and others totalling over two million—12 per cent of the population. Of the latter, the Albanians and Hungarians are the most numerous.[2] Of the 24 European countries, Yugoslavia, with 255,800 sq. km., takes ninth place in both size of population and average density (80·3 per square kilometre). Religions: Catholic, Orthodox, Moslem and Jewish; languages: Serbo-Croatian (Croato-Serbian), Macedonian and Slovenian. Following the 1971 constitutional amendments, in addition to these three

---

1. Serbia is the most populous with 8,921,000 inhabitants (5,457,000 living in what is called Serbia proper—the central part of the republic, 1,996,000 in Vojvodina, 1,486,000 in Kosovo); Croatia comes second with 4,551,000, followed by Bosnia-Herzegovina with 4,075,000, Macedonia with 1,826,000, Slovenia with 1,793,000, and Montenegro with 571,000.

2. Albanians 1,308,246, and Hungarians 467,586, according to the 1971 census.

languages, Albanian and Hungarian are also used in the federal administration and federal affairs. Two alphabets are in use: the Latin in the western part of the country and the Cyrillic in the eastern.

A high degree of national heterogeneity is to be found in Bosnia-Herzegovina, Vojvodina and Kosovo.[3]

Yugoslavia—home of many cultures

Greeks, Romans, Turks, Habsburgs, the influence of West European civilisation; Gothic, baroque, mosques, differences in customs and way of life—in short, a diversity that is impossible to understand without at least a passing acquaintanceship with the history of these nations.

The nations that make up Yugoslavia have a long trouble-filled history, though the state which unites them is a relatively new creation—only fifty years old. Its establishment was the outcome of centuries of struggles for their liberty by Croats, Slovenes, Serbs, Macedonians and Montenegrins—a struggle which led at the end of the First World War to the disintegration of Austria-Hungary and the formation of the common state of these Yugoslav, i.e. South Slav, nations.

The political history of the new state in the inter-war period was one of severe strain in international relations. The profound national, political and spiritual differences went unrecognised, while social and political conflicts, like the national ones, were most often forcibly suppressed by the police regime.

In 1941, occupied Yugoslavia was parcelled up among four states: Germany, Italy, Bulgaria and Hungary. Benefiting by the lessons learned from the country's tragic past and from the nation-wide resistance movement and revolution in the course of the Liberation War, the Socialist Federal Republic of Yugoslavia was created as a federal state with six republics and two autonomous provinces.

---

3. Bosnia-Herzegovina: Serbs form 37 per cent of the population, Moslems about 40 per cent, Croats 20 per cent; Kosovo's population is composed of Albanians—74 per cent, Serbs—18 per cent, Montenegrins—2·5 per cent, and Turks—1 per cent; Vojvodina: Serbs—52 per cent, Hungarians—22 per cent, Croats—7 per cent, Slovaks—about 4 per cent, Romanians—nearly 3 per cent.

At the junction of Europe, Asia and Africa

The geopolitical position of Yugoslav territories is such that history has been merciless towards them, as it has towards the whole of the Balkans, of which Yugoslavia forms a central part. In the last millennium and a half since the arrival of the Slavs, there have been few cataclysms that have not affected this region and its people. The natural route between Europe and Asia, this territory has ever been the dream of conquerors: Illyrians, Celts, Greeks, Romans, followed by warlike tribes from the eastern steppes—the Avars, the Slavs, the Turkish conquest and then the European . . .

The country's landscapes are just as diverse as its peoples and their histories: from the Danube and fertile Pannonian Plain, which marks the start of the great eastern steppes, across the extensive mountain areas, covering three-quarters of the country, to the Adriatic Sea and the blue lakes on the borders of Albania and Greece.

With its exceptional geographical position, Yugoslavia is a region of first-rate economic and political importance, a region intersected by major international routes. The main roads linking West and East, Western Europe with Asia Minor, Central Asia, North and East Africa, the central and eastern Mediterranean, have always crossed Yugoslavia. Not surprisingly, over a long historical period, this region at the crossroads of the known world attracted the interest of conquering powers and was buffeted by countless storms — the onslaughts and devastation of hordes and armies.

Yugoslavia is, in fact, a land bridge between Western Europe (across the Bosphorus and Dardanelles) and Asia Minor, North Africa and the Mediterranean region. This Mediterranean state with an Adriatic coastline two thousand kilometres in length has maritime links with the whole world.

'Via militaris'—the fatal Roman military road.
Almost one thousand years under alien rule

From the north have come many invaders and would-be settlers of Yugoslav territory and the Balkan peninsula, starting from the Illyrians, Thracians, Celts and South Slavs—right down to the Second World War.

For almost a thousand years, from the time the Hungarians

reached the Adriatic Sea (1102) until the creation of Yugoslavia in 1918, Croatia was alternately under Hungarian and Habsburg domination; Slovenia was held by the Habsburgs, while the other regions of Yugoslavia (Serbia, Macedonia and most of Bosnia) were subjected to the feudal rule of Turkey for about five hundred years.

In the time of the Roman Empire, the Balkan military road —*Via militaris*—was constructed through the interior via Belgrade, a link between West and East. It was this road that the Crusaders followed on their first, second and third expeditions to the Holy Land. It was the route taken by the Turks, only in the opposite direction, on their campaigns in the 14th, 15th and 16th centuries that carried them, again via Belgrade, to Budapest and Vienna. It was along the same route, in the autumn of 1915, that Kaiser Wilhelm II, with his Austro-Hungarian allies, pushed via Belgrade into Serbia and Macedonia. Here it was that the Franco-British Allied armies met when they came to aid the Serbs. And it was along this same route in 1941 that Hitler's forces penetrated south into Yugoslavia and Greece, their sights fixed on the middle East.

Along the roads from the East the influences of the earliest Greek civilisation—the oldest in Europe—travelled to what is now Yugoslavia. In the spring of 1971, Paris had an opportunity to view the Yugoslav exhibition entitled: 'Cultural Monuments on the Soil of Yugoslavia' which covered the cultural monuments and events that have left traces on this territory over a period of eight thousand years.

Via the Aegean, the influences of Creto-Mycenean and classical Greek civilisation reached these shores, to be followed by Roman civilisation, carried by soldiers and merchants along the Constantinople-Belgrade and Salonica-Belgrade roads.

The Adriatic cities (Dubrovnik, Split, Zadar) were important intermediaries for economic and cultural links with the West and western Mediterranean (the Roman Catholic Church, Latin alphabet, Romanesque architecture, trade, fleets and so on).

Between Byzantium and Rome

In the distant past, the present territory of Yugoslavia was inhabited by Illyrians in the west and south, and Thracians

c

in the east. Greek cultural influences spread among them in the 5th century B.C. along the Vardar river valley and via the Greek colonies founded on the Adriatic coast: Vis, Hvar, Trogir and others. During the 4th and 3rd centuries B.C. the Balkans were overrun by Celts, who mixed with the Illyrians to form Celtic-Illyrian tribes. The 1st century A.D. saw the extension of Roman rule over the Illyrian provinces from the Danube to the Adriatic. The towns built by the Romans in these provinces served as both military strongholds for the defence for the Empire and centres for the spread of Roman cultural and political influence: Aemona (Ljubljana), Scupi (Skopje), Salona (Solin), Naissus (Niš) and others.

The attempts to achieve the Romanisation of the Balkans and dominance of the Latin language were more effective in the western parts of the peninsula, the eastern areas remaining within the Greek cultural orbit. After the division into Eastern and Western Empires in 395, the dividing line ran through what is now Yugoslavia, roughly from Budva on the Montenegrin coast to the River Drina.

The South Slavs' medieval civilisation was shaped under the impact of two antithetical powers—Byzantium and Rome —in an area where two mighty autocratic empires clashed for centuries. These Balkan and Illyrian barbarians, as they were generally considered in the West, gave the Roman Empire more than thirty emperors and consuls. Diocletian, a native of Dalmatia, built his imperial palace, completed in 305, on the site of present-day Split, and spent his last years there.

South Slav civilisation in the turmoil of wars

In the course of the 9th, 10th and 11th centuries, powerful Slav states of various tribes flourished in turn. In the 9th century, the Macedonian Slavs under Tsar Samuilo freed most of the Balkan Slavs from Byzantine rule, his state stretching from Bulgaria and Epirus to the Dalmatian coast. The Croatian state founded in the mid-9th century reached its zenith in the reign of King Kresimir IV (1058–1074), when it covered the coastal region of Croatia and the Sava basin. It failed to withstand the invasion from the north and was incorporated in the Hungarian kingdom in 1102, thereby losing its independence for more than eight centuries, until 1918.

In the 10th century, however, Croatia was an important power in the Adriatic. The Byzantine emperor ordered the Dalmatian cities to pay tribute to the Croatian rulers. Tribute was likewise paid for almost a century by the Venetian Republic, in order to acquire the right to trade and navigation along the Adriatic coast. The Byzantine emperor and historian, Constantine Porphyrogenitus, records that Croatia could raise one hundred thousand foot soldiers and sixty thousand cavalry, and that it had a strong naval force of about one hundred vessels and five thousand sailors.

The Serbian state also came into being in the mid-9th century, attaining the peak of its power during the reign of Tsar Dušan (1331–1355). From the 12th to 14th centuries it was ruled by the Nemanjić dynasty, the descendants of Stefan Nemanja (1167–1196), who succeeded in laying the firm foundations of an independent Serbian state, struggling against Byzantium. It was in the time of Nemanjić rule that the Crusaders captured Constantinople and set up the Latin Empire. The Pope bestowed a royal crown on Nemanja's son, Stefan Nemanjić. Two of the leading figures of that time, King Stefan Prvovenčani and Archbishop Sava Nemanjić, were the first Serbian writers. Archbishop Sava, who organised the independent Serbian Orthodox Church, is particularly notable for his religious and other literary works, and may be said to have laid the foundations of culture in Serbia.

The Nemanjić kings exploited the rich silver mines and sponsored much building and artistic activity. From this period date the famous Serbian frescoes and monasteries (the renowned monasteries of Studenica, Sopoćani, Žiča and Mileševa were built in the 12th and 13th centuries). At almost the same time as Philippe II was building Notre Dame in Paris and Rouen cathedral, Nemanja in Serbia was raising his own church dedicated to the Virgin Mary at Studenica, and many other foundations with celebrated frescoes.

In the 14th century, the Serbian ruler, Dušan Nemanjić, conquered Macedonia, Albania, Epirus and Thessaly, and was crowned Tsar or Emperor of the Serbs and Greeks. At the Assembly held in Skopje in 1349, he issued the first part of what is known as Dušan's Code, one of the most important documents of medieval Serbia.

The Bosnian state, formed at the end of the 12th century, reached its peak during the reign of King Tvrtko (1353–1391), when it developed economically and became a Balkan feudal state of political and military significance. Bosnia was the seat of the Bogomils, a sect anathematised as heretical by the Pope, which deviated from both Catholic and Orthodox beliefs. In Bosnia the Bogomils strove to defend not only their autonomous church and religious faith, but also the state's independence: at that time Hungary justified its constant pressure on Bosnia on religious grounds. Their church was 'Bosnian', organised in the national spirit and using the national language.

Slovenian lands lost their independence at the end of the 9th century, and in the mid-10th century were incorporated in the German empire by the victory of Emperor Otto over the Hungarians. Slovenian territory was directly held by the Habsburgs for six and a half centuries, and was not freed from alien rule until the end of the First World War.

All Yugoslav lands suffered for centuries under foreign yoke with the exception of Dubrovnik, an independent republic until the early 19th century. For several hundred years, Dubrovnik carried on trade between Western Europe, South-East Europe and the Mediterranean. In the 16th century, it was a mighty naval power with a fleet of one hundred vessels for long voyages, some of which sailed as far as America. Napoleon's forces entered the city republic in 1808, and after the Congress of Vienna (1815), Dubrovnik came under Austro-Hungarian domination.

The Serbian state finally succumbed to the Turks with the fall of Smederevo in 1459 and Belgrade in 1521, whereby the conquerors firmly established themselves in the Danubian basin.

From the mid-16th century onwards, the present territory of Yugoslavia was again a battleground of East and West. The Yugoslav nations found themselves divided among three powerful states: the majority was under Ottoman rule (Macedonia, Montenegro, Serbia, Bosnia and Herzegovina and some areas of Croatia); another part (Croatia and Slovenia) was under the Habsburgs; the third—comprising most of the Adriatic coast with its cities—belonged to Venice.

The shield of Christendom.
The 19th-century liberation movements

In the 16th century, Austria turned Croatian territory into a military camp, a defence zone against Turkish invasion, with the Croats serving as frontier guards, as did the Serbs, Bosnians, and Montenegrins.

Rebellions and uprisings were frequent from the early days of foreign rule until complete national liberation was achieved in 1918. Starting with the Slovenian peasants' rebellion early in the 16th century, followed by the famous peasants' revolt of 1573 led by Matija Gubec in Croatia, and the movement of the noble Frankopan and Zrinjski families against the absolutism of the Viennese court in 1671, uprisings were virtually continuous.

The first Serbian insurrection, under Karadjordje ('Black George') Petrović, in 1804, marked the real start of the liberation of the Balkan peoples from the Ottoman yoke. In 1813, the Turks managed to drive out the Serbian insurgents, but two years later a second uprising was launched. Thanks to the experience gained from the first and to the nationwide support, this national liberation struggle was crowned by victory. From then on, Serbia began developing as a modern European state. Though dynasties and governments, constitutions and parliaments followed one another, sometimes in quick succession, a new consciousness and new bourgeois class came into being.

The French Romantic poet, Alphonse de Lamartine, returning from the East, travelled through Serbia after it had won its freedom (1832) and wrote his 'Notes on Serbia' in which he described this drama of the Serbian nation with deep passion and sincerity. Entering Serbia, he noticed a tower composed of human skulls, a monument into which the Turks had built the severed heads of fifteen thousand Serbian soldiers:

'These skulls and these human faces, worn away and bleached by rain and sun, held together by a little mortar, formed a triumphal arch protecting me . . . I greeted with my gaze and from my heart the remains of these brave men whose severed heads mark the frontier of their independent homeland. Serbia, which we were to enter, is now free . . . May this monument be left standing here! It will tell their children how much a nation's independence costs, showing them how dearly their fathers paid for it.'

Taking advantage of the crisis shaking the Ottoman Empire, in 1876 Serbia, together with Montenegro, declared war on Turkey. At the Berlin Congress, two years later, it was formally recognised as an independent state. Prior to the creation of Yugoslavia in 1918, Serbia and Montenegro were the only Yugoslav regions that constituted independent states.

It was not until the 19th and early 20th centuries that the Yugoslav peoples began to emerge as modern nations and started their development as part of European bourgeois society.

The socialist movement of the 1870s and later on the territory of the present-day Yugoslavia strove for closer ties with Western Europe, the source of revolutionary influences, particularly after the revolutions of 1848 and the Paris Commune of 1871.

The Montenegrins won their independence through continual warfare with the Turks throughout the 18th and first half of the 19th century. They never formally recognised Turkish occupation, and Montenegro was in fact considered an autonomous state. In 1797, during the reign of *Vladika* (Bishop-Prince) Petar I Petrović, it acquired its first code of civil law, organised courts and administration. At the Congress of Berlin (1878), Montenegro was finally recognised as a sovereign state.

The national liberation struggle of the Croats in the 19th century was also dramatic. Early in the century, Vienna supported the efforts of the Hungarian nobility to denationalise the Croats, even after the 1830 revolution, and an official Magyarisation campaign was conducted. A law was passed making Hungarian the official language of all territories, including Croatia, belonging to Hungary. Young Croatian intellectuals began their fight for the recognition of their language and national individuality, launching the Illyrian movement, whose programme of cultural and political emancipation had an impact on all the South Slavs. The leader and ideologist of the movement, Ljudevit Gaj, was in close contact with the national liberation movements in the other Yugoslav regions of Serbia and Slovenia.

The struggle of the younger generations against Hungarian cultural and political hegemony grew steadily in scope, gaining fresh impetus after the constitutional reform of 1867 that created the Austro-Hungarian monarchy. The Croatian national liberation movement was headed by Bishop Josip Juraj Štrosmajer and Franjo Rački, who opposed union with Hungary, striving for the political and cultural emancipation of the Croats and the political unification of all South Slavs.

In Slovenia, the conservative nationalists wanted only cultural autonomy and free use of the Slovenian language, while the democratic movement—to which the poet, France Presern, belonged—put forward far greater demands: complete Slovene independence, a national government, and complete equality of nationalities. Its programme, too, had the unification of all South Slav territory as one of its ultimate aims.

Several times in the course of the 19th century, the eyes of Europe were drawn to Bosnia and Herzegovina. These regions were frequently a hotbed of revolt: in less than one decade (1852–1861), three large risings broke out against the Turks in Herzegovina. These culminated in the Herzegovinian revolt of 1875 which provoked the great Eastern Crisis.

Turkish rule in Macedonia enjoyed the support of the feudal landowners, merchants and urban craftsmen, most of whom were of Turkish nationality. Moreover, Macedonia, in the south, lay close to the heart of the Ottoman Empire, so that military intervention at any sign of rebellion was always swift and effective. In the first half of the 19th century, a movement for national and social emancipation gradually gained strength. Among the first victims of the Macedonian struggle for liberation were the Miladinov brothers who were executed in Istanbul in 1862. A strong Macedonian revolutionary organisation, VMRO, led by Goce Delčev, was formed in Salonica in 1873 to fight for the country's liberation. In the Ilinden Uprising, which began on August 2, 1902, about thirty thousand poorly-armed rebels fought, with some initial success, against the Turkish army. The so-called Krusevo Republic was proclaimed, but lasted only ten days. Despite the heroic resistance of its defenders, the town of Krusevo was captured and reduced to ashes; of its fifteen thousand inhabitants, a mere three thousand survived.

Nor did the Balkan Wars of 1912, when Serbia, Montenegro, Greece and Bulgaria allied against Turkey, bring the Macedonian nation its long-desired independence. The victors, with the exception of Montenegro, divided up Macedonian territory among themselves.

The centuries-long struggle of the South Slavs had its bearing on the fate and prosperity of Western civilisation. In an academic address (on the tasks of science, in Zagreb, 1969), President Tito said:

'For more than five hundred years, the South Slavs, with hoe in one hand and sword in the other, were forced to defend not only themselves but also the West, which always regarded us as backward, thereby enabling it to engage in higher cultural activities. The peoples who defended the West from Turkish onslaughts were unable to devote themselves to learning, to take up the pen.'

'Teenagers' assassinate Archduke Franz Ferdinand

Germany and Austria-Hungary were far from pleased to see the Balkan and Slav nations drawing closer together. The assassination of the crown prince, Archduke Franz Ferdinand, in Sarajevo on June 28, 1914, by 'teenagers', as one American journalist described the young revolutionaries (members of the Young Bosnia—Mlada Bosna—organisation) responsible for this act, served Austria-Hungary as a pretext for declaring war on Serbia. Thus began the First World War.

Austro-Hungarian aggression against Serbia in 1914 was regarded by all Yugoslav nations as the signal to start their joint struggle for a common state. Montenegro entered the war immediately, while the other nations aided Serbia in various ways. The Yugoslav Committee, set up in London in 1915, carried on a campaign for recognition of the Yugoslavs' right to unification. The Corfu Declaration of 1917[4] stated that, on the basis of the right of nations to self-determination, the representatives of Serbia, Croatia and Slovenia were in agreement on the creation of a common state—the Kingdom of Serbs, Croats and Slovenes, headed by the Karadjordjević dynasty. In 1918, the Serbian army, together with French and British forces, drove the German, Austrian and Hungarian armies from the territory of Yugoslavia. Following the unification of Montenegro and Vojvodina with the Kingdom of Serbia, the new state—the Kingdom of Serbs, Croats and Slovenes as it was first officially named—was proclaimed on December 1, 1918. Through incorporating almost all the territory inhabited by South Slavs, this state was composed of regions with wide economic, social, legal and cultural differences.

The creation of Yugoslavia was the outcome of the long-standing national liberation movement. In 1918, Serbs, Croats, Slovenes, Montenegrins and Macedonians were united in one state for the first time in their history. Their right to independence was won by arms in the face of German, Austro-Hungarian, Italian and Bulgarian territorial pretensions regarding Yugoslav soil. Yugoslav losses in the Balkan Wars and First World War totalled 1,900,000 or 16 per cent of the population of the Yugoslav state established in 1918. Serbia's losses accounted for about one million of these.

National mosaic and a unitarist monarchy

The troubled political history of the new state in the inter-war period was the product of the deep economic, cultural and political differences between the various parts of the country, which the monarchy ignored.

Agriculture was the dominant branch of the economy, but even here conditions were far from uniform. In Serbia and Montenegro, the small peasant holding prevailed; in Slovenia, Croatia and Vojvodina much of the land was held by big landowners; in Macedonia, Bosnia and Herzegovina semi-feudal re-

4. The Corfu Declaration, signed on Corfu on June 20, 1917, by the Serbian Government (Premier Nikola Pašić) and Yugoslav Committee (Ante Trumbić), expressed a desire for the liberation of the Yugoslav nations from foreign rule and their unification in an independent state of Serbs, Croats and Slovenes headed by the Karadjordjević royal family.

lations still obtained. Industry was mostly confined to Slovenia, Croatia and Serbia. Together with crafts, it employed only 9·8 per cent of the working population.

The idea of a federal-type state in which no nation would have primacy was uppermost in the minds of those who desired unification. In Serbia's courageous resistance, the other nations saw a chance to throw off foreign rule and join together to form a powerful state. However, this idea was frustrated by the hegemonic policy of the Serbian bourgeoisie, which insisted on the liberating mission of Serbia towards the other Yugoslav nations, desiring their incorporation in a centralised state under the Serbian crown and not the unification of Yugoslav lands on terms of equality.

From the very start the Kingdom of Serbs, Croats and Slovenes did not recognise the national identity of the Macedonians, Montenegrins, Albanians in the Kosovo region, and others. The ruling circles endeavoured to conceal the existence of several nations. The unsolved nationality question, the only partial solution of the agrarian question, and the repercussions of the Russian and Hungarian revolutions gave rise to widespread unrest in the country in 1919 and 1920.

In the local government elections of 1920, the communists gained majorities in large towns and industrial centres, and in the elections for the Constituent Assembly the following year, the Communist Party won 15 per cent of the seats.[5] A government decree (*Obznana*) issued in December 1920 banned the Communist Party, confiscated the property of the trade unions, forbade the publication of several papers . . . From that time until the outbreak of the Second World War, the Communist Party and its organisations were illegal.

The January-6th dictatorship

With the *Obznana* in force, the *Vidovdan* (St Vitus' Day) Constitution was pushed through in June 1921 by a majority of 223 deputies to 196. This was centralist in spirit, making no

5. This revolutionary atmosphere brought about the unification of two workers' parties—the Social Democratic Party and group of communists —in the Workers' Party of Socialists/Communists, which took the name of the Communist Party of Yugoslavia early in 1920. The same period also saw the organisation of progressive trade unions and the League of Communist Youth of Yugoslavia.

allowance for regional-national autonomy. The national movement in Croatia which opposed the unitarist monarchy was led by the Peasant Republican Party headed by Stjepan Radić, who was shot and mortally wounded during a debate in the Assembly in 1928 on the instigation of circles close to the court.

Despite the various agreements reached between the bourgeois political parties in Serbia, Croatia, Slovenia and Bosnia, the nationality question dominated the scene.

But even the *Vidovdan* Constitution, which tolerated the parliamentary system, did not suit the regime. On January 6th, 1929, King Alexander Karadjordjević seized power and established a regime of personal rule known as the January-6th Dictatorship. The National Assembly was dissolved, and the Constitution suspended. All political parties were banned, all trade union, national and religious organisations disbanded, severe censorship was imposed, and the use of national names forbidden. Henceforth, the state was to be known as the Kingdom of Yugoslavia. The existence of a single nation was proclaimed with the slogan: 'One king, one nation, one state'. The dictatorship coincided with the worldwide economic crisis of 1929–1931, which had catastrophic consequences on Yugoslavia's industry, trade and agriculture.

The internal political struggles were so fierce that in the decade preceding the outbreak of war (1941), Yugoslavia had 23 different cabinets. King Alexander was assassinated in 1934 in Marseilles, during a state visit to France, the plot being laid by pro-fascist, extreme nationalist organisations. The French foreign minister, Louis Barthou, died together with the Yugoslav king.

On March 25, 1941, Prince Regent Paul and the Cvetković-Macek government signed the Axis three-power pact. This provoked nationwide revulsion and mass demonstrations, led by communists. A group of pro-British officers overthrew the government on March 27, ended the regency and proclaimed Peter II, a minor, as king.

Hitler was not long in replying to this affront: on April 6, 1941, Belgrade was heavily bombed, and without declaring war German, Italian and Hungarian forces invaded the country. The occupiers carved up the state, creating artificial frontiers: Slovenia was divided between Germany and Italy,

Serbia was placed under German occupation, Montenegro under Italian, and most of Macedonia under Bulgarian; Croatia was proclaimed an 'independent state' with a fascist-Ustashi regime; most of Kosovo belonged to 'Greater Albania' under Italian occupation, while the region north of the River Drava (the districts of Backa, Baranja and Medjumurje) went to Hungary.

The tragedy of the South Slav peoples is that their civilisation vanished in the toils of war, in the course of those six hundred years—from the 14th to 20th centuries—of Turkish, Austrian and Venetian rule, when they were divided by force of arms.

The dramatic struggle for national freedom, for freedom of language, belief, ideas and creativity, the struggle for physical and spiritual survival, began, perhaps, in the 9th century with the Bogomils, who wanted their national church and autonomy, thereby preceding, it may be asserted, Wycliffe, Hus and Luther.

By the way they wrote in their own alphabet, and worshipped in their own language, by their steadfastness in their beliefs, by the manner in which they strove for independence, by their behaviour throughout history, the nations which today constitute Yugoslavia are a living refutation of power and force. If the spiritual and moral structure of the present Yugoslav society has retained anything from the past then it is that tenacious and militant spirit.

Chapter 2

The Origins of Self-Management in Yugoslavia

Stalin and self-management

On a visit to Latin America in the spring of 1971, Edvard Kardelj was asked: 'If self-management in Yugoslavia is Marxist in spirit, why has it not been established in other socialist countries?' The question is certainly pertinent: how did it happen that self-management appeared and was accepted in a relatively undeveloped Balkan country, in Yugoslavia?

Many foreign writers take the view that it was precisely the conflict with Stalin and the Cominform that set Yugoslavia off on a new course in its internal development. To provide a fuller answer, one must look further back into the past.

From the very outset the Yugoslav revolution was quite autochthonic in its basic orientation. The very decision of the Yugoslav Communist Party to launch a nationwide uprising in 1941 was not completely in line with Comintern tactics, and was assessed by this body as reckless. Blinkered by dogmatism and Stalin's blueprints for revolution, the Comintern rejected the concept of a mass rising with national liberation and revolution as its aims.

Even before the occupation of Yugoslavia, and particularly after the invasion of April 6, 1941, the Communist Party of Yugoslavia was resolute in its course of resistance to fascism, encouraging and calling on the people to fight the occupiers. It regarded the occupation as a temporary state against which the Yugoslavs should take up arms.

Up to this time the Party had been illegal and had only 12,000 members, though the Communist Youth League had a membership of 30,000.

The resistance movement drew its internal strength from

its respect for national differences and its struggle for national equality, which had been ignored and suppressed by the prewar regimes. Its fundamental idea was the brotherhood and unity of all nations in the fight against the occupier.

This explains how the Partisan detachments in 1941 managed to attract 80,000 armed fighters, who tied down about 620,000 enemy soldiers in the Yugoslav theatre of war. The new front thereby established in Europe became an increasingly significant military-political factor in the anti-fascist coalition.

In 1942, the People's Liberation Army and Partisan Detachments of Yugoslavia numbered 150,000. These engaged 30 enemy divisions (750,000 men)—an army more numerous than, for instance, that which fought in North Africa. The Partisans were in control of free territory amounting to one fifth of the country—about 48,000 square kilometres.

By the end of 1942, the Liberation Army of 300,000 fighters was tying down 19 German, 8 Bulgarian and 3 Hungarian divisions. The strength of the Yugoslav army had reached 350,000 by the summer of 1944, at which time there were 400,000 men of the occupation forces and 250,000 quisling troops in the country.

Of the 58 states which took part in the Second World War, Yugoslavia suffered losses totalling 11 per cent of its population (1,700,000 lives), and in this respect comes third, after the Soviet Union and Poland.

The civilian population was frequently subjected to the most brutal reprisals. A particularly horrifying instance occurred in the Serbian town of Kragujevac in 1941, when German occupation forces shot 7,000 of the 38,000 inhabitants in one day, their victims including several hundred schoolchildren. On the site of these mass executions in Kragujevac, a striking memorial has been raised, resembling a bird with broken wings. A solemn march-past of about one hundred thousand people is held here every year on the anniversary of this tragic event.

A personal note is perhaps permissible here on the grounds that it illustrates those bitter and bloody times. In 1941, the author was a seventeen-year-old schoolboy living in Uzice (Serbia). Of the 38 pupils in the class, 26 of us joined the Partisans in that year. Only three of us returned, one without a leg. The Yugoslav revolution was the people's cause. Huge numbers participated in it, not only by extending their political sympathies and support but by actually taking up arms to fight for it under the most severe conditions.

There is no better way of gaining an understanding of life and reality than being placed in conditions in which human life is not respected—as in times of war and other types of violence. Over the past half century, history has afforded Yugoslavs many 'opportunities' of facing death and subjugation, of suffering unpunished injustices. It may be asserted that the Yugoslavs' bitter struggle during the Second World War enabled them to see more clearly the course their future should take.

Tito's message to Stalin in 1942

People's liberation committees were organised on free territory as early as 1941: there were about a dozen Serbian towns with such bodies. In the November of that year, the Main People's Liberation Committee of Serbia was formed for the whole free territory in Serbia. In the same period, similar organs of local government were established in Bosnia, Slovenia, Montenegro, Croatia and elsewhere.

Instructions regarding the creation of people's liberation committees were issued by the Supreme Command of the People's Liberation Army in February 1942. Known as the Foca Regulations, they were drawn up by Mosa Pijade, a well-known lawyer, painter and journalist, one of the leading figures of the national liberation movement, who was President of the National Assembly when he died in 1957. The foundations of social ownership were laid in these regulations, which stated:

'The people's liberation committees, as organs of popular government, shall confiscate the property of all enemies of the people: Ustashi, spies, traitors . . .'

They also provided for democratic procedure in the election of liberation committees, insisting from the very beginning on respect of law. The Foca Regulations bear a strong humanitarian stamp: they stress the principle of the individual's responsibility for his acts, provide for protection of the families of enemies of the people, and reject the idea of collective, tribal or family guilt and revenge.

In November 1942, in the liberated Bosnian town of Bihać, the leadership of the uprising formed its highest political representative body as the supreme organ of authority in the liberated parts of Yugoslavia: the Anti-fascist Council of National Liberation of Yugoslavia, generally known by its initials—AVNOJ. At this time the Germans were in front of Moscow and Stalingrad.

Today, the Yugoslavs themselves marvel at this temerity. When President Tito was interviewed by the author for the daily *Politika* in 1967, on the 25th anniversary of the formation of AVNOJ, he was asked what had motivated the leaders, at that grim moment in the war, to set up a body of national government. He replied:

'The liberated territories of Bosanska Krajina, and parts of Croatia, Dalmatia and Central Bosnia had been linked up, so there was already a huge area in which new fighters could be mobilised and the political authorities strengthened . . . We arrived at the idea of calling a meeting of respected political figures and patriots from all over the country.

The preparations for this meeting have their background. Since we were in contact with Stalin, I informed him that we intended to create a council which would have the character of a parliament and executive powers . . . Stalin was not opposed to the meeting, but did not favour the formation of any kind of government. However, we were already in a position to form such a body at Bihać and it seemed to me that we would not be making a mistake in doing so. Anyhow, we didn't insist; I abandoned the idea and at Bihać we only founded the Anti-fascist Council of National Liberation.'[1]

1. *Politika*, November 28 and 29, 1967.

At the Second Session of AVNOJ, held in November 1943, there were 208 delegates from all parts of the country, among them eminent public figures such as Dr Ivan Ribar, prewar president of the Yugoslav parliament, the 70-year-old Croatian writer Vladimir Nazor, Josip Vidmar, one of the best known Slovenian and Yugoslav writers, Nuri Pozderac, a prewar Moslem deputy from Bosnia-Herzegovina, and many others.

On November 29, 1943, AVNOJ elected a Partisan government—the Yugoslav National Liberation Committee, stripped the government-in-exile in London of its powers, and forbade the return of King Peter II to the country. It was likewise decided that the Yugoslav state should be organised on the federal principle. In accordance with the revolution's policy on the nationality question, national government bodies had already been set up in most of today's republics and provinces: in Serbia as early as 1941, in Croatia, Slovenia, Montenegro and Bosnia-Herzegovina in 1943, in Macedonia in 1944. The foundations of the new federal Yugoslav state laid in those troubled times have remained virtually unchanged down to the present day.

The shadow of Yalta

Yugoslavia's tribulations did not end with the war. On October 11, 1944, Stalin and Churchill reached agreement in Moscow on the fifty-fifty division of Yugoslavia as regards spheres of interest. This is how Churchill described the scene in his memoires:

'The moment was apt for business, so I said: "Let us settle about our affairs in the Balkans. Your armies are in Romania and Bulgaria. We have interest, missions, and agents there. Don't let us get at cross-purposes in small ways. So far as Britain and Russia are concerned, how would it do for you to have ninety per cent predominance in Romania, for us to have ninety per cent of the say in Greece, and go fifty-fifty about Yugoslavia?"

While this was being translated, I wrote out on a half-sheet of paper:

D

Romania:

Russia	90%
The others	10%

Greece:

Great Britain	90%
in accord with USA	
Russia	10%

Yugoslavia	50%—50%
Hungary	50%—50%

Bulgaria:

Russia	75%
The others	25%

I pushed this across to Stalin, who had by then heard the translation. There was a slight pause. Then he took his blue pencil and made a large tick upon it and passed it back to us. It was all settled in no more time than it takes to set down.'[2]

Later this proposal was definitely accepted at the Yalta Conference between Churchill, Stalin and Roosevelt, in February 1945. For the big powers, the Yugoslavs were just a minor matter, their destiny to be decided with no consideration of their wishes, despite their enormous sacrifices and losses in the fight against the occupier, and the fact that they had liberated themselves with their own army.

The shadow of Yalta, the desire of the powerful to control the fate of a small country, still falls over our land.

2. Winston S. Churchill: *The Second World War*, Vol. VI, *Triumph and Tragedy*, p. 196, Cassell.

Chapter 3

From Administrative Socialism
to Self-Management

'Administrative socialism'

The basic elements of a socialist system had already been constructed in the course of the war: bodies of state authority elected in the spirit of direct democracy, large voluntary armed forces, and socio-political organisations to organise the action of the masses. At the end of the war, the Communist Party of Yugoslavia numbered 100,000. Of the 12,000 members and 30,000 young communists who had entered the war, one half had lost their lives.

The first Constitution of the Federal People's Republic of Yugoslavia (January 31, 1946) gave legal form to the previous revolutionary changes, defined the new political organisation of society, and sanctioned the achievements of the liberation war and revolution: equality, and a socialist federal system.

In the immediate postwar years, several laws were passed which resulted in fundamental changes in society: on the confiscation of war profits (1946), the confiscation of enemy property (1946), and the sequestration of the property of foreign capitalists who had collaborated with the occupier.

One of the most important measures was the nationalisation of private enterprises in the main economic branches, which was proclaimed in the first Constitution (1946). The owners received a certain amount of compensation (in bonds or cash). Two years later, in 1948, large residential buildings and building land were nationalised. The management of enterprises was entirely in the hands of the state (the Federation, republic or commune, depending on the size and importance of the enterprise). All major decisions were taken at the centre: on the setting up and closing of enterprises, the production plan, distribution of raw materials and finished goods, wages of the employed, and assignment of personnel to posts and jobs. Production was stimulated by various devices: socialist competition, the shock-worker movement, the encouragement of new inventions and improvements in production, production councils, and so on.

A radical agrarian reform was implemented in favour of the small farmer and landless. In 1945 the maximum holding was fixed at 25 hectares, and in 1953 reduced to 10 hectares (about 25 acres). This reform and the appropriation of the means of production when used to exploit the labour of others were acts of far-reaching social and political significance. Rent and profit were abolished as forms of exploitation. The working class in industry, agriculture and other activities were released from their hired-labour relationship with the unproductive classes.

Moreover, the nationalisation of industry, trade, mining, transport and other branches (with the exception of crafts and other small-scale activities) created a powerful state-owned socialist sector which played a dominant role in the national economy. The new state, with which the political organisations —the Communist Party and others—became identified, exercised decisive control over the economic, political and cultural development of the country. This era is known in Yugoslavia as the period of 'administrative socialism', or 'revolutionary statism', the latter term being considered less pejorative, though not essentially different in meaning.

The revolution was authentic, but the first period of revolutionary development bore the clear stamp of Stalinist ideology, then in its 'golden age' and dominating the socialist countries of East Europe. Though later abandoned, administrative socialism, or something similar, was inevitable, and indeed progressive, in the initial period of Yugoslavia's postwar development. The powerful concentration of all resources and accumulated wealth was essential in order to overcome the enormous problems facing the war-torn country, ensure political stability, strengthen the new society and rebuild what had been destroyed. But such a concentration of resources could be achieved only by the centralisation of powers and decision-making, by strict central planning.

Wartime economic devastation.
The failure of collectivisation

Already scourged by backwardness, Yugoslavia emerged from the war with a completely paralysed and dislocated economy. The report of the Reparations Commission in Paris states that during the Second World War Yugoslavia lost about 1,700,000 inhabitants and suffered material damage of over 9,000 million dollars (17 per cent of the total losses of 18 Allied countries, excluding Poland and the USSR). The material damage inflicted upon Yugoslavia in the war was 1·4 times greater than that suffered by Great Britain, twice that of the Netherlands, and 72 times greater than US losses. To illustrate: 21 per cent of the total number of buildings were destroyed or damaged, 24 per cent of all farm stocks were wiped out, damage to industrial projects totalled 36 per cent of the overall value; the railways were left without 76 per cent of locomotives and 83 per cent of other rolling stock, while 56 of the 95 large vessels were lost; the bridges destroyed made up 65 per cent of the total length of bridges in the country; of the 210 hospitals in Yugoslavia at the outbreak of war, the enemy ruined or badly damaged 179.

In such a situation, planned distribution, strictly controlled prices and rational allocation of the available goods were essential. There were no great disparities in way of life or standard of living. A kind of wartime communism was perpetuated, requiring self-sacrifices and self-denial from all. It is easy to understand the need, under such conditions, for a monopoly of power in running the economy and administration of public affairs.

Administrative socialism suffered its first defeat when an attempt was made to end small-scale agricultural production, from which the majority of the population earned their livelihood. Partly under pressure from Stalin and the Cominform, which accused Yugoslavia of making concessions to petty-ownership attitudes in the countryside, the gradual collectivisation of farming was undertaken in 1949.

It soon became evident, however, that this was an economic and political mistake. The subsequent decline in farm production could not have come at a worse time, coinciding with the East European economic blockade and the ambitious first five-year plan of economic development. Four years later, in 1953, the attempt at collectivisation was abandoned and the peasant working co-operatives were disbanded. It was later admitted in the Federal Assembly that:

'Under our conditions, collectivisation of the land and collective tilling of the soil did not lead to an increase in labour productivity in agriculture.'

It was something which did not fit in with actual social and political conditions in Yugoslavia, and served as one more clear warning against belief in the magic powers of directives from 'on high' and in a single model of socialism.

The conflict with Stalin and the Cominform, 1948

Yugoslav society was very soon confronted with the problems of bureaucratisation: the growth of the administrative apparatus, slowness, inefficiency, lack of incentive by the workers to improve production. Moreover, the imposition of the Soviet model of social organisation, on which Stalin had insisted, proved unacceptable in Yugoslavia's specific conditions.

It is hard to gauge the extent to which the leading forces in society were aware at that time of the historic dilemma; to follow the trodden path or find one's own way? It is likewise hard to say how Yugoslav society would have developed had there been no conflict with Stalin in 1948. There was certainly much wavering, and the basic cause of these doubts (economic underdevelopment and a dogmatic attitude in some circles) has not completely vanished even today.

What was decisive, though, was the fact that the Yugoslav revolution, throughout its entire course, had been independent. Indeed, this had been a cause of friction with Stalin while the war was still in progress. Any attempt to ignore the mood of the people, to exact blind obedience to the Communist Party and state, and above all to any foreign power, would have brought the revolutionary forces into conflict with the masses. The Yugoslavs had to seek their own ways and means of ensuring that after the victory of the revolution the working people played an active part in deciding their own future.

The 'excommunication' of Yugoslavia by Stalin and the Cominform, military and political pressure, severe economic sanctions—all this was a real and unexpected catastrophe for Yugoslavia. For more than a year hunger threatened, and the country was forced, for its very survival, to seek aid from capitalist countries.

The economic pressure was steadily increased to the stage of total blockade. In 1947, the countries of the eastern bloc provided 56 per cent of Yugoslavia's imports and took 53 per cent of its total exports. In 1949, these countries accounted for a mere 14 per cent of the total value of Yugoslav foreign trade, and in the following year they completely suspended trade with Yugoslavia. To find new markets in just a year or two would have been a hard task for any country, let alone undeveloped Yugoslavia at the height of the cold war.

It is estimated that the direct consequences of the blockade alone cost the Yugoslav economy 430 million dollars (at then current prices), not counting increased military expenditures, the halting of investment projects and disruption of production due to lack of parts and materials.

Border incidents over a twelve-month period (1949–1950) obliged Yugoslavia to send 95 notes of protest to neighbouring socialist countries. In two years, 896 border incidents were recorded.

A young socialist society now stood poised at the crossroads. As the first motive for bringing pressure to bear on Yugoslavia, Stalin cited disagreement with some aspects of the country's foreign policy. This was, in fact, an attempt to restrict its independence in foreign affairs.

The second 'reason' was disagreement with Yugoslav practice regarding the role of the Communist Party. Stalin complained that the Yugoslav Party was being 'watered down', that it was not given the leading role in society. What he did not understand was that the Yugoslav Party could not allow itself to be separated from the broad front of progressive forces which had formed the basis of the success in the national liberation struggle.

The third complaint related to agrarian policy; that Yugoslavia had not undertaken collectivisation of the Soviet type.

Stalin also objected to deviation from dogma. In practice, the Yugoslavs had rejected a whole system of ideological relationships in the international communist movement; the concepts of a single road to socialism and of the state and Party as supreme judges in all domains, from culture and science to politics.

Finally, Stalin levelled the accusation of nationalism, a criticism that held within it the demand for Yugoslavia's renunciation of its independence with regard to internal development.

Acceptance of these criticisms and demands would have conflicted with the expectations of those broad sections of society which were the mainstay of the revolution.

One undoubted consequence of this pressure by Stalin was the breakdown of ideological taboos and the adoption of a more resolute course towards a specific form of democratisation—self-management.

Chapter 4

Self-Management – From Proclamation to Practice

The Yugoslavs opted for self-management because they were seeking a new logic of social development that differed from administrative and technocratic management.

This orientation was not a propaganda move, nor accidental, though in the early days it was to a considerable extent proclamatory. Before the introduction of self-management, Edvard Kardelj, taking part in a parliamentary debate (on the Law on People's Committees) in 1949, said:

'No perfect bureaucratic apparatus, however brilliant the leaders at its head, can build socialism. Socialism can only grow from the countless initiatives of the masses, together with the correct leadership of the Communist Party. Consequently, the development of socialism can take no other path but that of the steady growth of socialist democracy, in the sense of an ever greater degree of government by the working people.'

In November 1949, Djuro Salaj, President of the Trades Union Confederation of Yugoslavia, and Boris Kidric, a member of the government responsible for the economy, sent out instructions to 215 large enterprises on the formation and work of workers' councils. These pioneer councils were to concern themselves with the following: the drawing up of enterprise plans, making proposals for raising output, productivity and quality, measures to lower costs, personnel training, work discipline, proposals as to norms and the systematisation of working posts. Councils were to be elected by secret ballot of all the employed, the director being an *ex officio* member. If the latter and the workers' council failed to agree, a higher level in the state administration was to arbitrate. Workers had the right to recall unsatisfactory council members before the expiry of their term. Meetings were to be held out of working hours.

All 215 experimental workers' councils sent copies of the minutes of their meetings to Belgrade.

The idea met with widespread approval and support. Numerous enterprises began submitting requests for permission to elect a workers' council, with the result that before the Law on Self-Management was passed, about 500 councils were already functioning.

'Invisible' revolution

Prior to the passing of the first law on worker management in the Federal Assembly—on June 27, 1950—broad action had been undertaken to reduce the bureaucracy and decentralise administration, particularly in the state apparatus and socio-political organisations, in which large staff cuts were made. By the beginning of 1950, the number employed in government bodies and the socio-political organisations had been reduced by about 100,000.

At that time, the author was Secretary of the Central Committee of the Yugoslav Youth Organisation, which had about 5,500 paid political officials until the axe fell in 1950. The number was then cut to just a few hundred. Today, this organisation has only 270 professional functionaries in the whole country.

The introduction of workers' councils was not a purely pragmatic move. The Yugoslavs wanted to bring something new into the programme of socialist construction and into socialist relations. Some writers in the West thought they were unaware of the scope of the step they were taking, describing them as 'unburdened' by principles. But in a speech in the Federal Assembly on June 27, 1950, during the debate on the law on worker management, Tito made it clear that the introduction of workers' councils comprised a whole programme of socialist development:

'The state take-over of the means of production did not mean that the slogan of the workers' movement, 'Factories to the workers', had actually come true, for the slogan, 'Factories to the workers—land to the peasants', is not empty propaganda but a watchword with real meaning and substance regarding social ownership, and the rights and duties of workers. Consequently, it must be put into practice if we really mean to build socialism.'

The law went a stage further than the trial project in providing for a managing board—an executive body to be elected by the workers' council from among its members. It also stipulated that the number of council members could range from 15 to 120, depending on the size of the enterprise. If the total number of employed in an enterprise was under 30, no council was to be elected, for the whole collective would participate directly in management.

In addition, the enterprise statute (rules and regulations) was to be passed by the workers' council, subject to the approval of the relevant higher bodies. For the first time, enterprises gained the right to dispose of part of the profits, with the workers' council deciding on how it was to be spent.

The director of the enterprise had a dual role: he was both a state official and—as a member of the managing board—carried out the decisions of the workers' council.

The elections were secret, with democratic procedure in the proposal of candidates.

The first year or two abounded in ceremonies: the director handing over the factory keys to the workers' council, the unveiling of commemorative plaques marking this event, and so on. This action was conceived with long-term aims in view and was politically audacious, for at that time foreign pressure made it necessary to spend about 23 per cent of the national income on defence.[1]

The historical significance of this first step should not be exaggerated. It did not end, in a flash, administrative socialism

1. In 1976, defence expenditures totalled 6·3 per cent.

and bureaucracy, but it did signal the path that was to be followed and was important as an act of confidence: the 'risk' was taken of placing powers directly in the workers' hands. Naturally, it was not possible for the transfer of factories to worker management to be accompanied straight away by real, effective control and participation in the distribution of profits. The state continued to play an extremely important role in setting the legal and economic bounds within which the workers' councils operated, in levying various taxes, in determining wages and prices.

The self-management of the fifties was more a form of representative than direct democracy. Even the largest factories had only a single workers' council, the various departments and work units having no role in the self-managing organisation.

The introduction of workers' councils called for the construction of a new economic system that would allow the organs of self-management greater independence and freedom of action. It was necessary to change the existing system with regard to planning, income distribution and remuneration, and to establish new relations between the state organs and enterprises, thereby altering the function of the state apparatus in management of the economy. A series of minor 'invisible' revolutions were set in motion.

In view of the need for rapid completion of key projects in the country's industrialisation, the state still controlled the major share of investments.

Now, however, the national plan no longer prescribed what goods each factory should produce and at what price. The enterprises paid taxes and certain other contributions to the state, the amount depending on how well-equipped and profitable they were.

Banks began to engage in extending loan to the economy and gathering its unused resources, instead of simply being a distributor and keeping the records.

Nevertheless, in vital sectors of production and consumption, prices were administratively controlled, in basic industry, power production, transport, cereals.

All the same, the changes were considerable. Previously, the administration had determined workers' earnings according to hierarchy and rank, qualifications, difficulty of the job and norms. Now the distribution of earnings and enterprise funds became the concern of the employed.

Coupons for purchases were abolished and most foodstuffs and general consumer goods became freely available on the market. The price of cereals was held down by means of imports. Prices of footwear, textiles and sugar were considerably reduced. The system of compulsory purchase of cereals and other farm produce, whereby the farmer had to sell his goods to the state at low prices, was ended. Under this system, the state had supplied the urban population with cheap food, and was thus able to keep wages low. The political price, however, was widespread dissatisfaction among the peasants, who were told exactly what to produce as well as being compelled to sell to the state. This had been essential, however, in view of the million-strong migration of the population from rural areas to towns. The demographic changes of those years in fact constituted an 'invisible' revolution in themselves.

For the first six years or so, self-management can be said to have been on trial. Four years elapsed after the passing of the law before worker management was introduced in the railways and postal services, and subsequently to other public services: city transport, water supply, sanitation, and so on.

The task of bringing self-management to education, the arts, the health and social welfare services, and social insurance proved long and difficult, for the principle of material incentive could not be accepted.

Socialism—personal happiness and 'higher goals'

In the first decade of self-management, about 700,000 people, or every tenth adult in the country, served on a workers' council. Towards the end of this decade, the basic question no longer concerned the freedom of the producers to manage their enterprises but the level of material possibilities for exercising that freedom.

Two political gatherings were of outstanding importance in that decade: the First Congress of Worker-managers, held in 1957 with 1,872 delegates participating, and the Seventh Congress of the League of Communists of Yugoslavia, 1958, which approved its Programme, an original document marking the consolidation of Yugoslav socialism and its further direction along its own path of development. There were two sentences in this Programme, in particular, that met with wide popular acclaim:

> 'Socialism cannot subordinate man's personal happiness to any higher goals, for the highest goal of socialism is the personal happiness of the individual.'
> 'Nothing that is created must become so sacred to us that it cannot be superseded and give way to what is still more progressive, freer and more humane.'

Yugoslavs wanted, first of all, freedom to criticise, and then to participate. There is an old proverb: 'He who waits for the crowd to buy him a cap will go bareheaded'. By introducing self-management, the Yugoslavs merely wished to buy their own cap, and one made to their own design.

But when speaking of participation and freedom, it was not the chance to reject and oppose something that was uppermost in the mind, but the material basis that enables man actively to benefit by freedom.

The right to self-management—the 1963 Constitution

In the beginning, the share of work organisations in the distribution of their income was relatively small—about 30 per cent of the net product. It began increasing after 1963:

	Year	%
Share of economic organisations in the net product	1963	44·7
	1964	52·1
	1965	55·4[2]

Democracy was flourishing at the level of direct participation in the enterprise and on local level—in the commune, but the question was how to exert influence on the distribution of capital resources and funds, and on policy on the national

-----

2. In 1976—62·8 per cent. The highest level was 68·3 per cent in 1971.

plane. The only way to establish democracy in decision-making on this level was to create a system whereby the ordinary citizen and producer would have a say on the spending of the part of the surplus product (profits) which was 'alienated', being left to the Federation, republic or commune.

One of the basic concerns of the Yugoslav Constitution of 1963 was to ensure the stable socio-economic position of the worker-manager and his social security.

Ever since that time, the 'strengthening of the material base of self-management' has been an ever-present slogan in every debate on self-management and in the public speeches of politicians. Two things are involved here. First, that enterprises should retain more of their earnings in their funds for investment and for increasing personal incomes. Second, that the producers should exert a greater influence on the spending of available resources within the commune, republic or province and Federation.

The 1963 Constitution granted 'self-managing status' to all forms of socialised labour (or associated labour, as it is usually termed in Yugoslavia). All institutions[3] gained the right to elect their bodies of management and through these decide on matters concerning their work, income distribution, working conditions, remuneration, and future development. To find measurable social and economic criteria to evaluate work of this kind has always been extremely difficult. Self-management in education, the health and social welfare services and civil service had as many administrative as self-managing elements in it, since their financing was, until recently, administrative in character (that is allocations from various budgets and centralised funds), so that the system of earned income was harder to apply in those domains.

The 1963 Yugoslav Constitution proclaimed a completely new right, as an integral part of those traditional civil rights dating from the French Revolution of 1789. This is the self-management right of the working man and citizen to manage production and all public affairs, a right that is protected by penal legislation.

3. i.e. health and social welfare institutions, banks, the civil services, schools, universities, etc.

The 'deprofessionalisation' of politics

The principle of compulsory rotation of functionaries in leading posts was first provided for in the 1963 Constitution: the post of director had to be re-advertised at regular intervals (the incumbent being able to apply for reappointment), assembly deputies could not serve more than two consecutive terms. This rule was also applied to the leading functionaries of socio-political organisations. The practical purpose of this was to prevent bureaucratisation and give young and able people more opportunities of playing a prominent role in public affairs. The cadres from the war and revolution, most of them enjoying general public esteem, had stayed too long in the same posts. New times called for more educated and younger people, and the principle of compulsory rotation and re-appointment, though it might be questioned from the formal democratic viewpoint, legalised this social need. This step was taken without any personal attacks and groundless political campaigns of a dramatic character such as usually accompany replacement of cadres under undemocratic conditions.

The qualifications and educational level of many directors of economic organisations were inadequate, a state of affairs that rapidly improved after the introduction of compulsory reappointment. The number of professional politicians holding such posts was reduced, and qualifications and knowledge began to be valued more than a bureaucratic career.

Between 1965 and 1970, the number of directors with higher education rose by 11 per cent, but even so they still made up only just over half the total. Considering only directors of enterprises with over 30 workers, i.e. those that elect workers' councils, directors with higher education formed 57·9 per cent as against 47 per cent in 1947.[4]

There was also a sharp cut in the number of professional politicians in the federal and republican parliaments.[5]
(See Table 1)

4. In 1976—87·2 per cent of directors had higher education (university degrees or two-year college diplomas).
5. Until 1963, the Federal Assembly consisted of two chambers: the Federal Chamber—elected by general suffrage, and the Chamber of Producers—the representative body of the working people and work organisations.

Table 1
*Composition of Federal and Republican Parliaments,
1963 and 1969*

Body	Year	No. of deputies	No. of prof. politicians	%
Fed. Assembly	1963	572	142	24
Fed. Assembly	1969	618	65	9
Rep. Assemblies	1963	2,268	417	19
Rep. Assemblies	1969	2,137	214	10
Prov. Assemblies	1963	619	149	25
Prov. Assemblies	1969	614	79	12

These data show that in 1969 there were two and a half times fewer professional political functionaries than in 1963. In the republican assemblies their number was halved, and in the provincial assemblies more than halved.

The socio-economic reform of 1965

The Yugoslav economy would have inevitably been confronted with very serious problems had it not been for the economic reform of 1965.

Major results as regards quantity of output had been achieved by this period, the end of the third five-year plan of economic development. The national *per capita* income was now close to 500 dollars, and Yugoslavia was already among the European countries with a medium level of development: the annual rate of industrial growth was 12 per cent (among the highest in the world), while agriculture was increasing production by 5 per cent annually. Personal spending had risen over the seven-year period by 70 per cent.

It was not growth, therefore, that was causing concern, but prices and quality of goods, productivity, and competitive power on the world market. Every encounter with the industrially advanced states of Europe and overseas indicated ever more clearly that the Yugoslav economy was developing in the main on the closed home market, sheltered by high customs barriers and various protectionist measures. Exports had been to a great extent supported by subsidies, which were almost totally abolished by the reform. With a shortage of foreign currency, enterprises were encouraged to earn it by exporting:

E

the more goods exported, the higher the enterprise's foreign currency quota. This was combined with a central fund for those industries which could not export but whose development was desirable. The foreign currency left to an enterprise could be used for investment, loaned to another enterprise through a bank, or used for purchasing goods abroad, as required.

Enterprises could now trade directly with foreign firms, though the bank kept an eye on these programmes through the Central Foreign Currency Fund.

Aimed at influencing the conditions of price formation rather than prices themselves, the reform freed many previously controlled prices.

The artificially maintained low prices of transport, electricity, raw materials and even labour made the processing and manufacturing industries much more profitable than the others. Since Yugoslavia's economic regions for the most part coincide with the territorial-political division, the undesirable political implications were by no means insignificant (for instance, Bosnia-Herzegovina's main economic branch is coal and iron mining).

The reform was intended to favour the enterprise as the basic investment unit, and not various political bodies. At that time there was a large number of so-called political factories, running at a loss, that had been built without regard to economic criteria—as a reward to a region for its contribution in the liberation war, because of the need to solve unemployment, because influential politicians wished to do something for their home region, and so on.

The economic reform did not allow the problem of employment to be solved simply by the migration of labour from the country to the town. Between 1945 and 1965, employment increased at the average rate of 8·9 per cent annually; after 1965 the number of employed even fell by about 100,000.

The reform likewise cut the high rate of economic growth from 10–12 per cent to 6–7 per cent, the economy being forced to modernise and give preference in employment to skilled labour and qualified personnel. The entire increase in the social product (GNP) of 6·3 per cent annually (between

1966 and 1970) was achieved through higher productivity.

It was realised in advance that the economic reform would create many political, social and economic difficulties. The social problems were particularly in evidence: redundancy of workers in enterprises, coupled with the continuing influx of labour into towns, and surplus manpower in the countryside. In international trade, many economic factors were becoming uncertain, unpredictable, making it necessary to be well-informed and knowledgeable.

On the other hand, the reform helped to bring weaknesses and advantages in economic behaviour into the open, and to formulate more clearly questions relating to the economic function of the producer, which constitutes the basis of worker management.

Chapter 5

The Organisation of Worker Management in Yugoslav Enterprises

There is no single model of self-management organisation that could be successfully applied to all types of enterprises and in all environments. Even in one and the same enterprise the organisation of worker management has differed in various periods, in accordance with the development of the enterprise and of material and social relations. What is constant in all this is the constitutionally-guaranteed right of every working collective to self-management (worker management), a right that cannot be withheld. The Constitution likewise stipulates the obligations of worker-managers towards society.

The organisation of a self-managing enterprise is a doubly complex task: account must be taken of the method of decision-making, so that the producer is brought into this as fully as possible, while, on the other hand, the technical and economic requirements with regard to the links and relations between the various parts of an enterprise call for the highest possible degree of integration and efficiency.

The constitutional amendments of 1971 gave working collectives considerable independence in the organisation of worker management, with the proviso that as many decisions as possible should be taken directly by the workers. Naturally, part of the managerial functions of the working collective can and must be transferred to the management bodies: the workers' council (or councils in complex enterprises), managing board, and councils in work units.

Worker management in parts of an enterprise

At present, enterprises adopt one of three models of self-management organisation, depending on their size and complexity: (See Diagrams, pp 56–58)

1. One-level worker management (smaller and simpler enterprises);

2. Two-level worker management (in enterprises with work units);

3. Three-level worker management (in the largest and most complex enterprises—integrated enterprises, factory-farms, combined plants, the railways and so on).

The enterprise statute regulates the organisation and powers of each organ in accordance with the Constitution, but nothing can enter the statute without the prior approval of the collective. The procedure in this is strictly democratic.

The organs of worker management are: the working collective, the workers' council and the managing board.

The working collective A workers' income and future depend not only on the results of his personal work but also on the business success of the whole enterprise. If business results improve, so do his earnings and prospects. The idea of this is that the worker should become concerned about and responsible for the operation of the whole enterprise.

The working collective participates in management directly through referenda or meetings of workers in the various parts of the enterprise. Generally speaking, direct worker management cannot be achieved completely because of the large number of employed, physical separation (as is the case with the railways, river and maritime shipping, large building enterprises, mines with several pits and departments, etc.) or because of shift work. Direct decision-making on a large number of matters would, of course, be quite irrational and damaging, since it would slow down the production process. Such decisions are entrusted, in the first place, to the workers' council.

The collective elects the workers' council by secret ballot, and may recall it if its activities run counter to the interests of the enterprise and workers. The collective has the right to be kept informed of the council's work. From time to time, the council or individual members submit reports to the collective or work unit.

Meetings of the workers' council are public, and may be at-

Diagram I
THE ORGANISATION OF WORKER MANAGEMENT IN THE BOR MINING AND FOUNDRY BASIN (SERBIA)

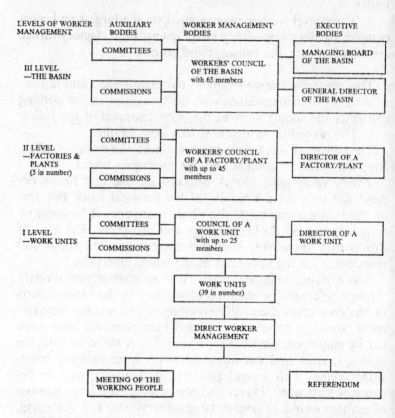

The Bor mines are the largest copper mines in Europe. From 1904 until World War I (1940), they were exploited by a French company. The Mining and Foundry Basin employs 11,500, engaged in the production and processing of copper and artificial fertiliser. The Basin is technologically divisible, some of its parts forming technological-economic entities.

Diagram II
THE ORGANISATION OF WORKER MANAGEMENT IN THE 'JESENICE' IRON AND STEEL WORKS, JESENICE (SLOVENIA)

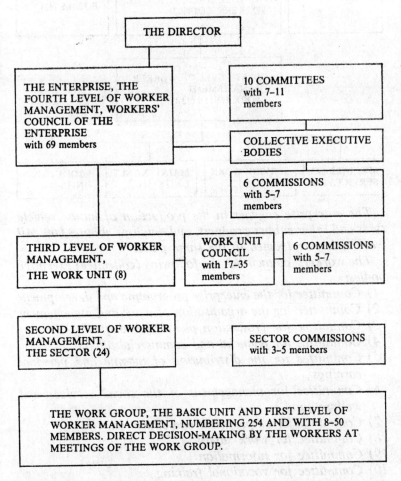

The Iron and Steel Works employ about 7,000. It is technologically indivisible—all parts are located in the same place.

Diagram III
THE ORGANISATION OF WORKER MANAGEMENT IN THE 'SAVA' ENTERPRISE OF KRANJ (SLOVENIA)

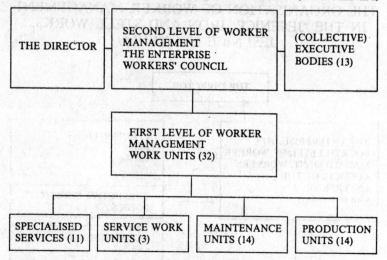

The enterprise engages in the production of motor vehicle tyres and other rubber products, and employs about 3,000. All work units are located in the same place.

The workers' council has the following (collective) executive bodies:

1) Committee for the enterprise programme and development
2) Committee for the organisation of work and management
3) Committee for production planning and quality
4) Committee for financial and commercial affairs
5) Committee for the distribution of income and personal earnings
6) Committee for management of the social services and welfare fund
7) Committee for employment and education
8) Committee for work safety
9) Committee for information
10) Committee for vocational training
11) Committee for the assessment and compensation of damage and injury
12) Committee for establishing dereliction of duty
13) Internal arbitration

tended by any member of the collective. As a rule, attendance is highest when matters such as housing, earnings and the living standard are being discussed.

The largest number of enterprises (91 per cent in 1970) have two-level worker management, while only 9 per cent have three-level decision-making.

In Yugoslavia there are few really large enterprises with complex organisation and three-level worker management: in 1970 they numbered 127.

The *Crvena zastava* Works in the Serbian town of Kragujevac (a factory turning out about 100,000 automobiles a year and employing 27,000 workers) has 14 workers' councils, 15 managing boards, 19 departmental councils, 134 committees for presiding over meetings of the workers—all together 1,431 elected members of management bodies, not counting the members of standing and *ad hoc* commissions elected by these organs.

In the *Mosa Pijade* Cable Works in Svetozarevo (with about 4,000 employed), 1,017 persons or every fourth employee is a member of a body of worker management. If the members of the auxiliary bodies of these organs (commissions and committees) are added, then the total is 1,500 or every third worker.

In the *Saponija* chemical factory in Osijek, 319 out of 1,400 workers are members of management organs and auxiliary bodies.

The workers' council—This is the most competent organ of worker management and vehicle of common interests within the enterprise. Its powers are very wide and precisely formulated in the enterprise statute. They usually cover the following:

1. Organisation of work: the passing of plans and development programmes and measures for their implementation;

2. Staff: the appointment of the director and other executives, personnel training, the employment and discharging of workers, if this function has not been transferred to the work unit councils;

3. The domain of financing and commercial matters: decisions on the type, price and quantity of goods to be produced, on investments, the use of funds, consideration of the annual balance sheet;

4. General organisation: determining—by democratic procedure—the self-management structure and powers of the individual organs.

The workers' council passes various internal regulations which have the force of law within the enterprise.

The *Konstruktor* building enterprise in Maribor, for instance, has 25 normative acts, of which the most important are:

—the enterprise statute,
—regulations on working relations,
—regulations on working relations for work in Austria,[1]
—regulations on income distribution,
—regulations on book-keeping,
—regulations on the allocation of flats and credits for housing construction,
—regulations on annual holidays,
—regulations on trainees,
—regulations on safety at work,
—regulations on the systematisation of working posts,
—regulations on the election and recall of the organs of worker management, etc.

The collective elects the workers' council by secret ballot, every employee, except the director, having the right to vote and be elected to this body. The elections are conducted by electoral commissions and committees. The list of candidates can be submitted by meetings of workers and by a certain number of voters. The term of office of the workers' council was at first one year, but was later extended to two. Now, the collectives have the right to stipulate in their statutes the length of their council's term of office. The majority have opted for a two-year term. To prevent 'professionalisation', no one can be elected for two consecutive terms.

Auxiliary bodies of the workers' council—After several years of experience, the workers' councils began setting up specialised commissions to augment the functions of the

1. The enterprise also builds projects in Austria.

director and expert staff, not in order to reduce their powers but to supplement and check on their work. Both commissions and expert committees prepare material to facilitate the council's decision-making: the commission for employing and discharging workers, the disciplinary commission, the commission for requests and complaints, the planning committee, the committee for financing and commercial matters, the personnel and social welfare committee, and others.

The managing board of the enterprise—This is primarily the executive organ of the workers' council, but it does have a certain degree of independence: it decides on some matters of enterprise operation, as provided for in the statute; it prepares drafts of the statute and other regulations; it draws up plans and programmes of work and development (at the proposal of the workers' council); it sees to the implementation of the council's decisions.

The workers' council elects the managing board annually from the ranks of its own members and others employed in the enterprise. The board usually has five to eleven members, depending on the size of the workers' council and enterprise. The council supervises and, if necessary, recalls the board members. The board usually meets once a week, since it has to consider every proposal put forward by any member of the collective and give a reply within one month.

In practice, the managing board exerts a great influence, both as the executor of the council's decisions and, even more, because of its responsibility for submitting proposals to the council. The director is an *ex officio* member of the board, but has no special rights in this body.

The director—The director is the only individual in the enterprise with special competences. Previously, these powers were determined by law, but since the adoption of Constitutional Amendment 25 in 1969, they have been set by the collective, in the enterprise statute.

Together with the expert executive team—the professional managers—the director carries out the decisions of the workers' council and managing board, organises and oversees the production process and running of the enterprise, and ensures discipline. It is he who bears the main personal responsibility to society for the legality of the enterprise's work. The director performs his functions independently, but is responsible to the whole collective and workers' council. He has the right to block, temporarily, the council's decisions if he considers them illegal, the final judgement on this being passed by a special arbitration body in the commune.

The workers' council and its organs do not interfere in the actual day-to-day running of the enterprise, in technological matters, but follow and assess the work of the director and expert executive team on the basis of their overall results.

The director is appointed by the collective or workers' council (depending on the enterprise's size) following public advertisement of the post. This procedure must be repeated every four years, thereby giving a chance for new candidates to apply for the job.

The director must possess the technical and economic knowledge and qualifications that are required almost everywhere for such a post, together with the knowledge and qualities demanded by self-management relations in Yugoslavia. He is not subordinate to the will of a government department, as in a statist system, nor is there any class confrontation between director and worker-managers, as is the case with the director/manager and trade unions in a capitalist enterprise.

Requiring directors to apply for reappointment at regular intervals proved an effective method of improving the general qualificational level of persons holding such a post. The number of directors with higher education in 1970 was considerably larger than in 1965, but they still constituted no more than 50 per cent of the total. Not counting small enterprises with under thirty employees, this percentage is about 57 per cent; forestry leads in this respect, with 83 per cent of directors with higher education, followed by agriculture—79 per cent, industry—67 per cent, building—65 per cent, transport—60 per cent, trade and catering—56 per cent.

The director is under the supervision of the workers' council, but his expert executive team, usually composed of highly trained staff, can assume too much power. There are cases of technocratic usurpation, when all major decisions are taken by technical personnel and economists. This has become more common since the adoption of Constitutional Amendment 25, allowing for the possibility of workers' councils founding one or more business boards instead of one managing board. The business boards are usually made up of highly qualified staff, generally in some executive post. It is here that the danger lies of technocracy dominating worker management.

The emergence of technocracy is inevitable in the constant search for a balance between democracy and efficiency. The chances of avoiding it depend on how up-to-date management methods are, and on the actual strength of worker management in a collective.

The meeting of working people—The meeting of all the workers of an enterprise is considered the most direct form of self-management, but is only practicable in smaller collectives. As the law stands at present, the entire collective is obliged to gather five or six times a year to approve periodic accounts, the annual financial report and production programme. Most enterprises now consider this requirement outdated, since there are few collectives that can in practice meet together at one time, because of their size, shift work or other considerations of work organisation.

However, there is strong pressure within enterprises in favour of direct management. A few examples will illustrate how some large enterprises have tackled this problem:

The *Merkator* trade enterprise of Maribor (Slovenia), employing 3,000, holds 'assemblies of working people' composed of delegates elected by the work units and numbering at least 10 per cent of the total employed in the enterprise.

The *Jesenice* iron and steel works (7,000 workers) had decided on meetings of the work units made up of 230 to 1,500 workers as a solution, but a number of technical difficulties (shifts, premises) gave these gatherings a rather formal character in which debate was either lacking or repetitive, and voting was a pure formality. The steel works then sought a way out in meetings of 'work groups', composed of at most 30 employees, who meet in working hours. Work in the organs of self-management is not considered 'political activity' but treated as part of an employee's duty.

Gatherings of the entire collective are in the main regarded as impracticable and ineffective, direct participation in management being better achieved in the smaller organisational and production sectors of an enterprise—in the work units.

The work unit—A need was felt for certain cells of direct democracy so as to avoid the age-old failing of parliamentary bureaucracy: the lack of control over the elected representative in the period between elections.

The smallest sector of a factory, a department, that can cost account independently, constitutes an independent work unit. The counterpart of the work unit in a capitalist enterprise is the economic unit, which serves to facilitate cost control and management, increase efficiency, and even to create a better working atmosphere.

Since production costs and accounts are worked out at the unit level in Yugoslav enterprises, each worker has an insight into everything on which the success of his enterprise and his personal work depend. This makes it possible to assess work results precisely, so that remuneration according to these results can be achieved.

The work unit can adopt its plan (through the unit's workers' council or directly), and its regulations on work discipline and organisation.

The work unit gives the individual greater opportunity to show creative initiative. He does not regard his position from the traditional trade-union standpoint, demanding higher wages, but is aware that his earnings depend on productivity, which in turn depends not only on his personal work results but also on the results of others.

Worker management through work units gives every individual a chance to make a real choice, and to be informed on the state of affairs in his enterprise and in a broader context. Even in the largest industrial and commercial systems, the individual thus becomes an active factor in work and management.

This concept has not so far been applied everywhere. According to data of the Federal Institute for Statistics, in 1970, of the 8,114 enterprises which were analysed, in only 1,458 had certain rights of decision-making been transferred to parts of the enterprise and smaller units.

Among the big enterprises, however, there are wide differences in practice regarding the powers left to work units and worker-management organs on this level. The central workers' councils and the councils of the individual factories and plants of the big enterprise retain most of the rights of decision-making. A trade union questionnaire showed that in 6 per cent of enterprises work units do not decide directly on matters of work organisation that fall within the scope of worker management, in 23 per cent of enterprises the work units do not decide on income distribution, and in 9 per cent they do not decide on personal earnings. Instead, this is done in their name by the workers' councils. In enterprises with three-level worker management, the situation is even worse: in 76 per cent of enterprises, work units do not decide directly on income distribution, and in 33 per cent they have no direct say on the distribution of personal earnings, this being within the competence of their representative bodies.

Thus, decision-making is primarily at workers' council level, a fact that cannot be justified on grounds of efficiency. Worker management in large and complex enterprises calls for well thought-out and precise organisation that will not allow any unwarranted limitation of direct decision-making.

It would be Utopian to believe that all decisions can be taken directly. Direct and representative democracy are not contradictory but complementary. Direct democracy does not mean simply conference-holding; it is intended to change the content of socio-political life by enabling everyone to exert an influence on the process of work and distribution, and on political life in general, without political parties and the bureaucracy as intermediaries.

The referendum—As a form of direct decision-making, the referendum is mainly used to decide major questions such as a proposed merger, a change of location of the enterprise head-office, a switch-over to a different type of production, and so on. It is still insufficiently used; in 1966, 82 per cent of enterprises with 1,000 and more employees did not hold a single referendum, and in 1969, no referendum was held in 90 per cent of enterprises with from 250 to 1,000 workers.[2]

In most cases, referenda are organised only when the law

2. Since the latest constitutional changes it has become a much more frequent practice. In 1976, only 40 per cent of basic organisations of associated labour held no referendum.

or statute make them compulsory. Otherwise, they are avoided, since they require complicated arrangements. Moreover, at meetings of the working people a proposal is more likely to be approved since voting is public.

In the *Krivaja* timber plant (Bosnia-Herzegovina), referenda are held to decide on changes in the location of the head-office, on integration (mergers) and withdrawal from mergers, changes in the basic activity of the enterprise, and dissolution of the enterprise organs of management.

In the *Politika* newspaper and publishing house in Belgrade, a referendum was organised in 1971. Approval was sought for a proposal whereby the annual holiday bonus (400 dinars) paid to all employees would not be distributed that year, the money to be used instead to provide flats for 12 cases of social hardship in the collective. Despite well-organised canvassing of support for this proposal, two-thirds of the employed voted against it.

Politika has the highest productivity per man of all economic organisations in Belgrade and ranks among those with the highest level of personal earnings. The failure of the referendum would seem, at first sight, a dismaying example of callousness. What, in fact, lay behind it? The result of the voting constituted a sharp criticism of the housing allocation policy. In the preceding years, the enterprise had distributed about 45 flats annually among the employed (1,500 in all), but the social hardship cases had not been lucky. The policy had been to allocate flats to those people who were most necessary to the enterprise (highly-qualified staff and journalists) and not those with the direct need for accommodation.

Recently, many collectives have been insisting that their statutes should make provision for referenda, and that the scope of questions to be decided by this method should be extended. They have realised that this is a very effective form of direct decision-making.

Educational and qualificational structure
of self-management organs

Self-management depends on how well-informed, educated and qualified to take decisions the worker-managers are. In an underdeveloped environment, where the level in this respect is low, there can be no social cohesion, the workers are not capable of perceiving even their true class interests, let alone working for long-term general interests, for a new, more stable and more moral system. For what is in question is not just institutional democracy, or simply personal interest in income distribution and remuneration, but the trends of a modern industrial society and greater demands in the sphere of production, organisation, management and social relations.

The number of qualified and highly qualified persons in self-management organs is growing steadily, as can be seen from the following data on the educational structure of workers' councils in 1970 compared with 1965:

with advanced professional education, 6 per cent as against 4 per cent in 1965;
with higher education, 4 per cent as against 2 per cent in 1965;
with intermediate professional education, 16 per cent as against 13 per cent in 1965;
highly qualified workers, 17 per cent as against 16 per cent in 1965.[3]

The structure of the workers' councils is better than the overall qualificational structure—a sign that collectives recognise the need for the highest possible qualifications, in both the social and professional sense, for successful worker management.

It is interesting that the number of so-called direct producers in self-management organs fell from 60 per cent in 1968 to 55 per cent in 1970.[4] At the same time, there was a 3 per cent increase in the number of those holding general administrative and specialised jobs, and a rise of 2 per cent in the number

3. In 1976—9·2 per cent of delegates to workers' councils had university degrees, 8·5 higher education (two-year colleges), 22·2 per cent secondary and 5·7 per cent primary schooling; 12·9 per cent were highly-skilled workers, 26·9 per cent skilled, 8·5 per cent semi-skilled, and 6·1 per cent unskilled.
4. By 1976, it had risen to 76 per cent.

F

of general executives in the management organs.[5] In trade enterprises, in particular, there is a high proportion of such staff —about 50 per cent—in the management bodies. The number of managing board members employed in direct production is 23 per cent lower than in workers' councils. In this body, members who work in specialised expert services and those in general executive posts outnumber the actual producers.

In the managing boards there is a constant danger of technocratic usurpation, particularly since Constitutional Amendment 25 now makes it possible for executive self-management organs to be formed in the way best suited to the day-to-day running of an enterprise. A growing trend is apparent for the managing boards (sometimes called business boards) to be treated as a kind of expert collegiate body.

Though Yugoslavia is still short of technical and expert personnel, the danger of technocracy does exist, and cannot be averted by institutional means.

Worker management and executive management

But there are other forms of usurpation, too: the self-management bodies may interfere in the technological-economic running of an enterprise, in the organisation of the production process, in other words, in the domain of the expert executive staff.

Both in theory and in practice there are frequent discussions of the cause of conflicts between worker-management and executive-management interests. In some research studies, sociologists have assessed this as extreme antagonism, as a struggle for the division of power and influence.

Other research workers at the Centre for Self-Management in Zagreb reached the conclusion that this phenomenon has three sources:

First, the interference in the domain of executive management derives, in their opinion, from the naïve misconception that self-management does away with the division of labour.

Second, in the first decade, the worker-managers' partici-

5. Meaning the technical services—the accounts department, clerical administration, sales department, and their chiefs.

pation in income distribution was little more than symbolic and they had no practical influence on investment and, hence, conditions of production. Self-management, therefore, existed but lacked vital elements, its economic basis. With the absence of true content, the self-management bodies occupied themselves with discussions and decisions concerning operative technical functions.

Third, some enterprises had a large number of insufficiently educated, mediocre, and even incapable executives, totally unfitted for modern production. These, in fact, undermined the importance of the organisational-technical functions. Frequently, the unqualified people holding executive posts were themselves the main opponents of modernisation and change. It was a question not simply of lack of formal qualifications, but of the dearth of creative ideas, of the backward, semi-handcraft concepts which go with this. In any case, the danger of the self-management bodies interfering in operative decision-making and the running of the technological process is most often present in enterprises where the executive management is professionally incompetent and lacks creative ideas.

Worker management and personal responsibility

Personal responsibility for failures! This is a topic often discussed in recent years, not only in economic organisations but by the general public. Two aspects of this have received attention: first, the nature of the responsibility of self-management organs for not carrying out tasks within their sphere of competence, and, second, the personal responsibility of directors and other leading executives for failures in professional, operational management. The debate has certainly not been academic in character, for the subject has been thrashed out by the public, press, trade unions, Socialist Alliance, Lawyers Association and others.

But for a number of reasons it is not a simple matter to settle, precisely and rationally, the question of the responsibility of self-management organs.

It is practicable to assert the legal responsibility of collective bodies, which under self-management socialism take the most important decisions. From the legal standpoint, only an individual, not collective, can be held responsible. This means that the workers' councils can be called to account only politically: legally they are immune, for a court can pass judgement only on a guilty person, in other words, an individual. We are left, then, with political responsibility: those who elect such a body may demand reports on its work, may call on it to account for its activity, and recall this body if necessary.

But is this enough? Is it effective from the standpoint of the general public interest?

More has been said and heard about personal responsibility of late because of a deterioration in the economic situation (illiquidity, inflation). Only the person who is to blame can be held responsible, but just who that is cannot often be readily ascertained. Losses may be the result of a general economic crisis, trends on the world market or ill-advised government measures. It is more often the case that enterprise directors and expert executives are, in fact, to blame, but are not obliged to bear any consequences: they take cover behind decisions of the workers' council, the scruples and misplaced humaneness of the environment, or the shortcomings and loopholes of the internal enterprise regulations which determine powers and responsibilities.

It is not all that unusual for the workers' council to pass decisions simply as a matter of form, everything having been decided, in fact, by the director and expert executives, for whose work the council merely provides a 'cover'. When the question of responsibility is raised, they can use the council as their excuse: 'This is within its competence; the workers' council passed the decision, and the director is obliged to carry it out.'

A large number of enterprises have their 'catalogue of duties', whereby competences in the various phases of decision-making: strategic, technological, operational and routine, are determined. The self-management bodies cannot be bypassed when it comes to fundamental decisions, but it would be incorrect to say that fundamental decisions are taken by the workers' council and all else is left to the executive management. All elements and all phases of decision-making can be linked up with worker management to the extent that the technical, technological and economic elements link up with the social—in particular phases of decision-making. If worker management were to be confined to major questions alone, if it merely charted future paths and left everything else to the professional management, it would be out of touch with life and the current interests of the working people.

In practice, the self-management organs are politically accountable for their actions, and the executives and workers personally accountable—and liable to disciplinary, financial and legal penalties.

The greater the independence of the executive staff, the greater their responsibility for their proposals and opinions. Those who have the task of drawing up proposals are answerable for professional and expert decisions. Thus, the proposers themselves are held responsible for decisions, while the director who allocates duties is responsible for their implementation.

Enterprises are at present considering whether to transfer as many executive, technical and specialist tasks as possible to individuals in the executive team or to regard the director as responsible for every decision passed by the self-management organs. For if he is not in agreement, the director is obliged to dispute a decision, to ensure respect of law, and to threaten his resignation in the event of the passing of a decision he regards as damaging to the collective or society.

In any case, most economic organisations are hurrying to get responsibilities precisely formulated.

The Zenica mining and metallurgical amalgamated enterprise (employing 23,000) ascertained that 70 per cent of its 17-million-dinar losses incurred in the first half of 1971 were the result of individual irresponsibility.[6]

The Vares iron mine (about 3,000 employed) decided that if losses were increased for three consecutive months the direct production managers should be replaced, and after six months of losses, the higher executive and director. This measure has not been adopted by other economic organisations, being regarded as totally one-sided. Losses may arise as a result of the general economic situation or for other objective reasons, and not only as a consequence of human fallibility.

According to *Politika*, August 21, 1971.

The statute of the Jesenice iron and steel works, employing 7,000, stipulates that workers who submit questions to the head office must receive an answer within 24 hours if the question relates to personal earnings, or 13 days if it concerns other matters. If they are not satisfied with the answer, they can appeal to the worker-management structure, and when all possibilities have been exhausted, they may resort to strike action. If workers should start a strike without resort to these various means of settling their complaints, they are personally accountable for their action and, according to the statute, may be discharged.

In the Bor amalgamated enterprise, a large copper mine with 11,500 employed, the regulations on production management lay down in detail the functions and responsibilities of every work post.

At the last Congress of Worker-managers, one speaker in a debate referred to a definition of social ownership in Yugoslavia as 'everybody's and nobody's', adding that some interpreted 'everybody's' as 'mine' when it was to their advantage, but 'nobody's' was the operative word when damage, losses and responsibility were in question.

Modern production and management demand strict division of labour and competences. Worker management or self-management means, in fact, that a man is responsible to himself. There is, one may say, a certain identity of subjects: he who suffers the losses and he who inflicts them are in principle the same subject—the organ of self-management. Such 'self-responsibility' calls for a high degree of personal and social awareness. Until that is attained, society must protect itself by modern organisation of work and the production process, and modern organisation of worker management, which implies detailed and precise division of powers, responsibilities, and other legal and political means.

In a society based on self-management, responsibility must not hide behind solidarity, humaneness, collective responsibility or imprecise demarcation of powers.

Self-management in Yugoslavia has not yet found all the modalities and answers in this domain.

Self-management in non-economic activities[7]

In order to achieve an integrated social system, an important aspect of self-management was its extension to other spheres not engaged in the production of goods such as universities, schools, hospitals, social insurance.

These organisations are gradually developing into autonomous self-managing institutions, thereby reducing state control over the life of society. If these institutions were not subject to public supervision, they might become strongholds of a decentralised bureaucracy.

Self-management in the domain of these so-called social activities involves not only those employed in these fields but also those who use their services, the worker engaged in production who provides the funds for them, and the general public.

In this sphere, income is not obtained through commerce. The price of services is not determined, or very little determined, by the law of supply and demand, and is usually not the real, economic price; the evaluation of work and services is rarely arrived at by mutual agreement. Because of state involvement in their financing and the character of these activities, the users of these services (education, health and social welfare, and others) are not in a position to know their price. In fact, most people think that they get them free.

Two questions are uppermost when considering self-management in these fields:

First, those employed in social activities have very little influence when it comes to determining society's need for their services or on the allocating of resources, but they are obliged to undertake all the tasks society sets them, sometimes regardless of the size of the funds allocated them.

Second, the producers have little control over the funds they set aside for non-economic activities.

This raises the question of how to extend the control of enterprises and the general public over expenditure in non-

7. This term covers: education, health and social welfare, the arts, scientific institutions—the so-called primary social activities. It also includes: banks, insurance institutes, the public accountancy and auditing service, the lottery and activities financed by the budget—national defence, security, administration, judiciary, etc.

economic fields, of how to make it dependent on economic trends.

The purpose of self-management in the non-economic activities is to ensure that the part of the national income set aside to finance them does not become 'alienated' from those who created it, that the producers and other users of social services can exert an influence on the spending of this part of the surplus product. Self-management in this sphere is intended to put into practice Marx's axiom: 'What the producer loses as a private individual he gains directly or indirectly as a member of society.'[8]

Self-management 'thinking' about the non-economic activities has mostly concerned itself with the question of how to free them as much as possible from dependence on the budget. From the self-management standpoint, freedom in the actual distribution of budgetary funds is not of great significance without influence over the sources of funds and without real links with the beneficiaries of these services.

In the efforts to achieve this, two conflicting demands have arisen: on the one hand, to halt the rise in social service expenditure, reduce the burden on the economy, and encourage modernisation of production, and, on the other, to improve the social services and their material position so as to meet the needs and level of economic development.

How can these activities be gradually freed from the administrative, bureaucratic approach?

In the first place, by the method of financing. A part of the income of social service organisations (about 30 per cent) comes from direct payments for services, and another part (about 60 per cent) from the social service funds of communes, republics and the Federation, and the budgets of socio-political institutions. A portion of these funds derives from contractual agreements with economic organisations, particularly in the case of vocational schools, engineering and economics faculties.

Payments received for services constitute 22 per cent of the receipts of the health service, about 14 per cent in schooling, 46 per cent in the arts, 58 per cent in social insurance,

8. Karl Marx: *Critique of the Gotha Programme.*

68 per cent in scientific activity, 2·8 per cent in public administration, and about 98 per cent in banks and insurance institutes.

In other words, the scope of budgetary financing is reduced, and increasingly confined to other fields: the administration, national defence and the judiciary. The budget is also used to aid communes and other political-territorial units if their own incomes are insufficient to cover essential needs.

Efforts to eke out modest resources by more efficient use have produced, in rare cases it is true, some examples of a certain commercialisation: it was considered almost a public scandal when a Belgrade school decided to lease out its yard to a circus over the summer; while another school rented its gymnasium as a warehouse during the vacation. In both cases, the motive was to earn supplementary cash to finance legitimate school expenses.

The resources given at present, particularly in the field of education, do not correspond to the 'real price' of services. The 1965 economic reform brought a certain redistribution of the national income in favour of personal consumption and the living standard. Personal incomes in most social activities are considerably lower than in the economy, despite the fact that

Table 2
Employment by educational categories, 1976

	Of the total employed	
	In the socially-owned sector of the economy	In non-economic activities
	%	%
Employees with advanced education	3·1	18·3
with higher education	2·5	16·8
with intermediate education	12·8	33·1
with primary education	7·4	10·1
Highly-qualified workers	7·3	2·1
Qualified workers	30·7	6·2
Semi-skilled workers	18·6	5·0
Unskilled workers	17·6	8·4

Source: Federal Statistical Institute

the qualificational structure is better in these activities. According to data of the Federal Institute for Statistics, at the beginning of 1972, schools, and health and cultural institutions ranked among the ten activities with the lowest personal incomes in the country.

Differences in personal incomes of those engaged in economic and non-economic activities with the same qualifications show that the primary social activities—education, health and social welfare, the arts—are lagging behind, and are thus not a sufficiently active factor in the society's overall growth.

On the other hand, personal incomes are much higher in the spheres of financing, insurance, and speculation, regardless of labour input. Lower earnings among teachers in recent years have given rise to complaints, protests, and even work stoppages.

The Federal Assembly intervened by passing a law curbing the unjustified growth of personal incomes in some economic and non-economic organisations. The trade unions undertook measures to ensure that the banks, insurance institutes and lottery, by means of so-called compacts, reached agreement on more equitable criteria for income distribution. The system of 'self-management compacts' has proved to be a successful device. The gap between the personal earnings of teachers and persons with similar qualifications employed in the economy has been reduced (in Slovenia from 25 per cent to 12 per cent in the past two years).

To ensure greater autonomy for the arts, science, education and health and greater influence on the part of beneficiaries, so-called unions for each branch have been organised in the communes, provinces and republics. The communal or republican assembly, for instance, sets aside a global sum with which these unions ensure the functioning of certain essential services. Room is left for negotiation with enterprises and others with an interest in the work of educational, health and social welfare institutions for the provision of additional funds to finance this.

Self-management in education

Schools have their councils composed of representatives of all those employed in them and of the pupils, or students in the case of universities. At the same time, there are territorial (communal and republican) education unions as the self-management associations of schools and universities. The self-management forums of these unions, their assemblies, are made up of elected representatives from two sources: from the schools themselves, and from the commune, republic or enterprises on their territory if these make a direct contribution to financing education. The union assembly elects its executive, mostly specialised, organs.

An innovation in this sphere is that their financing depends not only on the will of the administration but on compulsory contributions, i.e. taxes levied by law for a certain, longer, period of time.

The state organs have superiority and specialised powers.

The situation is somewhat different if a vocational school or faculty is founded by an economic organisation or has a direct contract with it. In such cases, the economic organisation which contributes funds has a say on the curriculum and type of qualifications the institution will provide, and has a certain number of representatives in the self-management organs.

Over the past ten years, new faculties and universities have been founded in leading industrial towns: the university in Nis (centre of the electronics industry, with a strong electrical engineering faculty, and a total of 10,239 students); engineering and economics faculties in Kragujevac (centre of the automobile industry, with 2,766 students); the technology faculty in Bor (a large copper mining centre, with 693 students); the university in Rijeka (shipbuilding centre, with 4,487 students); the universities in Sarajevo (23,306 students) and Novi Sad (13,669 students).

A direct tie-up between the economy and education is important for several reasons:

—It marks the start of the direct linking of productive and non-productive work.

—It corrects illegal territorial and financial distribution of schools and universities. Previously, universities were confined to the large administrative centres of Belgrade, Zagreb and Ljubljana.[9] Today, the policy of personnel training is more

9. Now 60 per cent of university-level institutions are located in the republican and provisional capitals, and the rest in 20 other towns.

closely tied in with the economic development programme. By 1985, the number of technical and scientific personnel should have increased tenfold, but to attain the present level of Western Europe, the results of their work would have to be thirty times greater.

—The more logical regional distribution is rapidly improving the social structure of the student body. Whereas students from families of manual workers make up only 13 per cent[10] of the 250,000 students at the eight Yugoslav universities taken together, they form from 22 per cent (Kragujevac) to 33 per cent (Nis) of the student body at newly-opened universities and faculties.

10. By 1976, the figure had risen to one third of the total enrolment.

Chapter 6

Income Distribution

Between politics and economics
In his book *Worker Management* published in Paris, Daniel
Chauvey states the view that the following four principles are
vital for worker management:

—the abolition of wage-labour relations;
—the organisation of work in enterprises on the principles
 of direct democracy and free discussion;
—a management committee elected by the workers;
—the removal of authoritarian bureaucracy in the enterprise.

What he says is true, but he has not said everything. What
is missing is perhaps the most important—a say in deciding
on the distribution of the surplus product.

No hard and fast line can be drawn, as people used to think,
between politics and economics. The struggle to free man
from bureaucracy and alienation, to build a modern democracy,
cannot be confined to the political field; it must be waged on
the economic and social fronts as well.

Yugoslav experience over the past twenty years shows that
worker management would have been regarded by the producers simply as a kind of formal democracy, had it not been
for the changes aimed at strengthening the material basis of
self-management.

What does this, in fact, mean?

A society does not spend every year the total value that it
has created, but invests some part of it in maintaining and
expanding the productive forces of society. This applies equally
to a completely centralised economy, to one based on self-
management, and to the capitalist system. The question is only

who gets this surplus product and who decides what is to be done with it. From the self-management standpoint, Yugoslavia's greatest dilemma was just this: who was going to control that part of the workers' earnings taken from them in order to expand the productive forces of society or maintain those who perform socially-useful but non-productive jobs? Should it be the state and its apparatus, some other political 'representative' of society, outside the enterprise and without the participation of the working man, or should it be that man himself?

The Yugoslav answer is that it should be, to the greatest possible extent, the working man. What bourgeois political democracy, based on private ownership of the means of production, was to the early stages of capitalism, self-management, according to the Yugoslav concept of democracy, is to socialism—a form in which the producer not only receives his personal earnings but controls the major part of income, thereby being in a position to influence directly his living and working conditions.

The state must not become an independent power above society and the working people, but their servant engaged in the task of the overall co-ordination and guidance of development.

The material interest of the working man, which comes to the fore through self-management, provides an incentive stronger than any other form and relationship among people. The worker has every reason to take an interest in the production process as well, for higher productivity means the raising of his personal income and that of society as a whole.

Who 'owns' the means of production?

The workers and their collectives are not the owners of the means of production they operate, nor can they become so. These means are the property of society (socially-owned), 'nobody's and everybody's' as the popular saying goes. Thus, they belong neither to the state nor to a group.

The economic function of the producers has been described by some sociologists in Yugoslavia as a specific type of undertaking—a 'collective undertaking'. The members of a working collective put in their labour, combining it with the means of production, which are public property, to produce a certain result: the income. They therefore bear the risk and gain the right to allocate the income for personal earnings and funds, appoint the executive personnel, and elect organs of management. But this interpretation is not really adequate.

Though social ownership predominates in Yugoslavia, there are also various forms of private ownership, particularly in agriculture. The forms of social ownership vary too, depending on a number of economic and legal relationships which are regulated not only by the Constitution, but also by agreements and contracts between enterprises.

Marxists have always been in agreement that the transfer of means of production from private to public ownership is essential for the attainment of revolutionary aims. The experience gained by socialist societies gives a warning, however, that this transfer in itself does not put an end to all forms of exploitation and alienation, nor does it abolish all the conditions and opportunities for manipulating the working class.

The viewing of socialist relations as the relationship between state and worker instead of private employer and worker is a form of anachronism and conservatism in socialist theory and practice. In this practice, and in theory as well, the state, economic and other types of administrative apparatus enjoy a high degree of independence, and political power, with which the Communist Party and its apparatus becomes identified. In time, these circumstances lead to the deformation of the ideological and political role of revolutionary organisations and their transformation into tools of power and government.

It was for these reasons that changes in the direction of self-management began to be considered in Yugoslavia.

In this country, as elsewhere, after the war the concept of social ownership was identical with the concept of state ownership. The state was the revolutionary expression of the interests of the working class. Though we were strongly influenced by this outdated theory and practice, the reason was not ideological prejudice but practical necessity. Everything was achieved by the power of the state: nationalisation, the reconstruction of the country, centralisation of resources, investment and planning.

Increasingly, self-management began to impose its own logic. It soon became evident that the social power of the working class depended on who held the economic power, who was to decide on income distribution, who was to manage the so-called socially-owned capital. The 1971 constitutional amendments provided for greater decentralisation, so as to extend still further the right of all to participate in government—both the working people and the socio-political communities.

In the self-management system, the worker is not a minor shareholder, as is sometimes asserted abroad, nor a group owner; neither does the state assume an ownership role on behalf of society and the working class.

All the same, as long as there is appropriation, there must also be ownership. The socio-historical purpose of self-management is to make appropriation on the basis of labour the sole type of appropriation. The worker should be freed from the hired-labour relationship towards any owner of capital, even if it be the state. However, this appropriation must be carried out not anarchically, but in accordance with the equal rights of other workers, in the spirit of working-class solidarity.

Social ownership in Yugoslavia is not a state monopoly, nor a monopoly of the technocracy, nor group ownership of the workers employed in a factory. Social ownership is a whole series of relationships—economic, political and legal—among people who make use of the common means of production. These means are the condition for their associated labour. They have equal rights and responsibilities in using these means, but they are not collective owners of them. The worker enjoys his right to a share in the income and his right to a say in the distribution of income on the basis of his work and not on the basis of some imaginary ownership right. But it is not only his share of the income—his personal earnings—that belongs to the worker. If everything else—accumulated capital—were not his, too, he would still be a hired labourer getting just a price for his work, and having no influence over the fate of the remaining part of the income. Concentration and centralisation are necessary in a self-managing society as well, but under the control of the worker-managers. No state institution or economic organisation in which socially-owned capital is centralised can use it as though this capital were its own property. Those who create capital must have a say in and control over its utilisation; these centres must be economically and politically responsible to every work organisation and worker concerned.

The Yugoslav system gives rise not only to socialist socio-economic relations, but also to forms of the previous capitalist and state-ownership systems, however much these may be considered superseded. Various forms of alienation and bureaucratic centralism, even within a single enterprise, the appropriation of super-profit, the formation of independent capital (for instance in foreign and internal trade organisations) unconnected with production and the enterprise's own business activity—all this shows that the movement and distribution of socially-owned capital is still not sufficiently under the control of those who created it.

In fact, two systems of managing income and socially-owned resources are confused in this country: one, the more prevalent, in direct production, in which the worker for the most part can exert control; the other, outside the sphere of production, in which self-management control is rather limited. The recent constitutional amendments have paved the way for more effective and fuller control over the distribution and movement of capital by those who have created it.

The right to self-management is not based on 'ownership' of the means of production, but on work and the fruits of labour.

'From each according to his abilities,
to each according to his labour'
The socialist principle—'From each according to his abilities to each according to his labour'—is not easy to put into practice. How can the real effects and results of work be recognised and measured? For the past decade, Yugoslavs have been trying to achieve objectivity and equity in this domain. In the first place—from each according to his abilities? This principle was degraded by certain old-fashioned concepts of 'experts' on the one hand, and 'the labour force' on the other, in which formal qualifications and degrees loomed larger than actual results, and position carried even more weight than qualifi-

G

cations. It was not unusual to find people holding posts of responsibility for which they had neither formal nor real qualifications.

Today, efforts are made, above all, to evaluate work and output, so that remuneration can be based primarily on this, and not on formal qualification. As a rule, there is a points system which takes into account results, working conditions, qualifications and experience. The general system of distribution in the country links individual incomes with productivity.

Sole consideration of position and length of service usually met with the disapproval of young people, most of them with professional qualifications, who were not paid according to their contribution and found promotion to responsible posts slow in coming. One of the main slogans of the youth movement in recent years has been: 'Let the most capable compete for every post'. Before the last elections for the republican and Federal Assembly, many posters urged us to 'Elect the Best'! One young wit extended this slogan to read: 'Elect the best, if they are candidates'. This was a justified implied criticism at that time, a protest against the reserve that was noticeable with regard to young people and experts.

The possibility of waste and prodigality

The independence of each enterprise and institution is ensured by the financial resources that it acquires as a result of its work. Each economic enterprise has a completely free hand in planning production and marketing at home and abroad. It is the right of the employed in every enterprise to decide, quite independently, how they are going to distribute the income[1] between the fund for personal earnings and the business funds, and how they are going to divide up the personal earnings fund according to results of work. Similar independence is enjoyed by all institutions for education, science, health and social welfare, though they are partially restricted by the budgetary financing previously described.

The principle of remuneration in accordance with work performed applies to members of work organisations, among

1. The income is what is left to the enterprise after production and capital depreciation costs and taxes have been deducted.

the parts of amalgamated enterprises, in the relationship between society and the working organisations, in inter-republican relations, and in obligations towards the Federation. Deviations from this principle can be made only by agreement, as a matter of solidarity and understanding of common needs, and under no circumstances by state compulsion.

The sole exceptions, therefore, consist of various forms of social assistance and solidarity.

The yardstick for income is individual output, the concrete value which is created by work. But since in a market economy (or socialist commodity production, as the Yugoslavs term it) the work of individuals attains 'social recognition' only on the market, when it is sold in the form of goods or services, it is not certain that the same amount of labour input will always be equally evaluated.

If enterprises are free to distribute their income as they wish between funds and personal earnings, is there not a danger—it will be asked—of economic organisations allocating it all on earnings i.e. eating the whole cake? This possibility, and danger, does exist.

There is certainly a risk of the workers ignoring expert advice or not understanding it sufficiently and deciding to allocate an unjustifiably high proportion of the income for earnings at the expense of investment. There are several ways of preventing this, however: 1) the influential position of the experts in the enterprise; 2) the political influence exerted by the trade union and League of Communists; 3) the work units may exercise control from below if distribution is not in line with the enterprise's prospects and if the expert services demand higher personal incomes to the detriment of investment.

In this connection, some interesting results were produced by a research study covering several years (1962–1966) and all economic organisations in the socialist sector.[2] In only three enterprises had there been no significant allocation of resources to funds, and in only five enterprises did the total personal earnings exceed the net income (and that only in some of the years covered). The majority of work organisations set aside

2. M. Korać: *Analysis of the Economic Position of Economic Groupings ... 1962–66*, Economics Institute, Zagreb, 1968.

about 30 per cent of their income for funds. Study of income distribution in enterprises showed that the economic branches with above-average personal earnings set aside a smaller percentage for earnings and a larger percentage for funds, while those economic branches in which personal earnings were below the Yugoslav average allocated a higher percentage for earnings, and less for funds.

The explanation is that those collectives that have higher incomes earmark more for funds so that personal earnings will be even higher in the future. As can be seen, this system of distribution functions rationally according to its own logic.

It is conceivable that economic enterprises which have high incomes might divide the lot as personal earnings.

Two factors, however, lessen the likelihood of such prodigality. In the first place, competition. In a competitive economy, capital has to be reinvested so as to expand and modernise production and keep up with home and foreign rivals on the market.

The other factor is the pressure of public opinion, and particularly of the trade unions. This has already been brought to bear, with the desired effect, in various economic organisations and branches: in electric power production, foreign trade organisations, banks and business associations, for example. Both the trade unions and the public (the press, public meetings) described such distribution as a 'deformation' and unjust. This was followed by administrative and political intervention—a wage freeze, the blocking of funds, and so on. An unwritten rule lays down the limits to which personal incomes can rise. If this limit is exceeded, various social sanctions come into operation: public criticism, political responsibility, so-called social compacts on the upper and lower limits of personal incomes in a particular economic branch, commune, or larger territorial unit, and, finally, financial and administrative measures.

This is provided for in the constitutional amendments and carries as much weight as a law. Some organisations with high incomes from somewhat dubious sources hasten to allocate a large proportion to funds, so as to avert public criticism.

The workers' say on investments

Workers decide on investments in their factory, but, it may be asked, what say can they have on national investments i.e. in the republics and Federation?

The 1965 reform favoured the enterprise as the rational unit for investment-making. Almost 60 per cent of an enterprise's income is now left to it to dispose of as it thinks fit. The result of this increased financial responsibility and authority of the enterprise is twofold. First, it has greater control over distribution (among personal earnings, investments, and social services and welfare); second, it has greater rights as regards the use of investment funds. The strengthening of the economic basis of self-management was a political as well as an economic decision.

The reform redistributed the national income so as to leave a larger share at the disposal of the work organisations.

In the early years, up to 1957, the so-called profit, which served as an incentive and was divided up within the enterprises, was a negligible amount—in 1955 only 5 per cent in excess of average earnings.

The transfer to the system of income rapidly expanded the material base of self-management. The workers' influence on business policy, and hence on the conditions of their work, thus became far greater, this giving a fresh impetus to production and the development of self-management.

Until self-management was introduced, the level and distribution of the fund for personal earnings were restricted. The situation gradually changed during the first decade, so that by 1959, enterprises had about 42·8 per cent of the total income they earned at their disposal. The percentage has continued to rise, as Table 3 indicates.

The economic organisations' share of the income has risen since the 1965 reform, with a few oscillations, and was standing at about 60 per cent in 1970. The abolition of certain taxes in 1971 led to a further rise in the enterprises' share—to 61·9 per cent.[3]

A true picture of the influence of the direct producers on expanded production (investment) can be gained if we consider

3. In 1974, the share was 59·2 per cent, in 1975—58·2 per cent, and in 1976—56·3 per cent.

Table 3
Income distribution between the Community and Enterprises,
1959–1968.

Year	Share in %	
	Community	Enterprise
1959	57·2	42·8
1960	56·7	43·3
1961	49·7	50·3
1962	52·0	48·0
1963	51·7	48·3
1964	45·6	54·4
1965	41·3	58·7
1966	38·1	61·9
1967	39·2	60·8
1968	40·6	59·4

the part of the surplus product that is invested in expanded production. The total surplus product is not, of course, invested in fixed capital assets. Such investment declined in the 1964–1967 period. Fixed capital investments in the economy amounted to 21·7 per cent of the gross national product in 1964, 16·8 per cent in 1965, 16 per cent in 1966, rising to 21·1 per cent in 1967, 21·9 per cent in 1968, and 22·7 per cent in 1969.[4] It is still the case that relatively little is spent on modernisation and reconstruction. Of total investments in the socialist sector of the economy, reconstruction and modernisation accounted for about half in recent years, while one third went on new projects.

In the past few years, one of the main political preoccupations with respect to self-management has been to raise the economy's share of the national income, so that larger resources would be available for modernisation and to strengthen the economic basis of self-management. The increases have fluctuated and the level attained is still not satisfactory, so that this remains one of the fundamental questions which the recent constitutional amendments known as the workers' amendments should solve.

4. By 1976 it had reached 24·6 per cent.

Diagram IV
GENERAL SCHEME
OF ENTERPRISE INCOME DISTRIBUTION

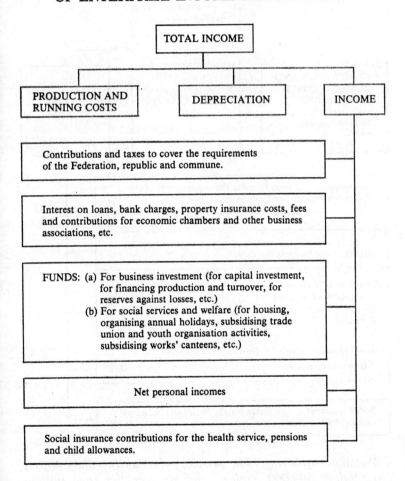

Diagram V
INCOME DISTRIBUTION IN THE 'POLITIKA' NEWSPAPER, PUBLISHING AND PRINTING ENTERPRISE

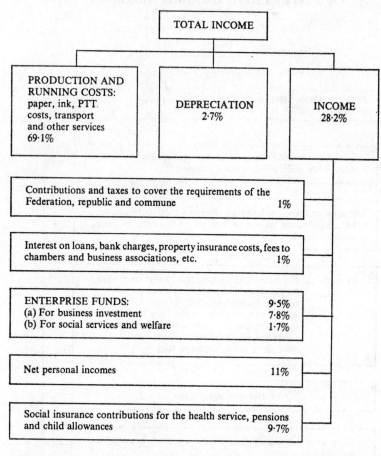

TOTAL INCOME

PRODUCTION AND RUNNING COSTS: paper, ink, PTT. costs, transport and other services 69·1%

DEPRECIATION 2·7%

INCOME 28·2%

Contributions and taxes to cover the requirements of the Federation, republic and commune   1%

Interest on loans, bank charges, property insurance costs, fees to chambers and business associations, etc.   1%

ENTERPRISE FUNDS: 9·5%
(a) For business investment   7·8%
(b) For social services and welfare   1·7%

Net personal incomes   11%

Social insurance contributions for the health service, pensions and child allowances   9·7%

Politika, *employing 1,700 people, publishes two daily papers (circulation: 500,000 copies), and six weeklies (one million copies). Its journalists number 320, while semi-skilled and un-skilled workers number only 250. It has its own printing house.*

Politika *has one of the highest capital formation rates in its branch, and even in the Belgrade economy as a whole.*

Income distribution within an enterprise

As already stated, the term 'income' is used for what is left to a work organisation after deduction of costs (apart from labour), depreciation and taxes from the total receipts.[5]

The income is, thus, the newly-created value that is produced.

An enterprise's obligations towards others are of two types: legal and contractual. First of all, it sets aside the money to meet contractual obligations—business costs and similar, and then the sums needed for personal earnings and part of its legal obligations (taxes and the like). It should be added that these latter are met only if the enterprise has any income (in the defined sense of the term); if not, it is freed from legal obligations.[6]

The ratio of funds to personal incomes is set by the enterprise plan, passed annually by the workers' council after consultations with all the work units.

Communal, republican and federal income tax is paid on the total sum set aside for personal earnings, this being used to finance non-economic activities: health, social insurance, education and assistance to underdeveloped regions of the country. This source ensures the minimum standard of operation in these spheres, additional resources and higher standards being secured on the basis of contracts and agreements between enterprises and services.

An enterprise is free to conduct its own independent credit policy, to borrow and lend through banks, even with foreign partners. Large enterprises have their own banks, which finance the major part of the enterprises' development.

The part that remains for personal earnings is further reduced by expenditures improving the enterprise's social amenities—sports facilities, day nurseries, annual holiday subsidies and so on, but only if this has been agreed upon by the collective and passed by the workers' council. Most enterprises establish a social services fund to cover such costs. This fund is exceptionally important since it is used to build housing, holiday hostels, canteens and other amenities that greatly cut the workers' costs of living. It provides all kinds of other

5. The Basic Law on Income Distribution in Work Organizations, 1968.
6. Art. 17 of the Basic Law.

assistance—from aid to new mothers to help with funeral expenses.

The institution of compacts, i.e. reaching agreement through joint consultation and discussion, has been introduced in order to achieve greater uniformity of personal incomes policy. Such compacts are of several types: between enterprises engaged in the same branch of activity; on a regional basis; and the so-called social compacts—agreements on a broader basis after consideration of suggestions put forward by socio-political organisations and representative bodies. On the basis of such compacts, written agreements may be drawn up or sanctions undertaken. An important role in this is played by the economic chambers, trade unions, and representative bodies.

Chapter 7

Socialism and Solidarity in Yugoslav Society

Sources of social differences

Yugoslavs live in a society that is still relatively poor. This is one of the basic causes of existing social inequalities, though not the only one. The differences in level of personal earnings, essential from both the economic and social standpoints, are more pronounced in regions that are economically and socially underdeveloped, and decrease as the level of development rises.

One of the major political concerns in Yugoslavia is how to eliminate differences that are not the result of work. At the time of student unrest in 1968, in Assembly debates, at the Second Congress of Worker-managers in 1971, at meetings of the trade unions and League of Communists, this has been an inevitable topic. Unjustified enrichment, mostly through speculation—the sale of building land near large towns, the sale of dwelling houses and flats, mediation in such transactions, possibly evasion of income tax—though not widespread or on a large scale, is morally and politically damaging out of all proportion to its scope. If a 'smart operator' manages to do better for himself by exploiting loopholes in the law than others who work in the socialist sector, then society may well be blamed for its carelessness and the poor organisation which hampers its attempts to prevent social deformations. This, then, is a cause of social differences, one of the 'burning topics' in Yugoslav political life.

There are, in fact, at least three sources of such differences: first, enterprises which enjoy a monopolistic position in the economy (electric power production and distribution, foreign trade, etc.); second, service enterprises that are not obliged to tie earnings to productivity, such as banks and institutions whose productivity is hard to evaluate: insurance institutes and the lottery are two examples; third, the sector of private initiative engaged in speculation—the buying and selling of flats, for instance.

In some environments, criticisms are voiced even of those differences in earnings that are the result of strict adherence to the principle of remuneration according to work performed—a type of egalitarianism that confuses economic and social aspects of the question.

Differences in internal distribution—Is the range between the highest and lowest personal incomes within one enterprise too great?

It is simultaneously too small and too great. The difference between the highest and lowest personal incomes in internal distribution (within the enterprise) is $4:1$[1]. This is the average for all enterprises throughout the country, and would seem to be a moderate range. It does not appear unfair that a top-ranking engineer or general director should earn four times more than an unskilled worker.

From the point of view of incentive, the internal income scale is an economic rather than a social problem. In the 1964–1970 period, the number of organisations with the lowest range—$1:1.9$ doubled; the number with a $1:2.9$ range rose by 50 per cent, while the number of organisations with a range of between $1:4.9$ or $1:5.9$ was halved. There is thus a clear trend towards diminution of differences.[2]

The difference between the earnings of unskilled workers and employees with university training was in the ratio of $1:2.7$ in 1966. Since then it has increased, but not much. In the period of administrative management of the economy, the ratio was $1:2$.

Thus, the range of personal earnings in Yugoslavia is not large. If anything, it could be considered as providing inadequate incentives.

In enterprises in the Soviet Union, according to official statistics, this range averages $1:4$; in France $1:5.9$ (1964); in

1. M. Korać *Analysis of the Economic Position of Economic Groupings (1962–66)*, Economics Institute, Zagreb.
2. Dr B. Sefer: *Social Growth in the Self-managing Society*, Belgrade 1971.

Denmark 1:4·3 (1965); in Italy 1:7 (1966); in Norway 1:2·4 (1964); in Sweden 1:3·2 (1963). These figures do not take into account the share of the profits that managers and executives may receive in capitalist countries.

According to data published in *Nouvel observateur*, the differences between the incomes of the poorest 10 per cent and richest 10 per cent of the population in various European countries was as follows: France 1:73·6; the Netherlands 1:26; West Germany 1:19·7; Denmark 1:15·9; Great Britain 1:14·6.

A large-scale enquiry carried out in 1968 showed that the ratio in Yugoslavia was 1:6·7.

There is no tendency for this scale to broaden: its annual fluctuations are negligible—from 0·01 to 0·03 points.

The coefficient of inequality in personal earnings ranges in Yugoslavia between 0·16 and 0·19, while in Great Britain it is 0·27, in the Netherlands 0·40, in West Germany 0·28, in France 0·35, and in Sweden 0·36.[3]

In Yugoslavia the best-paid categories of employed persons in the socialist sector are: commercial travellers and sales representatives working on a commission basis (an annual average of 100,000–120,000 dinars); enterprise directors (up to 100,000 dinars a year), national-team footballers (100,000–120,000 dinars), some engineers and architects (about 100,000 dinars), high-ranking officials, federal secretaries, federal and republican prime ministers and presidents of the federal and republican assemblies (from 60,000–90,000), pilots (about 80,000), university professors (from 60,000–80,000), high ranking personnel in the armed forces (60,000–90,000). These figures do not include fees for services performed outside the regular place of work and other supplementary receipts.

'*Millionaires*' *in Yugoslavia*—How are personal incomes and the total receipts of citizens taxed, and how many 'millionaires' are there in Yugoslavia?

In 1968, only 142,000 of nearly 4 million employed were liable to personal income tax. Progressive taxation began at 20,000 dinars (or two million old dinars). The majority of the 'millionaire' tax-payers had annual incomes of between 20,000 and 40,000 dinars, which average out at 170 to 340 dollars a

3. B. Sefer: *ibid.*

month. The richest earned about 80,000 dinars or in the region of 670 dollars a month before taxation. In the whole country there were only 223 persons in this income bracket!

Some individuals have extremely high incomes, far in excess of the highest personal earnings from a regular job, and this gives rise to considerable public resentment. The level and sources of these high incomes are often difficult to ascertain precisely. The secrecy of bank accounts is guaranteed.

A number of examples have come to light illustrating how excessive incomes can be gained, since they are clearly not derived from one individual's work. For the most part, they are the result of various types of speculation, skilful exploitation of legal loopholes, and violation of the law: a café-owner in Sarajevo ran a number of establishments registered under the names of various friends; a road haulage contractor in Zagreb registered every adult member of his family of nine as a truck owner and driver; several sharp individuals in Belgrade bought up cheaply buildings without vacant possession, counting on the fact that within a year or two they would be demolished according to the urban reconstruction plan, and their owners would receive compensation from the local authorities many times the amount they had paid; some take a cut from foreign business partners in return for signing a contract (this being extremely difficult to check). Private craftsmen often register their business and report their income for taxation in a poor commune where taxation is light, but actually live and work in Belgrade. A legal instance of high earnings—the most popular pop and folk-song singers receive enormous sums from recording companies for their exclusive services.

Personal income tax above 100,000 dinars a year runs at 70 per cent. Some persons get round the law by having their fees paid in the name of relatives, thereby 'spreading the load'.

The poor control carried out by the inspection and tax authorities is one of the reasons for the ineffectiveness of the public prosecutor and courts when it comes to starting proceedings for the confiscation of illegally acquired property and wealth.

The level of consumption— The living standard of the indi-

vidual is also affected by: size of the household, number of
employed in the household, and age structure of the household.

The level of consumption (spending) is lowest in farming
households and highest amongst those employed in the socialist
sector of the economy.

Differences in the level of personal consumption per family
member:

	1963	1968	1973
Farming households	100	100	100
Mixed households	135	133	124
Non-farming households	184	200	179
All households	144	153	143

The size of family and number of employed are factors with
a strong impact on the living standard. The average family
has four members; non-farming families average 3·4 members;
farming households 4·3; and mixed households 4·8 members.
In mixed households (those which derive their income partly
from farming and partly from other types of employment),
every fifth member is employed, while in non-farming households, every third member.

From this it is clear that the way to reduce differences lies
in creating greater opportunities for employment, particularly
for members of large families.

Differences arising from the position of particular branches
—The position of the various economic branches and the conditions under which they operate differ because some are better
equipped as regards capital assets than others, because of differences in the concentration of know-how and brains, because
of changing conditions on the home and foreign markets, or
because of differences in treatment arising from the country's
current economic policy. In consequence, there are differences,
too, in the level of income.

Personal earnings are 10 per cent above the national average
in the following branches: electric power production and distribution, oil production and refining, ship-building, design and
assembly services, air transport, trade, business associations,
financing and insurance. Those employed in these activities

number 450,000 or 13 per cent of the total employed population.

Personal incomes were 10 per cent below the national average in: the timber and wood manufacturing industry, textile industry, farming, mining, forestry, building, the railways, the hotel and catering trade and tourism, which employed 23 per cent of the total. With the exception of the railways, these branches have a lower organic structure of means of production, or face strong competition on home and foreign markets.

A similarly unfavourable position is occupied by almost all the non-economic sector with about 500,000 employed: education, health and social welfare, the civil service and social organisations.

Differences in pension levels are a further source of inequalities. Although pensions—retirement, family and invalid—are a form of worker solidarity, they are partly based, too, on the right acquired through previously invested labour, so-called dead labour. Pensions are not always raised in line with increases in personal earnings. Some enterprises, however, make provision in their statute for retired workers to use the enterprise's recreation centre, holiday hostel or canteen, and even to receive a certain percentage of supplementary pay (bonuses) if the enterprise finds itself with a surplus. For the success of an enterprise is founded not only on the work of those currently employed but on that of earlier generations, who often made sacrifices for their enterprise's future prosperity.

Regional differences, very marked in Yugoslavia, are another cause of social differences. Comparing Slovenia, where the living standard is close to that of advanced West European states, and the province of Kosovo, which is on a low level of development, we find that incomes are not the same even for persons with similar qualifications and performing the same work.

Social differences, therefore, are the outcome of uneven development, an uneven distribution of knowledge and availability of information, and varying experience in modern business management.

These differences, taken as a whole, are not great. According to some estimates,[4] only 18 per cent of the total personal incomes would need to be redistributed to attain perfect equality.

In a socialist system, unfortunately, the 'bourgeois law of distribution' still prevails, however—for unequal work, unequal pay. The goals of socialism cannot be achieved by simply issuing decrees; they are reached by lengthy efforts to develop the production forces, without which the free and full satisfaction of human needs would be an eternal Utopia.

The society is very sensitive to any distortions in the sphere of personal incomes, to differences which are not strictly based on work. Not long ago, criticisms were voiced of the salaries of political functionaries, whose work is hard to evaluate. In September 1971, it was decided in the Republic of Slovenia that such functionaries, in the Assembly, the trade unions, League of Communists, Socialist Alliance, youth organisation and so on, could not receive more than 6,000 dinars a month. This was an attempt to fix the pay of functionaries in relation to the average earnings of working people, on the model of the Paris Commune.

What particularly irks the public is that a certain number of people enjoy high incomes not on the basis of their work but through speculation: selling land, dwellings and cars, obtaining key money for vacating socially-owned flats, and taking advantage of various loopholes in the law. There are however, other abuses, such as taking a cut of trade transactions and other corrupt commercial practices, which were the subject of discussion in the Serbian and Macedonian parliaments in the autumn of 1971, and have lately come in for attack again.

Solidarity

It could be said that there are two criteria in Yugoslav society for satisfying human needs, which are more and more assuming equal importance:

—distribution according to work performed, and
—distribution according to equal rights—solidarity.

4. Dr B. Sefer: *Some Features of Global Trends in the Range of Personal Incomes 1961–1967*, Belgrade.

H

Solidarity in the field of production results—equating the value of highly-productive work and that marked by low productivity—is both harmful and impossible. Such 'solidarity' would simply penalise progress. It is pointless to ask pathetically how long the socialist system will continue to give rise to various contradictions and social differences. It will go on doing so long after our time. Some cannot reconcile socialism with a market economy, remuneration according to work performed with self-management and democratic development. It cannot be expected that a society in the process of such a profound transformation will be devoid of conflicts and contradictory features, the sort of society in which the early Church and Utopian socialists believed. Yugoslavs cannot proclaim, like Castro, that they are simultaneously building both socialism and communism, and that remuneration is to each according to his needs, not to his work.[5]

But if remuneration according to work were the only type of distribution, those enjoying the most favourable economic position would get further and further ahead. The system must be modified to a certain extent, so as to avoid the distortions inherent in a cash-commodity economy.

Social immobility would be inconceivable in a socialist society, and contrary to its ultimate goals. The vital and humane aims of socialism are: affirmation of the human personality and the creation of social security and wellbeing. Solidarity tends to diminish social differences without lessening the economic and social incentive that the system of self-management provides.

Rapid urbanisation of the population has caused many social problems—shortage of housing, schools and child-care institutions, for a start. The Constitution guarantees a minimum living standard and also lays down certain rights: to eight-year primary schooling, health protection, employment. In actual fact, these rights are not fully implemented in every case and equally enjoyed by all. The social welfare policy in Yugoslavia is thus of broader significance than the usual social protection, since it should correct defects and cover all matters related to living and working conditions—from the

5. *Le Monde*, March 19–20, 1970.

personal incomes policy to education and social welfare.[6] The work organisation is also a factor in this domain, since it concerns itself with the range of personal earnings, housing questions, vocational training, the creation of new jobs, direct assistance during the employees' working life and even afterwards.

Social security

Social security is provided, primarily, by the minimum living standard guarantee, security of employment, freedom in seeking employment, and assistance to enterprises that get into difficulties. Whether the market will recognise the value of the labour input cannot always be predicted, so that the society must guarantee a minimum living standard and social security.

A minimum personal income—If an enterprise is running at a loss, the workers have the guaranteed right to a personal income, regardless of the business results of their work organisation. The amount of the minimum personal income, which applies to all, is set by law, though the republics may raise or decrease this within given limits. Consequently, there are differences in the amount of the minimum personal income, its level depending on the economic development of the commune or republic and living costs in the area.

These incomes are paid out of the enterprise's reserve fund, and if this is inadequate, out of the joint reserves in the commune or republic.

The law guaranteeing a minimum personal income provides an essential degree of social security.

Besides the minimum, enterprises running at a loss may pay out personal incomes reduced by 5, 10 or 15 per cent. This was the case in over 1,000 enterprises with 318,000 workers in the first half of 1970. By the end of the year, however, the situation had improved and only 150 organisations with about

6. 41 per cent of the national income is set aside to finance various types of non-economic activity, and earmarked as follows: education 5·2 per cent, science 1·4 per cent, the arts 2 per cent, health service 5·7 per cent, social welfare 0·8 per cent, pensions 7·1 per cent, child allowances and child welfare 1·3 per cent, veterans' and invalids' welfare 0·8 per cent, and housing construction 7·9 per cent. (Federal Statistical Institute, 1970 figures).

30,000 employed were paying the minimum. Those who did so for more than three months numbered about 40, and employed only about 3,000 workers.[7]

What happens to enterprises in the red?—In the period of centralised administrative management of the economy, the losses of some enterprises were covered by the profits of others. The state even made provision for so-called planned losses, and served as a kind of reinsurance agency covering all differences and deficits.

In the self-management system, at the present time, the problem of enterprises operating at a loss is resolved by assistance, provisional receivership management, and finally, as a last resort, liquidation.

The first move, an alarm signal, is reduction to minimum personal incomes. This is followed by assistance aimed at putting the enterprise on its feet, perhaps a change in the production line or similar move. Banks give loans for this purpose, which the enterprise returns when it recovers. If there are prospects of the enterprise pulling through, its losses are covered by the reserves (communal, republican), from special funds, the money being repaid later. If none of this is possible, the enterprise is placed under provisional receivership management, and finally goes into liquidation.

Receivership management is decided upon by the communal assembly, whereupon the mandate of the self-management bodies is terminated and the director relieved of his duties. The management is taken over by a receiver or receivership committee. An enterprise can be placed under this type of management for a year at the most and on condition that it has 'severely harmed the public interest', it is unable to cover its losses from its own reserve fund, it lacks the resources to meet its debts for a period of six months, or it has not drawn up and submitted its annual financial report on time. Creditors whose claims amount to more than 70 per cent of all claims against an enterprise can also demand that receivership management be instituted. When this type of management is terminated, the president of the communal assembly invites

7. Data of the Yugoslav Public Accountancy and Auditing Service: *Information on the Business Results of Economic Organisations in 1970*, April 1971, Belgrade.

applications for the post of director and new elections for self-management bodies are held.

If an enterprise operates at a loss for two successive years, and it has proved impossible to put it on a sound basis, no recourse is left but liquidation.

The biggest problem in such cases is the future of those who lose their jobs. Earlier on, this was not given much consideration, and dissatisfaction in affected areas was considerable. In the past few years, however, other enterprises, the commune and republic have undertaken to find employment for those put out of work in this way.

All enterprises that are operating profitably allocate part of their income to the joint reserves to cover possible losses, for assistance to enterprises in difficulties, and for payment of minimum personal incomes. When it was found necessary to cut the number of employed in coal mines, for instance, a fund was set up to cover early retirement pensions, the creation of new jobs, retraining of young miners, and so on.

In the past few years, about 10 per cent of Yugoslav enterprises have been losing money, the major cause being the great changes in the economic structure following the 1965 reform. But organisations under provisional receivership management constitute a minor group: only 1·1 per cent of the total number of economic organisations with 1·2 per cent of the total labour force.[8]

Social welfare

If the economy and society did not recognise the needs of institutions, public services and enterprises whose activities are not profitable, there could be no talk of socialism, and self-management would lose its meaning.

Every employed Yugoslav and dependent family members are covered by social insurance, which means health protection and other services in kind and cash in the event of sickness, injury at work and elsewhere, invalidity, old age and death.

By law and contracts, social insurance has been extended to all categories of citizens, including those who are self-employed such as artists, craftsmen, lawyers and priests of all

8. *Bulletin of the Public Accountancy and Auditing Service of Yugoslavia,* April 1971.

religions. Since 1962, private farmers have also been partly covered by social insurance.

Social insurance benefits are financed from contributions paid by work organisations (enterprises and institutions) or the insured person himself. These contributions, for health insurance, pensions and child allowances, cannot exceed 19·5 per cent of personal income, their level being fixed by the assembly of insurance beneficiaries in each commune.

Each fund is autonomous. The beneficiaries, organised in social insurance unions in the commune, republic and Federation, themselves manage the social insurance funds.

Health insurance—Health insurance covers all employed persons, including the self-employed, and the dependent members of their families. Insured persons have the right to medical treatment, in hospital if necessary, medicaments, orthopaedic and other aids, and other services, including monetary remuneration for the duration of sickness, rehabilitation and preventive medical measures. The duration of health protection and treatment is unlimited.

Medical institutions make contracts with social insurance institutions fixing the price of medical services. A patient has the right to choose his physician and medical institution. Health insurance for farmers is incomplete, its scope depending on the level of their contributions to the health insurance fund. This insurance, too, is based on the principle of self-management by the beneficiaries—here, the farmers.

Pensions and invalid benefits—At present, there is one pensioner to every 2·5 Yugoslavs employed in production (excluding peasant farmers), which is probably the highest proportion in the world. Over the past ten years, the number of pensioners has risen by 11·5 per cent and the number of employed by only 3·8 per cent. In 1968, 8·8 per cent of the national income went on pensions and invalid benefits. In the same year, 12·6 per cent of male pensioners and 10·1 of female pensioners were under 50 years of age. There are more invalid pensioners than old age pensioners. War veteran pensioners numbered 256,000 at the end of 1968.

The insured acquire the right to a full pension after 40 years of work for men and 35 years of work for women, regardless of age. The right to a partial pension is acquired at the age of 60 (55 for women) after 20 years of work, or at 65, after 15 years of work. Those engaged in strenuous occupations with health hazards such as miners, certain types of building workers and pilots require fewer years of work for a pension (eight months are counted as twelve).

In the event of the death of an insured person, dependent family members have the right to a family pension, regardless of how long the insured had worked. A widow acquires the right to a pension from the moment of her husband's death if she has reached the age of 40 or has children under the age of 15. Children have the right to a family pension until they complete their schooling, though not after reaching the age of 26.

War invalids and the families of those who fought in the Liberation War (1941–1945) receive special treatment depending on the degree of invalidity and financial situation of the family. Of the million or so surviving participants in the Liberation War, over 600,000 live in towns, and about 400,000 in rural areas.

The welfare of women and children—Women, young people and children enjoy special protection to ensure their welfare. Pregnant women have the right to 105 days maternity leave, which may be extended for up to three years if the child's health so requires in the opinion of physicians. A pregnant woman or woman with a child under one year of age cannot be employed in night work or overtime. Women cannot be employed for physically strenuous work. Hospital services for childbirth are free, regardless of whether the mother is employed.

Young people under 18 cannot be employed on physically strenuous work which might harm their health, and are also protected from night work and overtime. More than 150,000 apprentices in industry under 18 benefited by this protection in 1970.

Child welfare is ensured in various ways. Child allowances, their amount determined by the republics independently, are paid to families in which the *per capita* monthly income does not exceed 500 dinars. The number of child-care institutions (day nurseries, kindergartens, and other special institutions) is now over 2,000.

The right to rest and holidays—Workers are guaranteed a 42-hour working week. All employed persons have the right to a paid annual holiday after 11 months of employment. The length of this holiday—from 14 to 30 working days—depends on length of employment and type of work. In exceptional cases, annual leave may be 60 days.

Unemployment assistance and the right to work—When temporarily unemployed, a worker has the right to unemployment benefits if he has worked continuously for at least one year or for 18 months within the past two years. Temporarily employed persons have the right to health insurance and family allowances. The employment service gives professional advice and help with vocational training, since a large proportion of those seeking jobs have no qualifications whatsoever (in 1969, about 210,000 of the 259,000 workers seeking employment were unskilled).

In addition, mention should be made of free eight-year primary education for all, and scholarships, credits, restaurants and hostels for students and secondary school pupils, all of which is designed to lessen as far as possible the inequalities in educational opportunities.

Chapter 8

The Self-Governing Commune

A discussion of the commune should begin from the generally accepted principle that democratic participation is impossible if it is not achieved at the base. This applies equally to the enterprise and to local government. And for the citizen to enter into self-managing democracy on the broadest social and national scale, it is essential that the commune be the source and starting point of all actions, elections, legislative initiatives, and delegation to representative organs of the province, republic and Federation.

The mere transfer of powers to elected representatives—the so-called assenting democracy, centralism designed to preserve national unity—can become just a ritual by means of which the vital interests of citizens are alienated and their will manipulated. As against this, there is participating democracy—the self-governing commune in which the function of the citizen is not simply to vote, to criticise, to dispute or resist something, but to play a part in the whole process of decision-making.

The evolution of the Yugoslav commune

As early as 1941, the first regional people's liberation committees were formed in Serbia and Slovenia.

From September 1941 onwards, there was a large area of liberated territory in occupied Serbia incorporating a dozen towns and with about one million inhabitants. In this free territory, in addition to local committees, the Main People's Liberation Committee of Serbia was formed in Uzice[1] (hence the name 'Uzice Republic' given to this territory). This was the first revolutionary government in Serbia in the course of

1. A town in Serbia with about 8,000 inhabitants on the eve of the war.

the Second World War 'where we laid the first foundations of what we have today' as President Tito said in 1959.

The same idea was expressed in 1966 by Kardelj, who, like Tito, himself played a part in the formation of the first democratic organs of popular government: 'It can be said that in Uzice the concrete foundations were laid for the construction of our whole future political system.'

The work of the People's Liberation Committee in Uzice in 1941 was many-sided:

—the feeding of Partisan armed units was organised (also supplying of the front with footwear, clothing, arms and ammunition);

—industrial and handcraft production was encouraged (in the town Partisan factories of arms and ammunition, textiles and leather, and a printing press were operating);

—provision was made for 3,500 destitute persons, mostly refugees from the occupiers;

—the price of wheat and bread was fixed, reserves of goods essential for the population were bought up, a moratorium on all debts was proclaimed, a decision that no rents were to be paid for the months of October and November was passed, etc.

The postwar period—The first law on people's committees—in the commune, district and regions—passed in 1946 was, in fact, centralistic. The national income in 1947 was but a quarter of the 1970 national income. The indispensable concentration of resources could be most easily ensured by centralisation, which at that time was also the best guarantee of efficiency and a socialist orientation. All the same, the 1946 Law on People's Committees did retain some of the traditions from the Liberation War and was, in essence, based on democratic principles.

Decentralisation began in 1952 with the third Law on People's Committees, which introduced self-government into communal affairs (following the introduction of self-management in enterprises in 1950). This decentralisation was carried out in two directions: certain powers were transferred from the central organs to the commune, and economic organisations gained greater independence in respect of the commune.

But it was the 1963 Constitution that brought more radical changes. Article 73 provided for citizens' self-government in the commune, which was accorded certain autonomous rights and freedom of action.

The basic idea was to increase the independence of the commune both economically and politically by cutting the number and administration of communes, thereby strengthening their economic power.

The territorial division in 1946 was into 11,556 local committees, 407 districts, 77 towns with district status, 6 towns with regional status and 58 regions: all together five types of territorial organisation with 12,000 units. In 1952 there were 3,800 communes, and in 1970 only 500 communes, with an average of 55 settlements on 500 square kilometres. This greatly lightened the burden imposed by a massive administration, and one that was insufficiently expert. A local community covering a broader area with a degree of economic and cultural unity would more easily fulfil its functions.

The achievements of the Paris Commune have been a source of inspiration to all revolutionary movements since, including Yugoslav self-management (both worker management in the work organisation and self-government in other spheres). Even at that time, the question of 'abolition of the state to achieve freedom' was raised; during the short life of the Commune the unbreakable link between democracy and the building of socialism already became apparent. In its published programme, the *Declaration to the French People*, in 1871, the following idea attracts attention:

'The permanent right of citizens to have a hand in communal affairs through the free expression of their ideas and free defence of their interests . . .'

This freedom is attained through self-government, which, according to the Commune *Declaration*, is 'the inherent right of the Commune.'

Communal freedoms do not mean the destruction of national unity. Contrary to the Proudhonist concept of the commune as the antithesis of the state, the sound sense of the Paris communards and the logic of events set them on the path of a new unity which constitutes a new solution of the relationship between centralism and autonomy, order and anarchy, necessity and freedom.

Self-government in the commune
—more than autonomy

In the Yugoslav commune, self-government means more than just autonomy. The commune is the basis from which spring all other organs of larger territorial units, including the federal. In fact, the entire socio-political structure of Yugoslavia is founded on the basic structure of self-government in the commune. The citizens directly elect deputies to the communal assembly, and these elect deputies to the republican and Federal Assembly, except for the so-called political chambers (the republican chambers and Federal Chamber), whose deputies are also elected by direct general suffrage.

Experience has shown that communal delegation is the best way of ensuring the cohesion and unity of the system, and guarantees the influence of the base on the summit. The Federal Assembly is, thus, not only the supreme organ of government, but also the supreme organ of social self-government and worker management, from which it is directly derived through the commune. Or rather, that is what it must become—for this has not yet been fully achieved—if we want self-government to permeate the entire society.

The commune's statute lays down the composition, organisation, type and number of communal organs, their powers and interrelationships. It determines the number of chambers of the communal assembly and their size, tasks, rights, method of work, types of commission and administrative organs.

The commune's triple role

The listing of institutional arrangements, though perhaps rather wearying for the reader, seems unavoidable if one wishes to provide any kind of insight into the system.

To put it briefly, the commune has a triple role:

—it is an instrument of government, the part of a unified system which conducts affairs on the local level;

—it sees to the provision of public utilities and services (water, electricity, drainage, local trade, etc.);

—it links up the various self-government and worker-management organs and interests, from the working man, the economic organisation and social organisations to the republic and Federation, harmonising conflicting interests if they occur.

This last is in many ways a new self-government function of the commune and its most important.

Economic functions—The commune engages in a range of economic activities for the public benefit on its territory: supplying electricity and water, organising public transport, creating favourable conditions for the working population in housing, retail supplies, health protection, vocational training and so forth.

It co-ordinates economic activity on its territory through the communal plan of social and economic development, which is in fact a means of bringing into line and dovetailing the activities of all organisations and bodies in the commune, particularly in the economic sphere. It predicts economic development on the basis of the plans of the individual enterprises, concerns itself with raising productivity, establishes a balance between material production and public services, and harmonises all this with the actual needs of the community.

Responsibility for the living standard—The commune organises public services to meet the social and cultural needs of its citizens. In the field of housing, it organises and channels housing construction, sees to the maintenance and use of dwelling houses, and controls the use of land for house building. It also promotes public utilities (water and electricity supply, transport, public sanitation, urban planning), ensures the provision of free primary schooling and creates conditions for secondary schooling and vocational training.

General political function—Citizens exercise all their basic freedom and rights in the commune: the right to self-government, the right to vote, the right to work, freedom of expression and belief, the right to free expression of one's nationality and use of one's language, freedom of the press and of scientific and cultural creativity, religious freedom, the right to health protection, the special rights of mothers and children—in short, all the basic rights laid down in the Constitution.

Forms of direct democracy

Local communities—The increase in the size of communes created a growing gap between the various villages (in rural communes) or neighbourhoods (in urban communes) and the organs of the communal assembly and their policy. It was found essential to form a smaller unit—local communities, which the Constitution defines as the most direct form of territorial-political democracy. They have no governing function nor professional administrative apparatus, so that they are truly self-governing communities.

Up to the end of 1969, 8,936 local communities had been formed as territorial units—an average of one to every two or three settlements (in rural areas).

It is in this basic territorial unit that specific interests meet up and the working people get together to settle many of their shared problems.

Voluntary contributions of citizens are the only source of financing for local communities. In order to encourage people to dig into their own pockets to finance common local needs such as roads, water mains and electricity supply, some communes partly or fully waive taxes in local communities which have undertaken to build some sizable project at their own expense.

In the poor commune of Prijedor (Bosnia-Herzegovina), for instance, where the *per capita* income is well below the Yugoslav average and the capital accumulation level of the economy is low, voluntary contributions and voluntary loans by the inhabitants have financed the construction of about 60 per cent of all projects built on its territory over the past five years.

Meetings of voters—Meetings of voters are one of the forms of direct participation in decision-making on social and political affairs. They take the initiative in putting forward various proposals and exercise a kind of control over the activity of communal representatives. The decisions reached by meetings of voters determine the decisions of government bodies on matters such as the collecting of voluntary contributions, the founding of new communes, the abolition or integration of existing communes or the changing of the seat of the communal administration.

Some decisions cannot be taken without the approval of the meetings of voters: demarcation of a commune's territory; adoption of the commune's statute, economic and social development plan, budget, and urban plan; and decisions relating to the financial obligations of citizens like taxes and voluntary contributions.

In practice, the meetings of voters have served more often as a rubber stamp, confirming proposals and decisions submitted to them, than as a place where initiative can be shown and direct influence on decision-making exerted. In towns, especially, the significance and prestige of voters' meetings has begun to decline, for they bear more similarity to parliamentary political life than to self-managing democracy. Moreover, the habits and living standard of the town dweller are such, that he does not take kindly to anything that impinges on his leisure time, particularly if it is minor matters that are to be discussed. In consequence, the percentage of citizens attending voters' meetings is falling. In Bosnia-Herzegovina, for instance, it dropped from 20·1 per cent in 1963 to 12·8 per cent in 1969.

Neither the commune, nor the local community, nor the meeting of voters has proved itself an ideal community where the citizens are just waiting to participate in decision-making on public affairs, confronted by a multitude of different proposals on which they have simply to make up their minds.

There is every indication that the further building of democracy on this terrain will be sounder if citizens, each of whom have certain interests and concerns, send their delegates to all those bodies where decisions on such questions are taken. Some large communes, such as the industrial town of Nis, which also includes extensive surrounding farm land, propose that the communal assembly should consist of three councils or chambers: (a) the local communities council (which would, in fact, be an extension of direct self-government from the local communities to the communal assembly); (b) the economic council, with representatives of the socially-owned sector of the economy; (c) the agricultural council, to which the private farmers would send their delegates to settle problems of vital interest to them. In the past, farmers have had little representation in the economic council of the commune, so that their interests and views have not always been adequately put forward.

Communities of interest—In one commune or several together, according to need, so-called communities of interest are formed, usually for the spheres of education, health and social insurance. Amendment 21 of the Constitution lays down that such communities should consist of the workers in public service organisations and the users of their services, who determine their mutual relations by agreement and contract.

This means that the composition and character of these communities will differ, depending on their purposes and the type of activity involved. The idea behind this kind of organisation is to enable those who use various services to exert some influence on their operation and control their expenditure.

Until now, every tax-payer, like it or not, has had to pay a certain percentage for the health and education services. It is proposed, however, that this percentage should not be fixed by law, but as a result of agreement reached between the beneficiaries (i.e. the tax-payers) and the providers of these services, though the republican assembly would, of course, set the minimum which work organisations are obliged to allocate for public service requirements.

Regional links—The regional linking of communes has also shown itself to be necessary, since there are many problems that are neither republican nor federal in character, and yet exceed the financial resources of a single commune. This led to the setting up of inter-communal councils, meetings of a certain number of delegates from each commune who may be permanent for the whole term of office of a communal assembly, or changed periodically. To save money and improve the quality of the service, neighbouring communes may agree to set up joint administrative services: an employment bureau, educational-pedagogical institute, prices institute, historical archives, joint social insurance, internal affairs service (police force), public prosecutor's office, building inspection service, unions for financing education and the arts, and so forth.

Some people in Yugoslavia believe that the future of a self-governing society lies in integration according to branches of activity and economic fields, and not according to the criterion of the community where people live and satisfy their needs. If this path were to be followed, it would very soon lead to technocracy and the dehumanisation of human relations, for people do not wish to live shut up in a particular sphere of social activity, as in a caste or barracks. The development of modern technology will gradually transform productive work itself into a kind of public service, for technology will be highly integrated and automated. The centre of gravity of self-management will shift from material production to the broader sphere of social life, primarily to the local community and the commune. The future of self-management lies in this direction.

In recent years, local communities, communes and work organisations have often got together and, on the principle of solidarity, agreed to provide the resources necessary to satisfy various local requirements. Such agreements (usually termed 'social compacts') were further encouraged by Constitutional Amendments 22 and 23 approved in the summer of 1971.

Work organisations are sometimes closed in upon themselves and try to settle as many problems relating to their workers' living standard as they possibly can. But since work organisations do not all have equal possibilities of doing this (some are much more prosperous than others), this trend could have a divisive effect on society and the working people. It was to avoid this that the whole solidarity and compact movement came into existence.

An example of this approach is the commune of Osijek (Croatia), which on a voluntary basis, through social compacts of enterprises and citizens, managed to extend the water mains, modernise the PTT services and trade network, build roads, and achieve uniform standards in schooling, child care and other services.

The commune was not in a position to carry out completely its task of providing all children with free eight-year primary education of a satisfactory standard. Voluntary contributions were collected and 17 modernly-equipped schools were obtained by building new or adapting existing premises. Now children in this commune could go to school in only two shifts instead of three or more, and the problem of primary schools was partially solved.

A pedagogical standard for elementary education was then drafted, with three variants: one requiring a levy from personal incomes of 3·6 per cent, another—3·8 per cent, and the third—4·26 per cent. A debate on this was organised in one hundred work organisations and all local communities. About 86 per cent of work organisations and the majority of citizens expressed themselves in favour of the third, which provided for:

I

—uniformity of working conditions in all schools on the territory of the commune;

—provision of free text books for all children;

—extended stay and a daily meal for school children;

—introduction of foreign-language teaching in all primary schools.

Similar steps were taken in the field of child welfare, when it came to creating new jobs for the unemployed, and when provision had to be made for the destitute.

Acting on the solidarity principle, Belgrade undertook a drive to build flats for persons employed in enterprises which cannot set aside any resources for this purpose. Financed by city funds, with the help of credits from banks and the contributions of work organisations of up to one third of the cost, 2,000 such flats have been constructed in Belgrade so far, and a further 10,000 should be completed over the next five years.

In view of the canvassing and publicity that precedes such 'social compacts' it may seem that an element of compulsion is involved. This practice is, however, essentially democratic and self-managerial in character: when tax-payers and work organisations see the connection between what they give and what is done with that money, when they see that it is earmarked for useful ends—a road, a school, a medical centre, a day nursery—they become more interested, find tax-paying easier, and participate more fully in self-government and worker management.

In principle, the socio-political organisations do not interfere in the sphere of self-management decision-making, involving the rights of worker-managers and self-governing citizens. But they do endeavour to exert an influence on the views and awareness of the working man, and thereby on his decisions. There has been enough democratic Utopianism: the belief that you only had to ask the workers, and they would come up with the best possible solution.

The communal assembly

Two basic groups of people may be distinguished in the commune: those who are employed, and all citizens grouped in local communities, including the employed. The interests of the former are represented in the communal assembly by the councils of working communities, usually two in number—the economic council and the cultural-educational, including health and social welfare, council. The representatives of the latter group (citizens) make up the communal council.

On many questions, each council of the communal assembly acts independently, but on some matters they pass decisions jointly.

There are, thus, two circles of interests within the commune—of work organisations and citizens, though these interests naturally overlap. Broadly speaking, the former are represented by the trade unions as a political organisation, and the latter by the Socialist Alliance.

Communal finances

The Yugoslav commune enjoys a large measure of fiscal autonomy. It is here that the decision is taken, by democratic agreement, on the level and source of taxation to finance the communal budget, and on how these funds are to be allocated. The economic and political limits are determined by the level of national income and social criteria. There could, of course, be no talk of the commune's autonomy if it was financially dependent on the higher administration and the good will of state organs.

There are three forms of financing communal needs:

—first, the budget, which gets its resources from taxes prescribed by the commune itself according to its requirements and taking into account the financial possibilities of its inhabitants;

—second, voluntary contributions of citizens, agreed upon by referendum, for particular purposes (it is not unusual for the resources in this fund to exceed those of the budget);

—third, sums allocated by a number of economic organisations or institutions, by agreement, for certain common purposes.

The national income in Yugoslavia is overburdened by fiscal obligations towards the Federation, republic and commune. According to some estimates these amount to about 37 per cent of the national income, the major share of this going to the Federation and republics.

Table 4
Distribution of budget resources and funds in some communes in Serbia, 1970.

| | Per capita national income in dinars | per capita in dinars | Communal income from budgetary sources and funds | | |
| | | | % of total income appropriated | | |
			Feder-ations	Repub-lic	Com-mune
Belgrade	11,792	3,390	52·5	9·6	37·9
Nis	8,941	2,593	53·4	14·6	32·0
Kragujevac	8,910	1,572	20·6	29·2	50·2
Zrenjanin	8,760	2,275	41·6	10·4	48·0
Valjevo	5,571	1,009	28·6	19·6	51·8
Pozarevac	5,549	1,000	19·2	26·8	54·0
Novi Pazar	2,600	400	17·7	21·6	60·7
Sjenica	1,802	237	18·1	21·4	60·5
Djakovica	1,792	340	15·2	14·2	70·6
Urosevac	1,666	319	15·0	16·6	68·4

The economically more developed communes naturally give larger contributions towards the general needs of society. The communes of Belgrade and Nis, for instance, strong industrial and consumer centres, give around 53 per cent of the total fiscal income collected on their territory to the Federation. Other communes give less to the Federation—15 to 20 per cent, but their taxes for republican needs are higher—10 to 20 per cent. The more developed communes are left 32 to 37 per cent of their total fiscal takings to cover the needs of the local community, but in less developed communes the amount is over 50 per cent, and in the most backward, up to 70 per cent.

Most of the funds are on communal or republican level (funds for schooling, roads, social insurance), but the communes do not always have a decisive say on their use since, in the case of republican funds, they are managed by committees composed of delegates from several communes. Those communes that contribute large amounts to the funds and those that give much less have the same rights, so that, logically, there is a clash of interests between those who provide the major share of the resources and those who spend them. Some are trying to give as little as possible, while others are endeavouring to get as much as they can.

Communes with a deficit

As part of its constitutional obligations, every commune must have the necessary resources for education, culture, health insurance, social welfare, and for the work of the communal assembly and its organs. If the commune's own income is insufficient, the resources are provided from republican funds. The amount of communal subsidies is not fixed. The right to a subsidy is enjoyed by those communes in which the *per capita* income is below the average for all communes in the republic. Subsidies may also be given because of special circumstances. For instance, in a nationally-mixed commune, resources may be provided from outside for bilingual schooling, for the cultural activities of the various nationalities, to cover the costs of bilingual administration, judiciary, and the like.

According to the law of the Socialist Republic of Serbia— the position is similar in other republics—communes with a deficit are defined as those with an income insufficient to finance the work of the local administration and judiciary, and the communal assembly, the functioning of the health and social welfare services, the implementation of national defence measures, the work of libraries and archives, the preservation of public and cultural monuments, the drafting of urban plans, and the activities of the socio-political organisations.

The amounts of subsidies are fixed annually, by agreement, on the basis of the law and previous experience.

The differences in level of economic development of individual communes is so great that *per capita* budgetary expenditure covers a range of 1:4, (of the 179 communes in Serbia, in 1969 55 per cent or 106 were receiving supplementary financing. These communes had a population of about 4 million or 48·2 per cent of the total Serbian population).

The supplementary resources allocated to communes, taken as a whole, are modest, forming only 5·8 per cent of the total budgetary expenditure in the republic. Subsidies make up from 2 per cent to 79 per cent of the budget of a commune.

In Serbia, on an average about 25 per cent of their income is left to communes to use as they deem fit. In some communes, however, this percentage exceeds 50 per cent after legal and constitutional obligations have been met.

The commune facing changes

By the end of 1972, a somewhat turbulent period of constitutional changes had come to a close. This was the so-called second phase, which considerably strengthened the position of the republican centres. The republics have acquired new powers, which give rise to new institutions—and higher expenses.

But the character and effect of these recent changes will depend on whether they stop short and simply reinforce republican statism or whether the powers and material basis of communes and enterprises will be expanded thereby.

It is widely agreed that the strengthening of the republics would be harmful if it were achieved at the expense of local self-government. It is therefore expected that the republics will increase communal autonomy.

It has been observed, in any case, that the practice of continually 'undermining' the independence of the commune has taken root. To take housing construction as an illustration: the commune is responsible for urban planning and housing policy and building, while rent prices are set by the Federation. The valuation of all housing was carried out in 1954, and the level of rents set on the basis of this. This, however, bears no relation to present prices and cannot cover maintenance costs.

Federal authorities criticise the communes for wishing to add higher rents to many other recent price increases, so that they can accumulate capital for projects that serve to glorify communal officials. The communes, on the other hand, claim that the Federation is favouring those who already have flats by insisting on cheap rents, and thereby delaying new housing construction indefinitely. The outcome of this is that higher rents based on the cost of building, maintenance and depreciation are being gradually introduced.

The communes are continually complaining that there are too many laws and too little guidance, awareness and self-government. The original law on communes subsequently gave rise, by some counts, to about 1,500 federal and republican laws on the commune and several thousand other decisions and regulations. The commune could very well suffocate in this multitude of laws and regulations and excessive institutionalism. And that in a system which attaches such importance to the awareness of each individual, to his being well-informed and participating in the exercise of government.

The system as a whole

The idea of self-management would have been condemned to failure if a new system had not been gradually built up as well—from the enterprise and local self-government right up to the federal parliament (the Federal Assembly).

Self-management is a pyramid of links from the basic units to the parliament. The fundamental question of self-management was and remains: how to ensure the influence of the producers on the work of representative bodies. Otherwise, the workers' councils would be simply a formality, something which could be manipulated from various power centres.

In principle, elections are carried out without the mediation of political parties—from the assembly in the commune to the Federal Assembly. All working people have a say in the procedure of selecting candidates and in the actual elections. This ensures direct links between the working people and their representatives which are more effective than the links that can be provided through political parties.

The multicameral structure of the assemblies, from communal to federal, allows various fields of work and life to be equally represented in political decision-making. The Federal Assembly at the present time has five chambers. Three of them represent the self-managing work organisations in the basic fields of social activity (the economy, education and culture, and health and social welfare). The fourth chamber, elected by direct general suffrage, represents the interests of the local communities, while the fifth, the National Council, is composed of deputies elected and delegated by the republican and provincial assemblies, on a parity basis. The National Council ensures the equal say of the various nations in the formation of federal policy. The Government (Executive Council) is, in fact, a specific type of Assembly committee entrusted with the implementation of laws and realisation of the policies set by the Assembly. This constitutes a radical reduction of the powers of the executive, which are everywhere in the modern world tending to expand at the expense of parliament.

In the various bodies of self-management—from the councils of work units in enterprises to the federal parliament—about one million working people and citizens are at present playing an active role.

Chapter 9

Underdeveloped Regions in Yugoslavia

The dualistic structure of Yugoslav society

The presence of underdeveloped regions, their economic and general situation and progress, are essential features of Yugoslavia's physiognomy.

The regional differences are indeed enormous. Over 40 per cent of the total area of the country is considered underdeveloped. This 'poverty belt', as it was once called in the *Economist*, stretches from Lika in Croatia, through Bosnia, Herzegovina and northern Dalmatia down to Macedonia in the far south.

Underdeveloped areas—those in which the *per capita* income is less than two-thirds of the Yugoslav average—can be found in four of the six republics that make up the Yugoslav federation.

Despite heavy investment to develop these areas, the differences have increased, in both absolute and relative terms. For every one dinar increase in income in these regions, there is a 2·1 dinar increase in developed areas. The ratio for *per capita* income between the developed and underdeveloped areas in Yugoslavia was 1 : 0·55 in 1947, and 1 : 0·52 in 1967. The income gap between the most developed and least developed regions has widened still further; in 1947 it was 3·3 : 1, and in 1967—5·1 : 1. (on the basis of *per capita* income). The Republic of Slovenia has a *per capita* income of 1,000 dollars, while the Autonomous Province of Kosovo has scarcely 200 dollars. Incidentally, Kosovo, in which most of the inhabitants are ethnic Albanians, has the fastest growing population in Europe—30 per cent in the past ten years.

Optimism concerning the rapid evening out of economic

development levels has proved justified only in industrially developed countries—the German Democratic Republic and Czechoslovakia, for example. It has not been achieved in the less developed countries—such as Albania, Bulgaria, Romania and Yugoslavia. In fact, the differences have become more pronounced. Some Yugoslav economists consider that more even growth becomes possible only when a medium level of development has been reached—i.e. a *per capita* income of about 400 dollars.

Paradoxes

The picture is also very uneven with regard to employment. In Slovenia, every third person is employed; in Kosovo, every twelfth. The average number of dependents per employed person in Slovenia is 1·7, and in Kosovo 4·1. This explains the inadequate effects of investment and the higher unemployment level in the latter region.

Average personal incomes of those working in the socially-owned sector of the economy in Slovenia are 33 per cent higher than in Kosovo. This figure should be viewed in the light of the fact that the employment level in Slovenia is four times that of Kosovo, and that the *per capita* income of the non-farming population is 2·8 times higher, and of the farming population 5·5 times higher in Slovenia.

In Kosovo there are 2,300 inhabitants to every physician, but only one third of that number in Slovenia. The number of persons to every hospital bed is 3·5 times greater in Kosovo, and the infant mortality rate 4 times higher than in Slovenia. In Kosovo, the illiteracy rate approaches one third, and in Bosnia-Herzegovina over one fifth (the Yugoslav average is 15·2 per cent). Over half the inhabitants of Kosovo have no school qualifications, while 15 per cent have had only four years of primary schooling.

The number of old age pensioners reflects the degree of development of the individual regions in the past. Yugoslavia as a whole has a large number of pensioners since pensions are acquired not only on the basis of work but according to other social welfare criteria (about 38 per cent are invalid pensions, 37 per cent old-age i.e. retirement pensions, and 24 per cent family pensions). In Slovenia, over half the pensioners are receiving old-age pensions, and one-fifth invalid pensions. In Kosovo, Montenegro and Bosnia-Herzegovina, the figures are the reverse.

The basic economic feature of underdeveloped regions is their inability to expand their productive forces. Their agrarian population exceeds 50 per cent, and in Kosovo 60 per cent of the total. In Yugoslavia, the underdeveloped regions are, at the same time, the producers of raw materials, while the developed areas have most of the manufacturing industries. The problem lies in the onesidedness of the economic structure. Before the 1965 reform, the prices of raw materials and farm produce did not permit expansion of production. The sharpest disparities were for the most part reduced after 1965, but the situation has still not fundamentally changed. Raw materials are still price-controlled, and their import free, while the prices of manufactured goods are mostly not fixed, and their import discouraged by protective tariffs.

There seems to be a lack of economic, not to mention political and social, logic in all this, which has given rise to certain minor political crises in the past few years.

What has changed?

Throughout the postwar period, the rate of investment in the underdeveloped regions has been above the Yugoslav average, but their share in national investments has been lower than their share of the total population. The higher population growth rate in underdeveloped areas has reduced the effect of investment, and the gap has widened.

Most of the underdeveloped regions of Yugoslavia have considerable natural resources: there are rich lead mines in Kosovo, iron and coal mines in Bosnia-Herzegovina, bauxite in Montenegro, nickle in Macedonia. In view of this, the heaviest investment has been in the extractive industry.

But this could not serve as the basis of further growth since the manufacturing industries were not developed: there was insufficient capital for this, and in any case the developed regions already had adequate manufacturing capacities. It was only after the decentralisation of resources and the economy that some branches producing raw materials in heavy demand began to play a significant role in promoting economic growth.

No region of the country was unaffected by the rapid changes in the population structure. In twenty-five years of postwar development, between 1946 and 1971, the agrarian population fell from about 76 per cent to 36 per cent. Four relatively developed regions absorbed about 1,197,000 new workers, and four undeveloped regions—all together 24,000! In fact, the actual size of the agrarian population has remained unchanged because of the high birthrate.

Social assistance or economic sense

At the present stage of the country's development, balanced growth is a political and economic imperative, for two main reasons: first, to maintain political harmony among the various nationalities, and second, economic reasons call for a higher degree of interconnection, communication and integration, fuller utilisation of the country's natural wealth. Exploitation of this wealth, including the human factor, offers prospects of a brighter economic future, and these resources are to be found, in the main, in the underdeveloped regions. In order to improve her foreign trade balance, Yugoslavia will have to make better use of her own natural riches.

Direct assistance is still being extended to the underdeveloped regions: about 2 per cent of the national product is set aside for this purpose, in a centralised federal fund. Kosovo's share of this is about one-third, which means that by 1975 it will have received about one thousand million dollars.

The underdeveloped are dissatisfied with the way this help is handed out and complain because it is labelled 'aid to the underdeveloped', while the developed regions, for their part, do not give all that willingly since they are short of capital themselves. Investment in roads and railways is perhaps more necessary than anything else, particularly in Montenegro, which is somewhat cut off from the rest of the country, not lying on main routes, or in Macedonia, which is also at a geographical disadvantage when it comes to communications and transport costs. The Belgrade-Bar railway, 700 km. in length, which is being completed with funds collected by a voluntary loan of about 50 million dollars, should be ready by 1975. This will help to integrate the economy of Montenegro with other parts of the country and will reduce its huge transport costs, as well as those of the Serbian economy, which will have a more easily accessible Adriatic port (Bar).

The regional policy of economic development is important for several reasons:

—the underdeveloped regions very often coincide with the national structure, i.e. the geographical distribution of the various nationalities;

—the economic interests of both the parts and the whole make it impermissible for the more developed regions to hold the others in a position of inferiority for any great length of time;

—self-management organisation and decision-making in both enterprises and territorial units require a higher economic level and greater autonomy.

Apart from social and political considerations, the progress of the underdeveloped regions is to the economic interest of all, including the 'rich'. Present efforts must be directed towards narrowing the gap, with gradual levelling off as the following stage.

Chapter 10

Constitutional Reform

Before its 1971 summer recess, the Federal Assembly approved 23 constitutional amendments, and the second phase of constitutional change is now in progress. These amendments relate to various spheres of life, but all have one basic aim: far-reaching decentralisation with transference of federal powers to the republics, provinces and communes.

Since the Second World War, Yugoslavia has had three constitutions, adopted in 1946, 1953 and 1963. These were preceded though by what was in effect a constitutional act—the Declaration of the Second Session of the Anti-fascist Council of National Liberation (a kind of provisional wartime parliament), held in the Bosnian town of Jajce in November 1943. This Declaration laid the foundations of the future Yugoslav state—a community of equal nations on a federal basis, and its new social system—the rule of the working class and working people. The essence of this was retained in all subsequent constitutions.

The 1963 Constitution introduced major changes in the direction of self-management, but being a reflection of the prevailing level of social awareness and relationship of forces, it was not devoid of a certain centralistic spirit.

A 'Utopian' plan for direct participation

Of all the European states with a federal or regionalist structure, regardless of political system, Yugoslavia is undoubtedly the one that has made most conscious effort to find the best solution of that exceptionally complex question—the relationship between the centre and the component parts.

Much ground has still to be covered before the citizens will fully govern the communes, the teachers and students run the universities, the insurees manage the insurance system, and all the working people exert control over the socially-owned capital. The 'Utopian' plan for the equal and direct participation by all in the management of public affairs has not been put fully into practice even in Yugoslavia. The recent constitutional amendments, which some see as ushering in the second phase of self-management, should broaden such participation from the base to the summit.

It cannot be claimed that Yugoslavia has achieved a fully integrated socialist system founded on self-management or that the working class exercises authority without the intervention of bureaucracy and technocracy. There were powerful elements of central decision-making, the repercussions of which can still be felt, and there are elements of anarchy, egoism, and even a certain danger of the restoration of capitalist elements, all of which call for the continual renewing and change of the organisation of society.

The constitutional reform means, in effect, the strengthening of self-government on all levels, the more consistent decentralisation of power and decision-making, while aiming at the same time to make the whole of Yugoslav territory a single market, to guarantee the free movement of goods, money and labour, to facilitate the development of free competition (a market economy) and the integration of socialised labour, and to prevent monopoly on the market. What is basic is the extent to which we can speak of government stemming from below, of the free circulation of political ideas, and of full, and not only economic, self-management by the workers. The system must act both vertically and horizontally, for it is not an end in itself but a method by which the common will and the contribution of the individual may find expression.

It is a matter, then, of the stabilisation of the position of the worker-manager and the efficiency of the economic system. To quote Edvard Kardelj, the working people cannot have political power unless they have economic power over socially-owned capital, over their 'own personal work'.

The Federation has retained those functions that are inseparable from the common interest: foreign affairs, national defence, national currency, distribution of foreign currency, joint development through the socio-economic plan, and management of the Fund for the Underdeveloped Regions.

If constitutional decentralisation were to stop short at republican level, the danger of centralism would be no less, for this would allow the creation of a number of small centralised states, each with its own bureaucracy, which would have legal reason to shut out their neighbours.

Freedom of decision-making, but inadequate means

In its early days, self-management was more or less confined to production and the distribution of personal incomes. The responsibility of the self-managing citizen was restricted, in the main, to his work unit and enterprise. All investment capital was concentrated in the Federation, banks, insurance societies and large foreign trade organisations.

At that time the question of how to allocate capital among the republics was constantly on the agenda. Conflicts between enterprises and the state over the division of capital earnings, 'state capital', became ever more frequent. The actual development of self-management democracy was being hampered by this state of affairs. The economy enjoyed freedom of decision-making, but was left with insufficient resources for this freedom to be exercised. Business circles and the worker-managers complained that the economy was overburdened by taxation.

The social and economic reform inaugurated in 1965 created conditions for self-management to cover the whole field of expanded production (investment). But in actual practice various pressures often came into play.

The republics, naturally, reacted to all measures of federal economic policy which, directly or indirectly, unfavourably affected the material position of the republic and its economy. Indeed, the prosperity of a particular economic branch, a whole region or a republic, is very much dependent on the credit policy, tax and tariff rates for a particular commodity, foreign trade controls, money supply policy and so on.

In the political sense, these conflicts of interest sometimes amounted to a crisis of the system, giving rise to discord among the various Yugoslav nations.

At any rate, relations became more complex. Having emerged from the war and revolution as agrarian nations for the most part, the Yugoslav peoples, though differing considerably in level of development, became modern nations seeking all the necessary conditions for full economic, political and cultural affirmation. Undeniably, for a nation to feel really free, it must have economic as well as political and cultural equality.

But a certain objective difference of interests does exist. On a single unified market, the developed and underdeveloped republics, agricultural and industrial regions, the producers of raw materials and the producers of consumer goods, do not enjoy an equally favourable position. Federal measures applied to the whole country do not affect all regions in the same way and are the source of conflicts. Such conflicts could not be eliminated by ideological formulas or administrative measures, but only temporarily suppressed.

The principle of parity

According to the constitutional amendments, the Federation is not separate from the republics, but its basic organs are formed directly by the republics and autonomous provinces on the principle of parity: equal representation regardless of size of population (a range of 1:16 between Serbia and Montenegro, for instance). The bodies formed on the parity principle are: the Presidium of the Socialist Federal Republic of Yugoslavia, the National Chamber in the Federal Assembly, the Executive Council (Government) of Yugoslavia, the civil service (administration), diplomatic service, and others.

The basic functions of the Federation for the most part cover three spheres:

—ensuring the independence and territorial integrity of the Socialist Federal Republic of Yugoslavia; protection of sovereignty in international relations; organisation of the system of national defence;

—determining the country's foreign policy, and economic and other relations with other states and international organisations;

—ensuring the unity of the socio-economic system, solidarity and social security, unity of the market and co-ordination of joint economic and social development; determining the socio-economic plan of Yugoslavia, the planning system, the monetary system and means of payment.

K

Even these three domains are not entirely within federal control. The republics, for instance, directly participate in the formation of foreign policy, particularly where neighbouring states and economic relations are concerned, in planning, national defence, etc.

National defence

In addition to the regular armed forces, there are territorial defence units in the republics, regions, communes, cities and enterprises. This is a type of organised civil defence involving the whole population, based on Partisan experience.

This nationwide defence system, as it is called, is regulated by the Law on National Defence, passed in February 1969. It has transformed Yugoslavia's 'weakness'—its multinational character—into one of its greatest strengths. Nationwide defence is auxiliary to the regular armed forces and is based on the awareness of the massive resistance force that can be generated if every factory, every village, every local community is organised. One foreign journalist commented: 'Yugoslavia is returning to her old love—Partisan warfare'. Indeed, the Yugoslav concept of nationwide defence is derived, primarily, from the country's own experiences, but also from the experience of other nations that have successfully organised national resistance against a numerically and technically far superior enemy.

The Law on National Defence and the Constitution explicitly forbid anyone to sign the country's capitulation: 'No one has the right to sign or recognise the capitulation or occupation of the Socialist Federal Republic of Yugoslavia or any of its parts. No one has the right to prevent the citizens of the SFRY from fighting an enemy who has attacked the country. Such acts are contrary to the Constitution and punishable by Law as treason and crimes against the nation.' (Amendment 41). The regular training of the youth and citizens in schools and places of work, and the fact that territorial units number about 600,000 men and women, are clear enough indication that the country is organised to resist in the event of invasion. This serves to deter aggression, since any invader would be met by a rifle around every corner and would become involved in an endless campaign against a ubiquitous army.

The whole defence of the country is under the central military command, but numerous operative actions are under enterprise, local and republican headquarters. It is of interest to note that enterprises and communes, even those of modest means, are open-handed when it comes to the equipping of enterprise and local units.

Naturally, this system is only as strong as the people's patriotism, their belief in their political institutions and need for a common state.

The market and the Federation

One of the basic functions of the Federation is to ensure unity of the market.

In practice, this means ensuring the free exchange of goods and services, scientific achievements and technical experience throughout the whole of the Socialist Federal Republic of Yugoslavia. Unity of the market implies free association of labour and means of production and freedom to pursue economic activities throughout the country; free competition on the market; the reaching of agreements and social compacts on the advancement of production and integration; prevention of monopoly on the market.

In agreement with the republics, the Federation determines the basis of the social and economic development plan and regulates relations in such fields as the monetary system, emission of money, foreign currency regulations, foreign trade and credit arrangements with foreign countries, customs and tariffs, the control of prices and services and crediting the development of underdeveloped republics and regions.

In a decentralised economy increasingly oriented towards the strengthening of independence, initiative and the work unit as the basis of the economy, these linking elements are indispensable in order to prevent uncontrolled growth, and check egoistic and particularist interests.

Federal legislation has been reduced to the spheres of national defence, international relations, the unity of the system of socialist self-management, and unity of the market. Legislation on all other matters is the responsibility of the republics and autonomous provinces.

Foreign observers of the Yugoslav scene often ask whether

the Yugoslav economy in the self-management system is a unifying factor in the country.

Underdevelopment, shortage of capital and a still insufficiently developed market certainly prevent it from being so to a greater degree. Local patriotism and particularism are indeed present, but as the economy strengthens, the dominant tendency is towards a higher degree of economic and social integration.

The 'veto' of the republics and provinces

Decision-making at the summit is conditional upon the agreement of eight partners—the six republics and two provinces—in the Federal Assembly, the Federal Executive Council and the federal administration, whenever 'vital matters' are in question. The fact that the previous approval of the republics and provinces must be obtained before important decisions can be taken means, in fact, that they have the right of 'veto', though this term is not used. At the same time, the republics, together with the federal bodies, bear responsibility for the execution of the functions of the Federation.

This principle has been the subject of considerable dispute, mostly regarding its effectiveness, the fear being that the need to seek republican and provincial approval would slow down decision-making to such an extent that the system would cease to function properly. What is in question, however, are interests of great importance to every republic, which cannot be bypassed or neglected.

In the past, when serious disputes and clashes between the republics arose, decisions were swiftly passed by a majority vote, but they were not always effective, for in practice their implementation was obstructed by those whose interests were threatened.

An extremely important innovation of the constitutional reform is the voluntary compacts on all current economic questions resulting in agreements and contracts between enterprises, communes, and republics, up to federal level. Self-management agreements and social compacts, have proved, on the basis of the brief experience to date, the most equitable way of co-ordinating interests. The inter-republican committees, whose task is to harmonise republican interests, and the so-called workers' amendments, which extend the self-management rights of the producer to the domain of investment and control of the movement of socially-owned capital, are the most important features of the constitutional changes.

There are many shared, but also many specific interests in Yugoslavia. The institution of inter-republican compacts provides a constitutional and political form by which the individual republican and other interests can find legitimate expression. An opportunity is given for each republic to put forward its own interests and become more familiar with the concerns of others in a completely democratic manner, instead of by backstairs canvassing and lobbying, as was previously the case. In the political domain this has much greater significance than just discussion of practical questions, and will certainly have a stabilising and unifying effect on relations between the various nationalities and ethnic groups that make up Yugoslavia. Co-ordination of interests in this direct manner, by discussion and without false alarms, demagoguery and upheavals, will certainly contribute to better mutual understanding, and greater tolerance and patience.

What remains to be settled is the relationship between the inter-republican committees and the Federal Assembly with regard to their competences, for the former cannot be allowed to undermine the prerogatives of the latter by their inter-republican compacts, but neither must the committees become a pure formality.

In any case, the practice of mutual consultation and compacts from enterprise to republican level is a form of co-operation which will assume increasing prominence, since in a self-management system many matters cannot be settled by state compulsion, acts and laws.

The system of co-unanimity introduced by the 1971 constitutional amendments imposes greater responsibility, for if even one republic (or province) says 'no', this means, in fact, that a decision cannot be passed. Such a move means the assumption of heavy responsibility. Thus, the right to veto carries with it not only the power to defend one's own interests, whatever the cost, but the obligation to co-ordinate one's own with other interests.

To illustrate, at the present time the republics are arguing about how the expenditure of the Federation on administration, defence etc. is to be financed. Some are for taxation based on the gross national product of the socially-owned sector of the economy, while others favour taxation on the basis of the national product of the entire economy. A compromise here is possible, but the province of Vojvodina, a predominantly agricultural region, considers that the tax basis should be consumption, the turnover of goods and services, and refuses to budge from this position, since any compromise would cost it many millions of dinars. Though a relatively developed area, Vojvodina considers that, as an agricultural region, it is not developing at the same rate as some others, and that the consumption of its population is lower. It would be unfair, it is argued, for Vojvodina to bear the same tax burden as those who have a rapid growth rate and high consumption. A strong point in its favour is the fact that for years Vojvodina, the Yugoslav granary, has suffered the adverse effects of the policy of low food prices.

In such circumstances, it is essential, from both the economic and political standpoint, to harmonise interests and views. It is, of course, impossible to achieve agreement at all times and on all questions. Differences are bound to arise in consequence of uneven development. From the standpoint of the interests of Yugoslavia, as it is today, equality is the only path to unity.

The Presidium

The most important innovation in the constitutional amendments was the institution of the Presidium of the Socialist Federal Republic of Yugoslavia. This is an independent organ of the Federation formed, on the principle of parity, of 23 members. Its task is to ensure the realisation of rights and duties laid down by the Constitution but without recourse to decision-making by majority voting.

The Presidium should use its political authority to resolve any conflict of interests between republics that may arise. It also has the right to initiate legislation.

The relationship of the Presidium to the Federal Assembly is such that neither can impose its will on the other. Both forums must give their approval when major questions are to be decided. If agreement cannot be reached, both bodies are dissolved and elections called. Certain changes are to be made in the federal parliamentary structure so as to adjust it to this new concept, the fundamental principle being: equality of participation and decision-making, without outvoting.

The Presidium also has the functions of a collective head of state. On the proposal of all the republics, in autumn 1971 President Tito was, exceptionally, re-elected President of the Republic and Chairman of the Presidium.

The Presidium represents Yugoslavia in the country and abroad. It is the highest organ in the command hierarchy of the armed forces. Considered as a whole, the Presidium is an independent constitutional body which corresponds to the multinational and self-management structure of Yugoslavia.

National relations

Observers have raised the question of whether Yugoslavia is suffering from an overdose of nationalism.

The debate preceding the 1971 constitutional reform was certainly more lively than anyone had expected, and it seemed to many that the divisions followed national boundaries more closely than before. Would this lead to the domination of national interests over class interests, would nationalism take precedence over socialism? many asked.

Immoderate nationalism was certainly in evidence at that time in various forms and discussions about the constitutional changes, economic system, national historical traditions, variants of the Serbo-Croatian or Croato-Serbian language, and even about the national anthem.

In this serious political climate, absurd importance was sometimes attached to seemingly minor matters. An amusing example of this was the case of the proposed magazine to be published by the association of composers of Yugoslavia. Shortage of funds precluded its publication in all the languages of the Yugoslav nations, so after considerable debate Serbo-Croatian was eventually chosen. But this raised new problems: which regional variant should it be and which alphabet—Cyrillic or Latin? Months passed. In the meantime, the composers began to publish a journal for foreign readers—in French. It occurred to someone that this could be circulated among Yugoslav composers as well, most being good linguists, and the language problem was solved!

A lesson can be drawn, however, even from such a trivial and ludicrous incident.

The essence of the matter, though, is more serious in character. The fact that Yugoslavia is composed of six nations and about 18 ethnical minorities speaks for itself. In a multinational environment, every major socio-economic problem assumes national overtones. National investment provides an illustration of this. Before the constitutional reform, about 20 per cent of investments were in the hands of the Federation. The administrative sharing-out of this capital gave rise to dissatisfaction, both well-founded and groundless and left scope for bureaucratic disregard of the interests of particular nations and for particularist excesses.

The constitutional amendments of 1971 provide for a higher degree of integration and centralisation within the framework of large-scale and complex work organisations. A constant watch must be kept, however, to guard against the flow of income from work organisations to the centre, which under Yugoslav conditions would mean favouring one republic at the expense of another republic or province. Any forced redirection of the social product, by economic or other means, would give rise to serious political conflicts. The economic logic must be respected, for clear-cut economic relations can serve as the main spur of integration beyond regional and republican boundaries.

The solidarity of the working people, nations and ethnic groups of Yugoslavia, which is a matter of exceptional importance in this country to ensure more balanced regional growth, the faster development of the economically backward regions and so forth, is also an economic question. Solidarity, too, must have its economic justification. It must not be a form of charity that encourages a parasitic attitude, but a type of assistance that stimulates the workers' creative impulses and promotes political stability.

In the present age, the national question has emerged as something basic to the freedom and equality of peoples, not only in a socialist system and not only within the borders of one country, but in the context of international relations. This is all the more reason why equality and free development of all nations in a socialist state should be a fundamental requirement. What is socialism if it does not ensure the free self-determination of nations and expression of nationality? If it does not ensure economic and cultural equality, if it tolerates majority domination and hegemony?

The nationality question in Yugoslavia was settled during the war in an elementary manner—by the abolition of national oppression and voluntary unification in a federal state. However, problems concerning the relations between nations in the Yugoslav state are ever present, colouring the country's whole life and development. It is natural that things should come to a head from time to time. The sources of differences are the uneven development of the country, differences in culture and traditions, differing interests, and to a certain extent backward mentality. But all this is the Yugoslav reality, the existing state of affairs which has to be taken into account and lived with.

It is true that the cohesion of the Yugoslav community is threatened by nationalist tendencies, whether unitarist or separatist in character. These cannot be sidestepped, nor banished by concealment or repressive measures. Equality and negotiated agreement will certainly render them less dangerous or quite pointless.

In recent decades, all socialist revolutions have had their 'national-liberation dimension', from the October Revolution, the Yugoslav and Chinese to the Cuban. Now what is left to be done is for the socialist system to ensure equality in internal relations among nations—not by state compulsion from the centre but through democratic participation, respect of national rights and self-government. It is this latter course that Yugoslavia has chosen, paving the way by the constitutional reform.

Centuries of centralism questioned
Even in countries with no multinational composition or self-government, decentralisation has become a major political issue in recent years, and an excellent political platform for party activity.

The need for decentralisation is felt to a growing extent in the modern industrialised society. This is a reaction to man's increasing subservience to the technological set-up and a kind of solution in the face of ever greater demands for self-management and local autonomy. In France, for instance, the need for decentralisation is extremely pressing because of the rigidity of the almost two-hundred-year-old administrative system.

In Italy, too, there is a clear conflict between the cumbersome, expensive and inefficient state machinery, almost a century old, and contemporary economic development and social aspirations. The socialist leader, Pietro Nenni, used the term: 'democracy without people' to describe the profound differences in Italy between the North and South, industry and agriculture, the centre and the periphery, the methods of urbanisation, building homes, schools, medical institutions and so on. As a means of bridging this dangerous gap dividing the command centre in Rome from those it governs, 20 administrative regions have been formed, to which many of the central powers have been transferred.

But all the regional revolutions that are announced: Pompidou's, Schreiber's, Nenni's, will be inadequate without social as well as communal reform, unless it is desired to add a further echelon of government and power to those already existing.

What is actually new in all this is the realisation of the need for decentralisation, the search for ways of giving the local, or national, communities a greater say and more rights.

The papal encyclical *Populorum progressio* likewise considers that '. . . nothing is more in accord with justice than the actions taken by authorities to improve the living conditions of ethnical minorities, particularly with respect to their language, culture, customs and the *economic sources of industrial undertakings.*'[1]

1. *Le Monde,* August 3–7, 1971.

Chapter 11

Socio-Political Organisations and Self-Management

A polycentric system and integration

People's interests are naturally connected with economic, social and political matters, and are for the most practical, even private, in character, rather than intellectual and cultural.

The Yugoslav system is in many respects polycentric, while contemporary socio-political life calls for linking up, channelling and integration. We find conflicts of interest between various social and professional groups, regions, nations, villages and towns, sectors and branches of the economy. The relationship between the department and the enterprise as a whole, the producer and the expert, planning and the market, the trade unions and management bodies—all this constitutes a complicated system of relationships that must be constantly kept in balance by the efforts of conscious forces—in the first place, the socio-political organisations.

Different interests and pressures, in opposition to one another, must always be given careful consideration. The individual worker, the League of Communists and the trade unions all have roles and responsibility that are not in every case the same as in other countries of the world.

There are three types of institution playing an integrating role in these circumstances: the Confederation of Trade Unions, the League of Communists and the Socialist Alliance. Other organisations—the Veterans' League, Students' League and Youth League—which have considerable social significance, are collective members of the Socialist Alliance, but carry on their activities quite independently.[1]

1. Collective membership in practice means simply acceptance of a joint programme of socialist construction.

The functions of the socio-political organisations are 'legalised' in the Constitution. The scope of their activities naturally differs, ranging from the channelling of development and initiation of political activity (the League of Communists), and the unifying and protection of the interests of the working class (the trade unions), to manifold activities connected with the organisation of direct democracy and public control over all institutions and organs (the Socialist Alliance).

Society, State and the League of Communists

Yugoslav experience and that of many great revolutions teaches us that new ideas and relations do not wait upon favourable social conditions before cutting a swath for themselves. A party soon becomes inert and lazy in its thinking when it comes to power. It quickly identifies itself with authority and the process of bureaucratisation sets in.

It may be said that the League of Communists, from the start, 'sponsored' self-management, making it its ideological and practical political platform and regarding it as a factor working for integration and synthesis.

What suits the interests of society as a whole is not automatically and spontaneously thrown up by the confrontation of interests. If Yugoslav democracy were to be organised structurally solely on an interest basis, leaving the process of social awareness to chance, the society would undergo serious upheavals. Hence the importance of organising the propagation of ideas from socialist and humanist positions, particularly in a society founded on the consciousness and initiative of each individual, and which places so much stress on human relations.

It is here that the role of the League of Communists begins.

Integration is impossible if in each separate centre of independent initiatives and decisions men and women have not reached the level of acting consciously on behalf of society. The League of Communists thus has a dual role: (a) to encourage initiative through information and education, and (b) to achieve a synthesis of creative powers, to be the factor linking and guiding development.

It became essential to separate the state (its government apparatus) from the Party and its role, to reverse statist trends and prevent state and Party from merging, so that the latter became the direct manager of all public affairs. It was for this purpose that the decision was taken, and quite successfully implemented, that the same people should not hold high office in both the Party and the state administration simultaneously, as had often been the case. The practice of the Party deciding current policy questions in advance, after which the state and representative bodies would go through the motions of decision-making, was also abandoned.

In 1953, the Communist Party of Yugoslavia became the League of Communists (the name first given by Marx to a communist organisation in 1847). But the change was not simply in the name of this organisation, with over one million members, but in its essence. The strength of the League of Communists does not lie in numbers, though, or in the enforcement of its will, but in its power to influence people, its ability to perceive and link up particular aims and interests with the historical interests of the working people.

The League of Communists has, in any case, a certain fund of confidence among the people on which it can draw. It had the strength to lead the way amidst the chaos of 1941, and enough character to reject the easy way out of crises. It had the courage to go to the brink in 1948 and withstand the challenge. This stand of the League's was of enormous importance in the country's postwar development.

Against a transmissive role

The term 'vanguard' is on the one hand abused, and on the other rejected for its associations with the old dogmatic scheme of things. But for the Party to take the role of vanguard in a self-managing society called for profound changes in its conception, a radical break with what is called the 'leading role of the Party' in a centralistic system and with the transmissive role of the political organisations in relation to the Communist Party.

In his famous work *Problems of Leninism*, Stalin, giving his definition of the dictatorship of the proletariat, states that socialism is a political system which ensures the three following:

—the taking of all major decisions by the Party leadership;

—the passing down of these decisions through the state apparatus and all social organisations (the system of transmission);

—the implementation of these decisions by the working people.

The Yugoslavs did not accept this concept of Stalin's. Their aim was that the Party should not be identified with its apparatus, nor the latter with the state. The Party does pass political decisions and concerns itself with current policy, but this is linked to strategic aims; it formulates positions, but does not impose them as directives from above. It is less an organ of political power than a force for social cohesion. The authority of the League of Communists ought to be based on powerful arguments, and cannot usurp the right of the working class to speak on its own behalf nor claim a monopoly of understanding and the foresight.

In political theory today, the division of political systems into multi-party and one-party is considered a fundamental distinction.

These are the prevalent but not the only possible forms of political organisation. The Yugoslav system does not fit into either category: it lacks elements of the one-party system, since the political organisation is not a factor in government, but at the same time, the multi-party system is considered anachronistic in Yugoslav conditions.

It has been insisted upon for a long time that besides the multi-party and one-party systems there is no other way. But a third road does exist: direct, self-management democracy. The Yugoslav ideal is not any kind of party system, but the supersession of this form of mediation and alienation of politics from the people.

Not by bread alone

The working class is not concerned solely with its material welfare, but with its position as a whole, with the general state of society. It no longer puts forward only certain narrow class demands, but interests itself in the whole of social relations and the character of the state. The rebellion that has manifested itself among the youth in fact reflects characteristic needs and aspirations of modern man. In a world in which material goods are becoming ever more plentiful and widespread, property and one's personal living standard are ceasing to be the sole criteria of value amongst increasingly broad sections of the population. Most political movements are introducing some kind of response to this demand in their programmes.

One of the most acute needs of contemporary socialism is to link socialism and democracy, freedom and socialism. According to Marx, man and his position must be the first and last consideration of the new society. The search for and free choice of paths, and not the imposition of a particular concept and model, are essential to contemporary socialism. The idea is not, of course, new.

In Dostoievski's novel *The Brothers Karamazov* Ivan Karamazov sets out his concept of freedom and choice of paths

> 'That need to worship together has been the greatest source of suffering to every single man, and to the whole of mankind since time out of mind. So that all should worship just one and the same god, people have destroyed one another by the sword. They have called to one another: "Leave your gods and come and kneel to ours. Otherwise death to you and your gods".'

Through self-management, Yugoslavs wanted to avoid 'worshipping one and the same god', and so they were not able to avoid suffering.

The League of Communists has been the initiator of the renunciation of a power monopoly by political organisations, though naturally in a process that cannot be completed overnight. Many have taken this to mean that the League of Communists is withdrawing completely from the political stage into an ivory tower of ideas, to emerge only for great political events and fateful decisions. This is certainly a great error, which began with Djilas, but is still occasionally voiced even today.

Why both trade unions and worker management?

Information a condition of self-management—Confronted by the demands of economic efficiency and modern technological progress, the worker-manager must be able to receive and interpret specialised information, himself put forward proposals, and base his decisions on the interests of his fellow-workers in accordance with economic criteria. If this balance between the individual's interests and economic sense were to be disturbed, Yugoslavia would have to sacrifice either its self-management system or its future economic progress. Information and knowledge clearly play an exceptionally important role.

The introduction of self-management and the progress of technology called for understanding of and the ability to tackle professional, economic and industrial problems on the part of the workers. The influx of manpower from rural areas made it necessary to organise adult general education courses and vocational training, so that the newcomers could adapt to urban life and industry.

The so-called workers' universities (adult education centres) began to be established in large numbers in the fifties, at the time of the introduction of worker management. In 1969, there were 456 institutions of this type in the country, offering a wide range of subjects and courses. In that year, 449,000 people completed seminars and courses of varying duration—from 12 hours to nine months. Here workers prepared to take examinations to obtain higher qualifications, completed their primary education and secondary vocational schooling (technical and economic-commercial), prepared for entrance examinations to universities and colleges, learned foreign languages, etc. Education can be organised on a contractual basis. Enterprises can 'order' the type of course their workers need.

Every sizable enterprise has its own paper. There are about 1,200 factory papers,[2] their task being to inform workers about technological and economic problems, managerial and worker-management proposals and decisions.

2. In 1970 there were 1,394 enterprises with over 500 employees in the country.

Table 5
Survey of Enterprises by numbers employed, 1970

	Over 500 employed		Over 1,000 employed		Over 2,000 employed	
Total	no. of firms	employing	no. of firms	employing	no. of firms	employing
1394	9%	62%	4%	47%	1·5%	29%

The managerial and expert services in an enterprise are obliged to present the material submitted to the self-management bodies in an acceptable and understandable manner, while the rules of the workers' council strictly stipulate the amount of time necessary for the worker-managers to study the material.

Observers often ask whether there is a need for both the workers' council and trade union—a query that recalls a much earlier discussion on the need for trade unions in a socialist state.

Self-management deals primarily with the interests of the enterprise, of the collective as a whole, which are certainly vital. But the fact that an enterprise is well managed does not automatically solve the problems of all the workers. Self-management concerns itself with one enterprise or group of enterprises, protecting thereby the interest of a part of the working class. The interests of the individual worker and of the working class as a whole are protected by the trade unions. These are also protected by self-management as a system of direct democracy, but, in the division of labour, self-management is in fact a production relationship, and this leaves room for the work of trade unions. It would be hard to ensure unity of the working class and to safeguard it from technocracy and bureaucracy without trade union organisations. In industry a qualified technocracy could dominate, and in the public services a bureaucratic hierarchy.

The trade unions' activity in the sphere of workers' education and culture is also highly important in Yugoslav conditions, since technocracy and bureaucracy find it easiest to gain a hold and usurp management in a backward environment.

L

Through worker management, the workers exercise their 'authority' over production and income distribution, their right to make decisions, while through the trade unions they exercise their right to unite, protecting their own interests in an organised and united manner, to act independently and fulfil their social and political function. The difference between these two functions was stressed by the President of the Trades Union Confederation, Dusan Petrovic, at the 1969 Congress of the League of Communists:

'The trade unions must not become identified with the self-management organs, nor perform a transmissive role, simply explaining the decisions and stands of other bodies.'

The protective role of the trade unions

If the Trades Union Confederation did not perform a protective function with regard to the working people, what purpose would the unions serve and what use would they be to the workers?

The trade unions work for the integration—mergers—of enterprises in line with the demands of modern technology and productivity, but at the same time they safeguard the interests of the 'weaker' from monopolistic behaviour by stronger enterprises. They are for the introduction of modern production methods, but against 'redundant' labour being left on the street. The unions strive to ensure full employment, but know that this cannot be achieved overnight. With this as their ultimate goal, they endeavour, in the meantime, to see that at least all qualified and trained persons find employment. Relying on the workers' strong feeling of solidarity, the unions have put forward the demand that the problem of redundant labour should not be solved by discharging workers. They demand that any modernisation programme should include resources and plans for employing those whose jobs will become unnecessary in the new production process.

The trade union also has a major role to play when it comes to income distribution. After settling its financial obligations to the community, an enterprise divides the remaining income into two parts: one which is spent immediately on personal incomes, housing construction, factory meals, rest and recreation facilities and so forth and one which is invested in the expansion of production, modernisation and growth of the enterprise. Taking into account the long-term interests of the workers, the unions try to see that a reasonable balance is struck between the two types of expenditure. They favour low personal income tax, so that highly qualified workers and other personnel will have incentive, but at the same time lay stress on solidarity, the protection of those with low earnings. While aiming at the socialist principle: from each according to his abilities, to each according to his labour, the unions realise that it is a rather complicated matter to put it into practice. They endeavour to ensure that incomes are dependent upon business results, that the workers really do exert an influence on the enterprise's personal incomes policy, that the range between highest and lowest earnings is great enough to stimulate expert and high-quality work, but that the lowest earnings are sufficient to cover minimum living costs.

There is a growing demand for the unions to undertake the task of protecting individual and group interests in an enterprise, for instance, representing a worker penalised for infringing work discipline if he appears to be the victim of an unjust decision or bureaucratic error.

The trade unions organise elections and submit proposals for candidates for the workers' council. They also take the initiative in passing votes of no confidence in the workers' council, managing board or an individual member of these bodies, should circumstances and the general mood of the collective point to the need for this step.

On the federal level, the unions are engaged in proposing new laws and take part in debates on the social and economic development plan. They operate both as a 'pressure group' and as an organisation—through their functionaries in the Federal Assembly.

The unions are not in a position to participate directly in solving production and distribution problems, nor is this their function, but the self-management bodies are obliged to consider their recommendations, comments and views. They may call for the holding of a referendum, convene meetings of work units, and take the initiative regarding changes in the statute or other regulations passed by the enterprise.

The influence and effect of the trade unions naturally depend on the degree of independence they display, and the initiative they show in day-to-day affairs.

Under the new conditions, the unions are not always effective in their traditional role—defence of the direct interests of the working class. In some places they still cling to their old role, typical of statist systems, of political tutors, leaving the workers to organise wild-cat strikes in order to protect themselves from particular cliques threatening their material and self-managing interests.

The Socialist Alliance

When discussing forms of direct democracy in the commune, mention was made of the basic political functions of the Socialist Alliance. It might be added to this that the Alliance is a forum for the exchange of ideas, in which each citizen can put forward initiatives. It is the broadest political organisation in the country, membership being open to all who accept the general programme of socialist construction. Having developed from the Popular Front, this organisation of eight million members constitutes a kind of link between all the socialist forces of Yugoslavia.

The Socialist Alliance accepts the programme of the League of Communists of Yugoslavia, but has its own independent activities and role as a means of public control over government and self-management institutions. It represents the political interests of the broadest sections of the population, organises elections for the representative bodies, exercises control over the work of deputies, and may, if necessary, initiate their recall.

The common programme is intended to show that the Alliance is not a rival political machine in opposition to the League.

But the need is felt for greater independence and initiative on the part of the Alliance, so that it may truly become an equal partner of the League. Many crises, mistaken tendencies, nationalist and hegemonistic features are not perceived in time by the organisations of the Socialist Alliance.

There is certainly a place for the Alliance, for the League of Communists has declared itself against the monopoly of one group or one party which assumes the right to interpret the wishes of all and represent everybody. Radical decentralisation of decision-making, with the abolition of the hierarchic structure and relations in which every cell of the social organism is subject to or dominated by another, has resulted in the creation of thousands of independently active centres. The socialisation of politics, in the process of the emancipation of labour, cannot be achieved without 'rivalry' of the action programmes of socio-political organisations, working in fact towards the same goals, in the course of which every citizen who is for the development of socialism in Yugoslavia can express his views and make his mark.

Chapter 12

The Economic Confirmation of Self-Management

Is the only purpose of self-management socialism to ensure the most equitable distribution of the available goods, or does it contribute, on the technological and economic plane, to the rational and scientific requirements of growth? Does this original model bring a high rate of growth?

Self-management has shown itself to be a stimulant, a vital and rational economic system. The best evidence of this is the concrete results. Moreover, it should be borne in mind that this progress in Yugoslavia, seen from the standpoint of man and humanism, 'costs' much less than in most other comparable countries.

Over a twenty-year period, this system has made fast economic growth possible, and shown itself capable of solving numerous complex problems and contradictions in the economy and society.

The following shows the annual growth rate of the gross national product in Yugoslavia compared with the developing countries and the industrialised Western states.

Yugoslavia	1950–1970	7%
	1957–1970	8·2%
The world:		
Developing countries	1950–1967	4·8%
Advanced countries	1950–1967	4·3%
Europe	1953–1967	5%
Southern Europe	1953–1967	6·4%
Advanced European states	1953–1967	2·8%–3·5%
Socialist countries	1950–1965	7·5%

To get a true picture of growth in Yugoslavia, we should follow its development from 1956 onwards, i.e. after it had overcome the difficulties that arose in its international position as a result of the Cominform Resolution and subsequent crisis in relations with the East European countries. This period reliably indicates that the system of self-management has contributed enormously to the country's economic development, though in day-to-day affairs there are still many reasons for dissatisfaction. This result is all the more impressive in that it was achieved in very complex conditions.

The growth of production in this period has made it possible not only to reduce the difference in the development levels of Yugoslavia and more advanced countries, but to ensure even faster progress in that direction in the future.

Because of the swift progress of science and technology, rapid growth is one of the characteristics of the modern world. But the pace of growth also depends on social conditions and relations. Twenty years ago, Yugoslavia was at the level of development reached by the developing nations today. When Yugoslavia began its modern industrial development, that process had been underway for over a century in the advanced countries. An encouraging fact in this respect is that in the period under consideration, the rate of growth in Yugoslavia was incomparably higher than that in the advanced countries when they started to industrialise.

Comparative data on the national product *per capita* in the USA in dollars clearly indicate this to be so.

To give a few more figures:

From 1950 to 1970, the gross national product of Yugoslavia rose by over 3·5 times—an average of 7 per cent annually. Industrial output went up by 10 per cent annually, which means that it doubled every seven years. In consequence of industrialisation, the farming population declined from about 75 per cent in 1946 to 36 per cent in 1971.

Agricultural production, the greatest headache of the socialist system, had almost doubled in 1969 in relation to the average output for the 1951/1955 period. The average annual rate of growth in farm production is appreciably higher than in most other countries. As regards yields of some of the most important crops like wheat and maize, on the socially-owned farms 'we have reached and even surpassed some of the most advanced capitalist states and all the socialist countries'.[1]

The volume of spending, both personal and public, rose by 3·7 times in the 1952–1969 period.

Yugoslavia is the only one of the insufficiently developed countries that has managed to narrow the gap separating it from the advanced states of the world. Most of the Yugoslav republics that are still not sufficiently developed now have a higher *per capita* income than the most advanced republic had twenty years ago.

Higher labour productivity accounted for about 10 per cent of the increase in the national product in the 1953–1957 period, 43 per cent in 1957, 53 per cent in 1961, and about 77 per cent in the five-year period (1966–1970) following the inauguration of the social and economic reform. This last, it is true, is partly a consequence of the decline in the employment rate after the reform.

It is impossible to express by global indicators alone all the achievements of the economy and production. Yugoslavia's development is marked not only by a growth in the volume of production, but by qualitative changes in its structure.

Today, Yugoslavia produces some key commodities that were not produced at all before the war, such as: coke, oil, automobiles, tractors, trucks, car tyres, etc.

Compared with 1939, furniture production has increased 25-fold, garment manufacture by 52 times, canned food production by about 70 times.

There are now about half a million passenger cars on Yugoslav roads (compared with 13,500 in 1939), 12,500 buses (943 before the war), and about 100,000 trucks and vans (4,286 on the eve of the war).

In 18 years (1952–1969), 886,000 dwelling houses were constructed with about 1·5 million flats, 40 per cent socially-owned and 60 per cent privately-owned, which works out at 3·8 square metres to every inhabitant. At present there are 11·9 square metres of housing space *per capita*, taking a nationwide average. This figure approaches that in the advanced countries.

Electricity has been brought to 75 per cent of rural house-

1. E. Kardelj, at the Second Congress of Worker-managers, Sarajevo, May 1971.

holds (compared with 48 per cent in 1960). In Slovenia, the figure is 93 per cent, on a par with that in advanced European countries.

According to the 1931 national census, 45 per cent of the population over ten years of age were illiterate (32 per cent of men and 56 per cent of women). Despite a large-scale drive to reduce illiteracy in the postwar period, according to the 1961 census, 19·7 per cent of the population, mostly older people, were still illiterate. The 1971 census recorded a decline to 15 per cent. The number of secondary school pupils has increased by 2·5 times since 1939, and the number of students by 15 times.

Progress has created fresh problems, though, particularly with regard to demands for the more even growth of the various regions of the country, which vary greatly in their level of development.

Over the last thirty years (1947–1977), the social product (GNP) has risen sixfold, or an average of 6·2 per cent annually. Total production doubled every eleventh year. Industrial production went up 9·1 per cent annually, on an average, placing Yugoslavia among the world's leading countries regarding economic growth over this period. Today, industrial production is fourteen times larger than in the immediate postwar years. Agricultural production has gone up in the same period by an annual average of 3·3 per cent. A total of 2·7 million dwelling units have been built, so that 43 per cent of the total housing is of postwar date. In the same thirty-year period, 2,665 kilometres of railway have been laid, and 36 per cent of the railway network has been electrified. There are now 1,732,000 passenger cars, 40,000 kilometres of road have been constructed or modernised. Between 1952 and 1976 personal consumption rose more than fourfold, or a yearly average of over 6 per cent. Every second household has a television set, and every third an automobile. About 90 per cent of the population have electricity in their homes, and about 40 per cent mains water supply. Over three million children attend eight-year primary schools, which is about 95 per cent of all children of primary-school age. The number of secondary school pupils has risen by 6·6 times compared with 1947, and the number of students sixfold. Over the same period, 608,000 students graduated from universities and other institutions of higher education. The mortality rate has fallen from 15 per 1000 before the war to 8·5 today. Life expectancy has risen by 14 years for men and 12 years for women to 67 years and 72 years respectively.

Chapter 13

Self-Employment – The Private Sector

In the eyes of some critics, an undesirable aspect of the Yugoslav system is that the so-called private sector of the economy has been allowed to expand—in the domain of catering, crafts and services, transport and agriculture. There is also criticism because a 'group of citizens' can establish an enterprise with a considerable number of workers, because people may have foreign currency accounts in banks, their privacy guaranteed, because of the discussions over increasing the number of workers any one person can employ (at present 3–5 in most republics) and the amount of farmland allowed per household (now 10 hectares). Some foreign observers see in this the emergence of certain paracapitalist forms, leading to the restitution of capitalism, and consider that Yugoslavia is following the path of the consumer society.

A few facts and explanations are necessary to give a correct picture of the situation.

The aim of socialism, of course, is to abolish exploitation and private ownership of the means of production. There is no reason why the workers' movement should renounce these historic goals. Private ownership of the means of production, big capital and monopolies continue to exploit man's labour, despite the myth that economic and social power are no longer linked with private ownership and capital but with the technological structure and so on. There are, however, certain facts and social circumstance in Yugoslavia that should be kept in view.

Producers who own their means of production in Yugoslavia may be divided into farmers and those engaged in craft and service trades. As a rule, these owners do not use the labour of others, but themselves directly produce for their own needs and those of society. A section of them, however, do employ others, and this is, in a sense, a vestige of the hired-labour relationship.

Although exploitation and enrichment ('unjustified enrichment' to use a currently popular term) is prevented by laws, inspection services and taxation, loopholes in regulations and shortcomings of the inspection services in communes, and even on a higher level, give scope for abuses of various kinds. Public opinion is particularly resentful of unjustified enrichment, a subject on which President Tito has spoken several times of late. This is not because it represents a threat to the system, but because it strikes the eye, being contrary to the established system of values. 'In a world of equality, a minor injustice is perhaps felt more than a great injustice in a world of inequality'.[1]

The peasantry is still, absolutely and relatively, the largest social group, as in most of the socialist countries. In the advanced industrialised countries of the capitalist world, it constitutes only a small percentage of those engaged in farming. But under Yugoslav conditions, the peasantry is the basis of small-holding production. Whether we like it or not, socialism cannot rapidly transform this method of production, just as it cannot swiftly turn the peasants into the working class. In the past, Yugoslavs perhaps made the mistake of trying to do this too quickly.

The strength and scope of the private sector

As a rule, a peasant farming household cannot own more than 10 hectares. In fact, about four hectares (10 acres) is the commonest size of holding. Agricultural workers, who form 36 per cent of the working population, create only 20 per cent of the national income.

In 1969, there were 2,026 socially-owned farms with about 1·5 million hectares of arable land (1 hectare = 2·471 acres), this being 15 per cent of the country's total arable land. In 1967, the socialist sector created about 29 per cent of the gross product of agriculture, and produced 49 per cent of the

1. Duverger: *Introduction à la politique.*

total market supplies of farm produce (65 per cent of the wheat and about 50 per cent of the maize sold on the market).

The share of private small-holdings in wheat production for the market has been steadily declining—at present it is just over 30 per cent. However, average wheat yields on these holdings have risen from 15·9 to 19 metric centners per hectare (1 mc. = approx. 1 cwt.), while maize yields have reached around 30 mc. The private small-holdings are the major producer of maize—about 85 per cent of the country's total yield. The volume of produce marketed by private farmers rose by one-and-a-half times from 1968 to 1970, inclusive, though the proportion of the marketed farm produce they supply has declined from 50·1 to 34·4 per cent owing to the even faster rise in output of the socialist sector. The private farmers supply most of the market-garden produce (90 per cent), from 80 to 90 per cent of livestock, but only 10 to 20 per cent of eggs and poultry (as against 80 to 90 per cent in 1959).[2]

In all republics and provinces except Vojvodina, for every farm worker there is only 1 to 1·4 hectares of land, on an average (in Italy and West Germany about 4 hectares in 1968, in the Netherlands 5 hectares, in France and Denmark over 9 hectares per farm worker).

The private farms in Yugoslavia are family small-holdings, usually supporting too many members: in Kosovo there is an average of 7·3 members to a family holding, in Macedonia 5·5, in Bosnia-Herzegovina 5·3, in Montenegro 4·8, in Serbia 4·3, in Croatia 4, in Slovenia 4, and in Vojvodina 3·5.

At the beginning of 1969, 40 per cent of all persons employed in the socialist sector of the economy were peasant-workers, that is to say, persons living in rural areas, tilling their own small-holdings, and working in factories. Together with their families, these number about five million persons. This transitional social stratum thus constitutes one quarter of the entire Yugoslav population, a fact that has its consequences on both industry and agriculture. Absenteeism is

2. It is notable that after a long period of stagnation, with partial collectivisation, Yugoslav agriculture began to move ahead from 1953 onwards. Considerable efforts have been made to modernise production methods, particularly the use of artificial fertiliser (consumption rose from 4·5 kg. per hectare in 1945 to 220 kg. in 1968).

highest in this group of workers, particularly in the farmer's busy season.

Catering, crafts and service trades—The private sector in this domain is gradually expanding. This growth, encouraged in a number of ways, is particularly marked in catering. In 1966, there were all together 6,200 private catering establishments, and in 1970—21,000. The rapid expansion of catering is, of course, closely linked with the foreign tourism boom of recent years.[3] There are about 145,000 private-owned crafts and service shops in the country[4] with about 190,000 employed —the vast majority of them being the owners themselves. The number of such shops has been increasing at the low rate of 1 to 2 per cent annually since 1967. Throughout the country a shortage is felt in this field, especially of services to repair household electrical appliances, TV sets, etc. Import duty on equipment for such workshops was recently lifted.

For a long time the private sector was strictly limited by tax burdens and other restrictions. But as the living standard rose and the socialist sector became much more powerful, the need was, and is still, felt by the public for a higher standard of services. The growth of the private sector in response to this also meant, among other things, an increase in the employment level.

The tertiary sector of the economy is already attracting more of the working population than the primary and secondary sectors, although at the present time the primary is dominant, employing 50·7 per cent, compared with 24·3 per cent in the secondary and 25 per cent in the tertiary sectors; (France had relatively more people employed in tertiary activities in 1901 than Yugoslavia in 1970, while the USA had more in 1820 than Yugoslavia in 1953). The social and economic need for the development of services opens up prospects for the growth of the private sector, particularly crafts and catering. More-

3. By 1970, the number of foreign tourists was 17 times the 1939 figure. In that year, 4·7 million tourists visited Yugoslavia (22 million tourist days). The number of Yugoslav holiday-makers was ten times the 1939 figure. The growth of tourism has been particularly rapid in the past few years.

4. Of the 145,000 private businesses, 24,000 are engaged in metal working, 20,000 in wood working, 19,000 in work involving textiles, 26,000 in building and decorating.

over, the purchase of their own tools and equipment so that they may be self-employed is one of the ways in which Yugoslavs working temporarily abroad can return home sooner.

The economic power of the private sector

A true picture of the economic strength of the private sector in Yugoslavia will be gained from the following data:

The volume of production of the private sector has considerably increased in recent years: in catering more than threefold, and in road transport almost threefold. In crafts and service trades and in agriculture, the private sector predominates (63 per cent and 79 per cent respectively). In catering, road transport and building it is much smaller (17, 14 and 13 per cent). In fact, catering and road transport constitute only a small part (4·4 per cent) of the whole private sector. The share of the private sector, including agriculture, in the total national product amounts to 20 per cent, the share of private catering and road transport—each 0·4 per cent—being negligible. This is stressed in view of the fact that some foreign observers have mentioned these two branches as evidence of Yugoslavia's trend towards capitalism. The strengthening of the socialist sector, the rise in the living standard and the rapid growth of tertiary activities create a need and possibilities for a certain guided increase in private enterprise.

These data (Table 6) show a decline in the share of the private sector in the national product, the decisive influence here being the growth of industry. The share of the socialist sector has risen to 79 per cent, and the share of crafts fallen from 7·5 to about 5 per cent.

The number of those employed in the private sector is likewise declining. From 2·6 per cent of the employed in 1950, it fell to 2·2 per cent in 1970.[5]

The third group of data (Table 7) shows that from 1952 to 1969 the national product rose, at fixed prices, by 3·6 times, or about 8 per cent annually, while the private sector increased its output by 2·2 times or 4·8 per cent annually—this growth being mainly due to agriculture. The share of crafts here too shows a certain decline.

---

5. Federal Statistical Institute, 1971.

Table 6

The National Product by Ownership and Activity Sectors

	Total	Socialist sector	Private sector	Industry	Farming	Forestry	Building	Transport	Trade & catering	Crafts
				In million dinars						
1952	9,490	7,209	2,281	4,462	2,257	44	693	755	580	429
1954	12,991	9,408	3,583	5,588	3,203	236	938	946	1,011	749
1959	24,463	17,551	6,912	10,504	6,860	285	1,768	1,553	2,500	1,294
1964	61,001	48,050	12,951	24,749	15,584	911	4,846	4,825	6,826	3,261
1969	132,485	106,084	26,401	47,011	29,137	1,586	11,096	11,105	24,403	8,148
				Structure in %						
1952	100	75·3	24·7	48·4	24·5	0·5	7·5	8·2	6·3	4·6
1954	100	72·4	27·6	44·1	25·3	1·8	7·4	7·5	8·0	5·9
1959	100	71·7	28·3	42·9	28·0	1·2	6·0	6·3	10·2	5·4
1965	100	78·8	24·2	40·6	25·5	1·5	8·0	7·9	11·2	5·3
1969	100	80·1	19·9	35·5	22·0	1·2	8·4	8·4	18·4	6·1
			Structure of the economy calculated at 1966 prices in %							
1952	100	66·0	34·0	23·6	34·1	3·8	9·6	7·3	14·1	7·5
1954	100	64·0	36·0	23·4	37·3	2·5	9·6	6·9	12·6	7·7
1959	100	66·8	33·2	27·9	38·6	1·8	5·8	7·4	12·8	5·7
1964	100	77·8	22·2	34·9	27·8	1·5	8·2	7·7	14·9	5·0
1969	100	79·0	24·0	36·5	24·9	1·2	7·4	8·9	16·2	4·8

Table 7

Movements of the National Product by Ownership and Activity Sectors (in 1966 prices)

	Total	Socialist sector	Private sector	Industry	Farming	Forestry	Building	Transport	Trade & Catering	Crafts
1952	31,326	20,680	10,646	7,400	10,678	1,175	2,294	2,302	4,432	2,345
1954	39,243	25,125	14,118	9,199	14,635	991	3,770	2,702	4,940	3,006
1959	63,263	42,234	21,029	17,626	24,475	1,123	3,693	4,670	8,086	3,591
1964	91,025	70,855	20,170	31,758	25,343	1,359	7,460	7,058	13,536	4,511
1969	113,629	89,790	23,839	41,508	28,321	1,366	8,439	10,144	18,418	5,433
Indices										
1969/1952	362·7	434·2	223·9	560·9	265·2	116·3	281·9	440·7	415·6	231·7
1969/1964	124·8	126·7	118·2	130·7	111·8	100·5	113·1	143·7	136·1	120·4
1964/1959	143·9	167·8	95·9	180·2	103·5	121·0	202·0	151·1	167·4	125·6
1959/1954	161·2	168·1	149·0	191·6	167·2	113·3	98·0	172·8	163·7	119·5
Average growth rate										
1952–1969	7·9	9·0	4·8	10·7	5·9	0·9	6·3	9·1	8·7	5·1
1964–1969	4·5	4·8	3·4	5·5	2·3	0·1	2·5	7·5	6·4	3·8
1959–1964	7·6	10·9	−0·8	12·5	0·7	3·9	15·1	8·6	10·9	4·7
1954–1959	10·0	10·9	8·3	13·9	10·8	2·5	−0·4	11·6	10·4	3·6

M

The private sector in some other socialist countries

In some socialist countries of Eastern Europe, particularly the German Democratic Republic and Poland, the private sector in the domain of production and services is more developed than in Yugoslavia. In these countries, however, private ownership and capitalism have ceased to be identified with each other for a long time.

According to statistical data for 1970 (in which the entire structure of private ownership in production is not covered), the German Democratic Republic has 3,600 large private enterprises and factories. In addition there are 5,600 enterprises under joint private and state ownership. This semi-state sector accounts for 8·6 per cent of the net product (1969 figure) and the private sector for 5·6 per cent. Private enterprises employ 686,000 workers, and the mixed enterprises 490,000. Every seventh employed person in this country works in an enterprise which is wholly or partly privately-owned.

East Germany has a total of 116,500 private workshops with a turn-over of 8,000 million marks. Private trade is also considerable: of the total trade turn-over of 58,000 million marks in 1969, 6,700 million (11·6 per cent) was in private shops and 5,300 million (9·1 per cent) in semi-private.

According to official East German data for 1970, 77·2 per cent of the gross product of industry was created by the socialist sector, 6·6 per cent by the co-operative sector, and 16·2 per cent by the purely private sector.

The scope of private initiative is explained as a feature of a 'more developed system of socialism'. In Czechoslovakia, however, which must certainly rank among the industrially most developed of socialist countries, private enterprise is negligible.

In Poland, private ownership is strongest in farming. Of the total of 19·5 million hectares, 16·3 million (85·7 per cent) are privately owned, and 2·8 million (14·3 per cent) state-owned. The maximum land holding is 50 hectares, and in regions that were under German occupation, 100 hectares. The private sector of agriculture provides 85 per cent of all farm production.

Private trade in Poland is estimated to employ over 200,000 persons, and small private industrial enterprises 28,000, while 170,000 craft shops employ about 340,000 people.

There is no reason to doubt that this is in line with the social and economic requirements of these countries, or to imagine that East Germany and Poland, because of their developed private sector, could turn capitalist.

Group enterprises

What possibilities are there for capitalisation and abuses in enterprises formed by groups of citizens? Yugoslav law permits citizens to set up enterprises, under prescribed conditions, which after their foundation are treated as socially-owned enterprises from the point of view of management and income distribution.

Since global data are lacking, the figures for the Republic of Serbia will be given as an illustration:

On June 30, 1970, there were 122 such enterprises on the territory of Serbia, 132 fewer than a year previously. According to their annual financial reports for 1969, 118[6] of these enterprises (out of the total 5,457 economic organisations in the republic) created 0·2 per cent of the total earnings of the Serbian economy. This means that their role in economic life is minimal. At the end of 1969, they employed all together 3,226 persons, of whom most were unskilled, and only 63 had advanced education.[7] Only nine directors had advanced education, 36 had intermediate (secondary) education, and the rest were skilled workers.

Checks revealed that in such enterprises the organs of self-management were either non-existent or not functioning, that the director was not appointed according to specified procedure, and that the enterprises were mostly founded by close relatives. The business of the enterprises was frequently changed, under the guise of expanding its activity, they changed also their place of registration, without communal permission, did not keep proper books and records, or pay their taxes.[8]

6. Of which 76 were engaged in crafts, 20 in trade and catering, 13 in building, 3 in industry, 3 in agriculture, 3 in transport and other activities.
7. Advanced education (university)—63 persons, higher education—78, intermediate education—424, primary education—271, highly-qualified workers—733, semi-skilled workers—228, unskilled workers—1,107.
8. Report of the inspection carried out by the Public Accountancy and Auditing Service of Yugoslavia for 1970.

After this check, 40 of the 118 enterprises were refused further permission to operate.

The socialist or capitalist character of private labour

Criticism of capitalism is based on the fact that private ownership dominates and is founded on exploitation of others' labour. Under Yugoslav conditions, private ownership of means of production is different from both the social and the economic standpoint. The private sector accounts for a very minor share of the national income, and is dominant only in the agricultural branch of the economy. The share of industry in this income is rapidly increasing in relation to agriculture, and the socialist sector of agriculture is gaining strength. The co-operation of the private sector of agriculture with the socialist is leading to the transformation of the former, not the latter. If the whole trend of development is towards the steady consolidation and growth of the socialist sector, then a certain expansion of the private sector may be allowed, without risk of social distortions, in some deficient areas of activity—crafts, catering and the like. Society is obliged to prevent speculation, unjustified enrichment, wherever it occurs, but not by stamping out private initiative and preventing people from working with their own means of production. This is indeed a vestige of the old system, but at the same time it reflects the country's need at the present stage of development.

Constitutional Amendment 24 of 1971 guarantees freedom of the individual to work with his own means of production, and places such activity on a par with work in the socialist sector. Private enterprises are guaranteed the right to associate among themselves and with other enterprises, to self-management and income distribution.

The Constitution likewise allows the possibility of an increase in the number of workers one person may employ, and of the maximum land holding in mountainous regions. It is considered that the present 10 hectare maximum is insufficient in such regions for the individual farmer to earn a living—hence, the heavy influx into towns.

There can be no doubt that the socialist sector will continue to dominate the economy, and to an increasing extent, in view of its great concentration of resources and capital formation, but the work of the self-employed will also be encouraged, since it represents no threat to society. In any case, the communes have wide powers to control and channel such activity: it is they who grant permission for the opening of craft and service shops and enterprises, authorise the labour contracts of those working for private employers, levy taxes and carry out inspection.

Means of production

There are no restrictions on the purchase of means of production such as machinery, tools, equipment used in work, but the communal taxation policy has generally had a discouraging effect.

Farmers were faced with a seemingly insoluble problem here: a tractor does not pay on only 10 hectares, but rigorous taxation was imposed on those who hired out their tractor to others. Although Yugoslavia today has about 70,000 tractors, and it is believed that one tractor replaces 1,000 horses, there are just as many horses now as there used to be—around 1·1 million.[9] Tractors, in fact, are employed on the 15 per cent of arable land in the socialist sector, while the other 85 per cent is for the most part tilled with the aid of draft animals.

For this reason, the assembly of the Autonomous Province of Vojvodina, the granary of Yugoslavia, recently passed a law explicitly forbidding communes to levy any taxes on farm machinery, including tractors.

Co-operation in production with the socialist sector

It is precisely the need to use modern machinery that encourages the individual farmer to co-operate in production with the economic organisations in the socialist sector of farming. The main organiser of such co-operation is the agricultural co-operative, which has done much to promote the use of modern methods by private farmers. Co-operation is most highly developed in arable and livestock farming. The supply of high-quality seed, and fertiliser, stable prices, especially of wheat, guaranteed purchase, a favourable credit policy—

9. The number of horses in Britain has fallen by 70 per cent in the past 10 years, in France by one third, and in the Soviet Union by one half.

all this is part of the movement to advance agriculture, which
has undeniably produced good results, as already mentioned.

Self-management in agricultural co-operatives

The co-operative movement, in which farmers voluntarily
associate, has quite a lengthy tradition in Yugoslavia. Previously, though, there was a large number of small, economically
weak organisations. Thanks to integration, imposed by economic necessity, the number of agricultural co-operatives has
decreased over the past ten years from 3,700 to 1,100.

The co-operative councils, as the self-management organs,
are composed of members of the co-operative and workers
employed in the co-operative.

In 1970, members with from 2 to 5 hectares formed the most
numerous group (30 per cent) in the co-operative councils,
members without land made up 25 per cent.

The co-operatives engage in production and marketing, and
organise co-operation with the large factory-farms, the trade
network and other co-operatives. They help the individual
farmer to obtain tools and other requirements and to sell his
produce.

The links between the private and socialist sectors of agriculture are many and varied, as are the forms of trading and
supply between village and town, between the retail network
and the agricultural producer.

In Slovenia, the most developed Yugoslav republic, steps
have been taken to encourage peasants to remain in their farms
in mountainous and other tourist regions: tourist organisations
make arrangements with peasants (provision of private holiday accommodation, etc.) which are of benefit to both.

A number of special bureaus have been established in this
republic to arrange co-operation in an efficient manner. The
individual farmer comes to the bureau and proposes a certain
type of co-operation. Experts inspect his holding, assess its
possibilities and draw up a plan—which crops it would pay
him best to grow or, in the case of tourism, what adaptation or
building needs to be done, what kind of amenities to provide.
In other words, an expert economic analysis is given, on the
basis of which the peasant is offered a contract. If he accepts
this, he gains the right to a loan to help him implement the

suggested measures. A sum is earmarked for such loans in the budgets of the republics and communes. The credit bank in such circumstances approves loans with a specially low interest rate of 2 to 3 per cent. This, then, is a modern form of co-operation in which the socialist sector provides capital and expertise, a project and programme in accordance with the development of the socialist sector, while the private producer contributes his labour, production and land.

There are, thus, various forms of encouraging the individual's work and initiative, of linking the private sector with the socialist, and achieving a socialising effect on the former. Such co-operation does not lead to the reproduction of capitalist relations; on the contrary, it tends to socialise private work and enables people to enjoy a higher living standard.

Chapter 14

Worker Management and Technology

Worker management—a formula of the past or future?
'Is worker management suited to modern technology?' is a
question frequently posed.

Sceptics assert that it is the ideology of the early industrial
revolution, a theory and organisation for medium-sized enterprises. The new technological revolution calls for large technical and economic systems, while worker management, they
say, appears to be the type of socialist order for small units,
decentralised and loosely knit, dealing with the problems of
each individual enterprise, each work unit. The modern technical revolution, it is claimed, needs a 'general socialism',
tending towards joint organisation of production.

Some endeavour to prove that worker management hampers
modern technology and work organisation.

Yugoslav results to date, however, indicate the opposite:
over the past fifteen years, the country has been among the
group of states with the fastest economic growth rate in the
world. This is not sufficient proof, though. To be able to see
all the consequences of the techno-economic revolution and
test worker management properly, a broader time-span should
be considered, and at a higher technological level than that
reached by Yugoslavia today.

It is difficult for Yugoslavs to gain a full insight here, since
we have no great experience as regards association, integration
and organisation of big systems. What experience we have is
very modest in comparison with that of the advanced states.

However, there is no aspect that we have studied in science,
economics and technology that does not show the full conformity of worker management with the technological rev-

olution. Workers are in favour of technological innovations because higher productivity brings higher earnings and a better living standard.

A limiting factor is the level of education and vocational skill of the employed. Though this is changing fast, the educational structure cannot be transformed in a decade or so.

Backwardness, and not modern technology, is the factor hampering worker management. As long as the majority of workers remain poorly educated, they are not qualified to pass sound and fundamental decisions. The danger here is that technocrats and politicians begin to take decisions in their name.

It would be extremely harmful to the very idea of worker management if current practice were to become fixed in a mould and the forms of organisation sclerotic, ignoring technical and economic changes and changes in the system of management. Whatever structure and superstructure may be in question, if they lack a real material base they cannot last long. If worker management, as an idea and practice, failed to follow material changes, it could not be justified. How many times in history have noble ideas perished simply because they could not reach man, because they lacked a grasp of reality?

With the modernisation of production and improvement of public services and amenities, the need is already felt for workers' councils to 'come out of the factories', instead of being isolated within them, dealing only with production and enterprise affairs. There is a need for them to concern themselves with decision-making on all levels in the commune and further afield. Automation and technological advances will gradually transform production itself into a type of public service, which will be highly integrated and automated. Self-management will be transferred more and more from the field of direct production to the broader domain of public life—from the local community to the country as a whole. There is broad scope for the future development of self-management in that direction.

Contemporary technical advances open up prospects of faster human progress and the raising of the living standard. But at the same time there is a danger of these advances becoming a means of man's further alienation from the fruits of his

labour and from government. If industry is completely automated, as futurologists forecast, by the end of the century,
both workers and intellectuals will be placed in the situation
of either participating in a system of despotic technocracy, with
unlimited accumulation of power, a monopoly of information
media, and the loss of true democratic freedom, or establishing
a democratic system of direct public control and self-management on all levels.

One of the prime causes of the worldwide protests of the
younger generation is the growing gulf between the ordinary
man and all centres of political, economic and even cultural
decision-making and activity. The young are losing interest not
in politics itself, but in the way it is conducted. Their dissatisfaction is rooted in the awareness that political systems and
movements mostly expect young people to act but not think,
to carry out their duties but not participate fully in public life.

The danger of technocracy

The arrival of new, trained people, fired with a desire for
efficiency, increases the danger of technocracy in economic
organisations. When Constitutional Amendment 25, adopted
in 1968, permitted collectives themselves to decide on the
character, size and composition of their managing boards, it
was not long before they consisted mainly of expert executive
staff, those in charge of the actual operation of the enterprise.
The managing boards began to resemble expert consultative
bodies rather than organs of worker management.

It is not a function of worker management to decide on
specialised matters. There is a need for professional management, i.e. highly qualified and experienced executives, just as
much as in a modern capitalist industrial firm. Professional
management is a highly specialised occupation, particularly
when large systems and complex production processes are involved. Economists and engineers cannot be expected to fall
in with the reasoning of the majority if this runs counter to
their knowledge and experience.

The appearance of technocracy is inevitable. Whether its
domination can be avoided depends on the methods and forms
of government in a particular society. Self-management offers
one solution to this problem.

Engineers and experts often have a decisive say in worker-management bodies, not numerically but by their actual influence.[1]

Some fear that this trend favouring the professional management in fact means the emergence of technocracy. The workers, however, look at it differently. They regard knowledge, expertise, as a production force that is just as important as modern machinery. Every day, matters requiring knowledge greater than theirs have to be settled in an enterprise. Naturally, the workers await the opinion of those who know more about it than they do.

But the experts' influence is not unlimited. All decisions they reach must be clearly explained in language the workers can understand and placed before the workers' council. The experts have to convince the workers, get their support and approval. True, experts are not always keen to explain to the uninformed what a development programme and modern production mean and entail. But, at the same time, they know that the interest and understanding of the producers are vital for the successful implementation of any programme. The fact that engineers and other experts usually gain a high percentage of the votes in secret ballots for worker-management bodies indicates the workers' respect for know-how, and also confirms that the expert staff have not abused their position.

Professional management and worker management

Professional management should become, to an increasing extent, a technical service on which worker management relies. At present, studies are in progress on the following:

—how to create a unified information system in society as the basis of self-management decision-making;

—how to set up a system for following capital formation, so

1. The number of workers' council members with advanced (university) education increased from 3 per cent in 1956 to over 10 per cent in 1970. The number with intermediate (secondary) education rose in the same period from 12 per cent to 16 per cent, while the number of semi-skilled workers in this body fell. Workers' council chairmen with advanced or higher education increased from 4 per cent to 19 per cent in the 1960–70 period. There was a particularly marked increase in the number of managing board chairmen with higher education: from 7 per cent in 1962 to 29 per cent in 1970.

that the worker-managers get a full insight into the situation and base their decisions on this;

—how to improve, modernise the organisation of, and integrate existing entities in the economy from which complex economic systems, based on worker management, could develop.

The primary condition of self-management is that the self-managing society must be fully informed. At present, however, we are still too preoccupied with equipment and investment in equipment, and neglect the other components of growth. OECD research has shown that technological differences between countries are less the result of equipment than of other factors: the personnel structure, investment, the type and area of research and development, and the level of management. By management we mean, of course, the scientific discipline dealing with the application of modern methods and means, including computers, in preparing and carrying out decisions. Who actually makes the decisions, and in whose interest, depend on the social system.

In Yugoslavia, little research has so far been done in the field of management, the use of modern methods, and programming techniques. We lag further behind the advanced countries in this respect than in technological research.

For instance, the federal fund for loans to the underdeveloped regions primarily provides credits for equipment. If a credit is requested for a research project, it is turned down on the grounds that this does not come within the scope of the fund.

According to a 1969 analysis by the Federal Economic Chamber covering 917 enterprises, mostly industrial, of the total investment in research and development, only 4 per cent was allocated for promoting management methods and work organisation. It is also symptomatic that in 1968 only about 4 per cent of enterprises were using computers in planning, programming, operative management and organisation. In 1970 Yugoslavia had ten computers per million inhabitants,[2]

2. By comparison, the number of computers per million inhabitants were USA 390; West Germany 90; Japan 105; East Europe 19; of which USSR 23; Yugoslavia 17.

but the number is increasing rapidly (doubling every five years). According to information supplied by the Federal Economic Chamber, one third of all enterprises plan to introduce computers in the near future.

Industry undoubtedly shows the most understanding of the need to raise the level of management. In the non-economic activities—the civil service, education, regional development, and public services—not much has been done so far to improve efficiency by adopting modern management methods.

Research and development

The programming of development has usually been identified with the physical growth of production, with personnel, education and information taking a back seat.

According to analyses made in 1968 and 1969 in enterprises employing 60 per cent of the industrial labour force and giving about 60 per cent of the total value of industrial production,[3] over half the enterprises covered either had no development programme at all, or else a programme for only one to two years. Only 30 per cent of programmes are completely carried through, while about 60 per cent are partially implemented. The record in this respect is better among small and medium-sized enterprises (up to 500 workers), which means that larger enterprises are inclined to draw up programmes more because of adjustment to the home and foreign market.

Questionnaires also show that by 1975, 45 per cent of enterprises will have undertaken changes in the technological field, while about 56 per cent will have mastered new types of production. About 34 per cent of those questioned cited integration with other Yugoslav enterprises as the decisive factor in their future development, while 20 per cent gave integration with foreign partners.

One third of the total personnel engaged in research in Yugoslavia work in the economy (60 per cent of technical science researchers). The economy provides 47 per cent of the money spent on pure research activity (94 per cent in technical sciences and 62 per cent in biotechnical in 1968), and 59 per

3. Analyses of the Federal Economic Chamber for 1968 and 1969.

cent of the resources spent on all types of research in the country.

Table 8 indicates trends in investment by the economy in research activity.

Table 8
Comparative Investment in Different Branches of Research

—investment in technical sciences	85·4%
—investment in biotechnical sciences	9·8%
—investment in social sciences	3·4%
—investment in natural sciences and mathematics	1·3%
—investment in medical science	0·1%
—mastering of new products	30%
—studying new techniques and production processes	28%
—improving the quality of products	20%
—market research	4%
—management and work organisation	4%
—studying foreign production processes and purchase of licences	2%
—industrial design	2%
—information and documentation	2%
—sociological research	0·15%
—other research	7·85%

Source: *Programming, Research and Development in the Economy,* Federal Economic Chamber, 1969.

The bounds of necessity

A realistic picture of Yugoslav society should be kept in view—a society on a certain level of development and with a certain national income, which is multinational and based on self-management.

The present and future call for the linking up of science with practical life and work, permanent education, and the inclusion of the school system in the whole social framework of work and creative activity.

The management of big systems is a particularly acute problem, for the enclosing of such systems within regional boundaries and their irrational construction could have serious consequences for the country's entire economic development. A big system does not necessarily entail concentration of management in one place, but it does mean the activation of large-scale resources by modern methods. It is time we insisted not only on the science of production but also on the science of management. The fact that 55 per cent of Yugoslav enterprises are now modernised and automated simply heightens the need for this.

To an increasing extent the laws of economic growth must be observed in a world tending ever more towards integration. In Yugoslavia, for instance, there are five oil refineries. Their total capacity is 8·6 million tons annually, and the country needs five million tons. Why five refineries? They enjoy tariff protection, while market prices are such as to give the maximum possible profit.

Another instance of irrationality is the fact that Yugoslavia has eight ports, whose total capacity is on a par with that of one foreign port of optimum size. It has, in fact, more ports than some highly developed maritime states. For the most part there is no specialisation: each port handles all types of cargo. The volume of goods handled has grown rapidly in recent years, but without a commensurate increase in earnings, because of the competition. Worker management is not 'to blame' here: the interests of several republics are in question, and a compromise must be patiently worked out.

Difficulties were encountered in creating a large system in the sphere of electric power production and distribution. Power stations with high production costs were all for a link-up, while the others were against it on the grounds that integration would allow the flow of resources from the area of highly-productive labour to that of low productivity. The national element also entered into this problem, since the power stations are located in various republics. In Yugoslav society, relations cannot be founded on the destruction of the weaker by the stronger, but neither can low productivity be tolerated and protected by state measures at the expense of high labour productivity.

Self-management is not in contradiction with modern production processes, but a low level of development, insufficient knowledge and information, and anachronistic habits certainly are.

Chapter 15

Yugoslav Planning Experience

Self-management is incompatible with centralised planning. Production and development plans are necessary, but at all levels, from the enterprise (the planning nucleus) and commune to the autonomous provinces, republics and federation. The aim is to find out where interests (economic, regional and national) coincide and conflict, so that a joint programme of future development can be achieved by synthesis.

Every enterprise adjusts itself to market conditions, and decides for itself on the quantity, quality and prices of its products. Co-ordination is carried out through business associations and economic councils from communal to federal level. In this way the wishes of the economic base 'rise' and the guidelines and wishes of the summit 'descend'.

The plan does not have the force of a directive: it is indicative, providing guidance and stimulus. It indicates what it is particularly desired to achieve. It may, for instance, lay stress on power production, iron and steel production, non-ferrous metallurgy, the basic chemical industry, tourism or certain branches of agriculture. The society achieves the desired effect by its policy in the spheres of prices, earnings and distribution, foreign currency and trade, taxation, and credit.

Planning—different interpretations of the same idea

From the point of view of planning, the existing economic systems may be roughly divided into two types: in one the economy is regulated by centralised decision-making, and in the other—by the mechanism of the market.

Today, neither total planning of production nor complete freedom of the market can be found anywhere in their pure form, but there are considerable differences in the degree of planning, or the extent to which market laws are allowed free play. It is not so much a case of complete rejection of the market in one system, and of planning in the other, but of the balance struck between the two.

When judging the character of a system from the planning standpoint, certain questions arise: to what extent do relations between the producer and the summit, the enterprise and the state, differ? What are the motivating forces of economic activity and who controls industrial and public investment?

Without entering into an evaluation of political systems, we can distinguish three types of planning:

—planning as state management of the economy;

—planning in which economic management is decentralised, in which numerous means and factors are brought into play, and where a balance between production and consumption is not established once and for all by a planning decision, but gradually by studying the market and in conformity with it;

—an economy in which the employers and employees are separate from each other, the latter having only their labour, while the former are the owners of the means of production, and hence of the surplus product, and have a decisive say on all economic trends.

Integral planning assumes, at the very least, the absolute power of the planners. In such a planning system, it is hard to follow the criterion of profitability very closely. If the state determines the income of each and all, the only way of ensuring the smooth functioning of the system is for the state not to consult those it governs very frequently. When centralised planning is used as a means of speeding up industrialisation, as was the case in Yugoslavia just after the war, it is difficult to combine the building up of a democracy with this kind of planning.

The highly developed capitalist industrial societies of today rely on planning and guidance to a certain extent to reduce the risk and the likelihood of crises inherent in an unfettered capitalist market economy.

The traditional concept of planning

A few decades ago, it was widely held that planning was possible only in a socialist society.

Marx and Engels gave a basic definition of planning after

N

observing the traditional capitalist society. One of the vital functions of planning, Marx stressed, was the co-ordination of production and consumption:

'Only when production is under the real planned control of society does society establish a link between the amount of social working time used to produce various articles and the extent of the social needs they are to satisfy.'

Since Marx's time, many leading Western economists have reached almost identical conclusions regarding planning and the development of society. In practice as well as in theory, all the advanced capitalist states have accepted various forms of planning and guidance of the national economy.

Planning has become a 'movement', though its forms and intensity are certainly not the same everywhere.

Even in socialist countries, planning is not conceived as a means of solving all problems of economic development. The socialist countries with a centralised statist concept of planning realise that central planning cannot neutralise the effect of the laws of commodity production and the individual motives of people to produce and spend.

Professor Jevsej Liberman of Kharkov, a prominent Soviet economist, wrote at the beginning of 1971 about the over-emphasis on 'administrative methods at the expense of economic, which has encouraged, both morally and materially enterprises to adopt oversized production plans in the Soviet economy.' 'I have proposed,' says Liberman, 'that profit and profitability be recognised as the basic indicators of an enterprise's work,'[1] along with the obligation of fulfilling the production programme planned in natural indicators.

In the same period, Nicolae Ceausescu, General Secretary of the Communist Party of Romania, also spoke in favour of 'the liquidation of too much centralism and the transfer of responsibility for foreign trade directly to the producers'. He declared that 'an enterprise has carried out its plan only when the goods produced have been sold. On this the financial success of an enterprise, and the earnings of its workers, will depend'.[2]

1. Liberman: *Economic methods of increasing the efficiency of social production*, according to *Politika* of February 3, 1971.
2. According to *Politika* of February 2, 1971.

Three periods in the evolution of planning in Yugoslavia

Over the relatively short period of twenty-five years, Yugoslavia has tried out three different planning systems.

The first was the centralised planning of the immediate postwar years. 'The state sets the direction of economic life and development by a general economic plan, based on the state and co-operative sectors, but with general control over the private sector of the economy.'[3]

The Federation adopted the 'general state and economic plan', the republics—republican economic plans, and the autonomous provinces, districts and communes—their own plans.

The first period coincides with the First Five-year Plan (1947–1953), which had the force of law and formed the basis of state intervention in the economy. Planning was total and interventionist, with precisely set targets for every enterprise with regard to the volume, range and value of production.

This type of planning could only bear fruit in an extensive economy, and as time passed it began to hamper initiative in various spheres.

The theoretical foundations of this planning system were essentially Stalinist: that the market and plan were mutually exclusive, and that strict central planning was a principle of socialism.

The second period begins in the fifties with the introduction of worker management, when new relations between the state and economic organisations were established, the period when state monopoly was eroded by economic and political democracy.

At this time planning ceased to be a function of the state alone. So-called social planning was introduced, in which the economic organisations were the main actors. The Law on Planned Management of the National Economy (1961) provided for republican and other socio-economic development plans, and independent plans of economic organisations, in addition to the federal plan.

Social planning, in this period, set the basic proportions between production and distribution. The economic organisations

3. The 1947 Constitution, Art. 15.

drew up their own plans of operation, undertaking to keep to the proportions set by the socio-economic development plans.[4] These enterprise plans changed in line with market trends.

This method of planning, partly centralised and partly on a self-management basis, was still closer to the former than the latter.

The third kind of planning was laid down in the 1963 Constitution: planning is the function and need of producers and citizens, and co-ordinates production and consumption. The socio-economic development plans constitute special programmes which do not have the character of a law. The main purpose of this change was to end the existing state monopoly in the field of investment.

The Socio-economic Plan (1966–1970), which took three years to draw up and adopt, had two new qualities: in the first place, the raising of the living standard was among the economic goals; secondly, the conditions of economic activity were such as to prevent monopoly and stimulate branches of special concern to the society.

It is often asked whether there is any kind of guidance of the national economy in the Yugoslav, self-management system of planning.

The Basic Law on Social Planning passed in July 1970 precisely defines planning goals.

The socio-economic plans of Yugoslavia, according to this law, cover the following:

—the general lines of development,

—general policy in the domain of the living standard, employment and personnel training,

—basic relationships in the distribution of the national product and national income,

—basic investment policy,

—policy in the field of foreign economic relations,

—the policy relating to faster growth in the underdeveloped republics and regions,

4. The fundamental proportions took into account: (1) the extent of utilisation of capacities by branches and republics; (2) basic capital construction; (3) the salaries' fund, by branches and republics; (4) average rate of accumulation of capital and funds; (5) resources distributed by the budget.

—strengthening the country's defensive ability and security. The constitutional reform has since transferred investment from the sphere of planning to the economic base. Until recently, about 30 per cent of investments were controlled at federal level: the Central Fund for the Underdeveloped, and investment in the Djerdap hydro-electric and navigation system on the Danube (on the Romanian border), the 700-km Belgrade-Bar railway, the Skopje iron and steel works, the aluminium plant in Montenegro.

The 'hierarchy' of plans

The plans are not linked by any hierarchical arrangement. Enterprises have the right to abandon their plans at any time. Every decision is the outcome of dialogue and the wishes of the whole community based on knowledge and study of the objective laws of economic development—embodied in the plan—and the wishes and judgement of the people actually engaged in production. It is not a case of having no planning institutions or procedure. Provision is made for various types of planning and procedure, there is an institute for complaints if any plan adversely affects the interests of any of the concerned, responsibility for execution of a plan is provided for, a network of expert bodies engaged in planning has been established, and the self-management compact is available as a planning method.

Unstable trends in production, consumption, goods reserves and demand, the price movements, inflation, increase in imports and the trade deficit which have been features of the Yugoslav economy in recent years are not the result of self-management nor, primarily, of weaknesses and shortcomings in long-term planning. An inadequate technological level, low productivity, tariff and other barriers abroad, and changes on the world market have placed enormous difficulties in the way of stabilisation and incorporation in the international market.

Planning in a self-management system must take into account the action of the market; it must combine direct democracy in enterprises with the planned forecasts for the country, and must link up the national economy with the world economy and market. The multinational population, and federal and

self-management system of the country constitute strong
reasons for adopting decentralised planning, which is quite
justified economically since it encourages initiative, co-ordinates interests, and favours economic criteria instead of political
voluntarism and centralistic subjectivism.

The Yugoslav medium-term socio-economic plan (1971–
1975), which has already been brought forward for discussion
three times, has still not been passed because of the need for
further co-ordination with regional plans, and trade union
criticism that it protects those enterprises that maintain a business policy of extensive and low-productivity output by means
of the low personal incomes of their workers.

A long-term national development plan is at present being
drawn up, providing for a growth of production by about three
and a half times, and a rise in the *per capita* income to about
2,000 by 1985.

Chapter 16

Yugoslav Workers Abroad and Foreign Capital

Exodus from farming

In recent decades, Yugoslavia has experienced those population and manpower upheavals that are inevitable when an agrarian country sets out to industrialise rapidly.

In the thirty-five years prior to the adoption of socialism, the agrarian population had fallen by only 5 per cent, and formed 75 per cent of the total in 1945. In the twenty-five years since the war, it has been reduced by almost 40 per cent. All other sections of the population and occupations have increased in number; only the number of peasants has steadily declined.

A population shift from farming to other occupations is naturally limited by a country's level of economic development and rate of economic growth. From 1945 to 1949, the number of employed persons rose eightfold. The annual rate of employment growth from 1945 to 1969 averaged 8·9 per cent.

In 1939, there were 59 employed persons per thousand—a third of the figure for 1970. In the first five postwar years (1946–1950) the employment rate doubled, but it took a further twenty years before it had doubled again.

The average annual increase in total industrial employment in the world is around 2·5 per cent and shows a slight tendency to rise. In the socialist countries of East Europe (with the Soviet Union) this increase is stable at about 3·5 per cent. In other parts of Europe it has slowed down considerably. The Yugoslav rate of growth in industrial employment is above the European and world average, approaching that in the socialist countries. In the 1956–1969 period, industrial employment went up by 4·6 per cent annually on an average. A slow-down in the growth rate occurred after the 1965 reform was inaugurated; it was 7·5 per cent from 1956 to 1960; 5·1 per cent from 1961 to 1965; and only 3 per cent in 1961 to 1969. Only industrial employment is considered for the sake of comparison.

Slow-down in new employment

The 1965 reform sharply focussed attention on productivity, exposed all the previous weaknesses in employment policy and pointed to the need to free industry of surplus manpower. A new era began. Extensive investment was avoided, factories were modernised, and greater care was paid to cost-cutting and profitability. Analyses showed that one fifth of the employed (about 700,000) held jobs requiring a higher level of education or training than they had.[1] The improvement of the qualifications of those already employed thus imposed itself as an urgent need, and there was a consequent standstill in new employment. In the 1965–1967 period, there was even a fall in the number of employed, of about 100,000.

Throughout the postwar period, the economic and demographic development of Yugoslavia have been marked by great pressure of surplus unskilled labour from rural areas and the annual influx of from 80,000 to 100,000 young people leaving school and seeking jobs.

It is estimated that the surplus labour in rural areas is in the region of 1,300,000 even today. This is an enormous army of manpower which is ever ready to 'set out for the city'.

Like it or not, at the present moment Yugoslavia is not in a position to provide full employment. The difficulties arising from agrarian overpopulation and industrial labour redundancy—the country's great headache—are not, of course, exclusively Yugoslav problems. The migration of workers is not unknown in economic history. All agrarian countries undergoing industrialisation pass through this process. After the Second World War, Italy adopted a modern policy of economic development, with large-scale capital assistance from abroad (primarily the USA), but even so a steady stream of workers went abroad. Even from Great Britain about 250,000 leave each year to seek better jobs. There would also be a heavy

1. Dr S. Suvar: *A Sociological Cross-section of Yugoslav Society*, Zagreb 1970.

exodus from some other countries that put the blame for this phenomenon on Yugoslav self-management, if the workers in those countries were free to emigrate. The British economist P. Rosenstein-Rodan[2] asserted back in 1943 that the East European countries had a surplus labour force of about 20 million, thanks to the agrarian nature of their economies. In the meantime, large numbers of these have moved into industry, into the cities, but this huge labour reservoir could not vanish so quickly. This surplus is still present both in industry and in rural areas.

Yugoslav workers abroad

Labour mobility, modern information media, improved transport and the openness of Yugoslavia have all encouraged the labour exodus.

According to data of March 1971, 671,000 Yugoslavs were temporarily employed abroad, 68 per cent of them men. The largest number was in West Germany—411,403 (61·2 per cent), followed by Austria—83,000 (12 per cent), Australia—40,000 (about 6 per cent), France—37,000 (5·5 per cent), Switzerland, Sweden, the USA and some other countries.

It is noteworthy that the biggest exodus occurred after 1965, particularly after 1968 (80 per cent). They found better conditions of employment abroad and earned more money—sometimes two or three times as much as for the same job in Yugoslavia. This is why many seek jobs abroad even when they are already employed at home.

The majority of Yugoslavs going abroad, however, were not employed (59 per cent), though 45 per cent were farm workers.

Most of these workers are in their most productive period—up to 49 years of age. Those from 20 to 44 years make up 84 per cent of the total. More than three-quarters are unskilled workers, and 76 per cent have only primary schooling. The country is worst affected by the departure of highly-qualified experts and highly-skilled workers, though these form only a small percentage. Only 10,000 (1·5 per cent) of all who have gone abroad to work are university or college graduates. These

2. P. Rosenstein-Rodan, 'Problems of industrialisation of Eastern and South-Eastern Europe', *The Economic Journal*, Jan.-Sept. 1943.

make up about 3·5 per cent of employed Yugoslavs with these qualifications. (Of the total employed persons in the country, 8·7 per cent have advanced or higher education). Skilled workers also form 1·5 per cent of Yugoslavs employed abroad.

Many problems, both social and political, follow in the wake of this Yugoslav phenomenon. There is no likelihood that the country will be able by the wave of some magic wand to end economic emigration. However, steps are taken to assist those planning to leave and facilitate the return and re-employment of those coming back, attention is paid to their social insurance and health service rights while abroad, and vocational qualifications acquired abroad are recognised. Finally, returning workers enjoy customs duty concessions when importing household articles, tools and other equipment for work, foreign currency savings accounts in Yugoslav banks are encouraged, credits being given on the basis of these, and so on.

The Yugoslav long-term development plan provides for a 3 per cent annual growth of employment—only a third of the rate in the first two ten-year periods after the war. But, on the one hand, modern production does not allow employment without regard to economic criteria, while on the other, unemployment is one of the fundamental long-standing problems of every economically underdeveloped country. Remedying unemployment by providing jobs regardless of economic profitability is only a superficial solution which is bound to have, and in some countries already has had very bad economic and even social consequences.

Foreign investments in Yugoslavia

The inclusion of a scarcely moderately developed country into the international division of labour, under conditions of inadequate knowledge, information and capital, calls for tremendous efforts of adjustment, co-operation, linking and association. The shortage of capital—an ill by no means confined to Yugoslavia—was just one of the obstacles to be overcome in carrying through this programme. One reason for the slow-down in new employment is certainly restrictions on the investment front resulting from lack of capital to create new jobs.

This is why new possibilities were opened up for economic co-operation with foreign countries—the joint investment of capital in Yugoslav projects of up to 49 per cent of the total. Five years have elapsed since the Federal Assembly passed a law making possible joint investment by Yugoslav and foreign partners.

What actual results has this move given?

—In the past five years, 52 agreements have been registered, with a total investment value of 4,809 million dinars, of which about 1,260 million or 26·2 per cent consisted of foreign capital.

—In 1968, five contracts were signed involving foreign resources amounting to 210·1 million dinars; in 1969—12 contracts with foreign investment of 344·2 million dinars; in 1970 11 agreements with 286·4 million dinars of foreign capital; in 1971—17 agreements with 269·8 million dinars; in 1972 (up to mid-May) 7 agreements with 150·1 million dinars of foreign investment.

—The maximum foreign share of about 49 per cent of the total capital was invested in 18 cases, and less than 20 per cent in eight cases (in two agreements it was even less than 10 per cent).

—Italian and West German firms are the most frequent and largest co-investors in the development of the Yugoslav economy, providing about 50 per cent of the total foreign capital invested.

—Most interest has been shown in investment in the Yugoslav automobile industry, which received 53 per cent of the foreign capital. It was followed by the chemical industry— 16·7 per cent, the rubber industry—7·5 per cent, metalworking —4·9 per cent, the leather industry—4·7 per cent, and other industries together—13 per cent.

Although modest in scope, such investment to date has been a not inconsiderable feature of the country's economic development policy.

But why, it may be asked, so much restraint on the part of foreign investors? A certain confusion and lack of clarity with regard to guarantees for foreign investors, and the ownership of the invested capital equipment, coupled with indecision about management and control, made foreign investors very hesitant. Yugoslav regulations on foreign capital investment were extremely rigorous and unfavourable to foreign investors, who had neither essential guarantees nor the freedom to do as they wished with their profits.

This is what prompted the Yugoslav government, in the summer of 1971, to propose to the Assembly urgent amendments to the Law on Foreign Capital Investment, coupled with the guarantee that future changes in the law could not harm the interests of foreign investors. Namely, the foreign partner was given legal assurance that he can use or withdraw his resources at will. Whereas he was previously obliged to reinvest 20 per cent of his profits in Yugoslavia or deposit that much in the National Bank—an arrangement that was clearly unattractive—he can now do as he likes with all his profits.

The law imposes only one new obligation on foreign partners: their capital investment must not be less than 100,000 dollars (exceptions may be made with special permission).

Yugoslavs have been criticised for allowing the investment of foreign capital on the grounds that it gives money priority over the rights of man, interferes with self-management, restricts self-management rights, legalises profit in the capitalist sense of the word, and so on. The foreign partner's right to a share in the earnings (profit) in proportion to his investment and the results achieved in production and sales does not carry with it any other managerial, social or political rights. When drafting the law, the prime concern was to ensure the impossibility of any outside interference in the social, self-management and political set-up. Hence the strictness of the regulations. The foreign partner is not a factor in self-management but simply shares the profits.

It is of interest to note that this type of foreign capital participation can be found in other socialist countries: Fiat is building a car factory in Togliattigrad in the Soviet Union (to the value of 875,000,000 dollars); a similar car factory is being built in Romania, along with six synthetic rubber plants (Pirelli), etc. 'Today, there are about 150 factories in East European countries built by West German firms alone, with either a licensing or profit-sharing arrangement'.[3]

Yugoslavia is more to be criticised because its participation in international economic exchange is below the level of its economic development. While the European share of world trade is 54 per cent, Yugoslavia accounts for a mere 0·55 per cent, although in size and population it makes up 7 per cent of Europe. This means that with the present average level of European development, Yugoslavia should account for 3·78 per cent, or almost seven times its actual amount. The country's economic possibilities do not lag behind the European average to anywhere near the extent that it lags behind in world trade.

Technical progress in Yugoslavia depends to a great degree on our activity in international economic co-operation. In our present situation, it is equally conservative, even reactionary, to speak of integration within one republic as it is to shut ourselves inside the state frontiers. Yugoslavia cannot advance rapidly unless great efforts are made towards incorporation in the international division of labour; this is clearly a logical demand of economic and technological progress. It goes without saying that such co-operation must not permit the domination of big monopolies. Judging by the policy that is being followed, there is no likelihood of such a danger in Yugoslavia.

3. Ernest Mandel: *The Socialist Answer to the American Challenge*, in the magazine *Pregled* (Survey), Sarajevo, November-December 1969.

Chapter 17
Work Stoppages (Strikes) in Yugoslavia

Work stoppages* in Yugoslavia have given rise to many questions, and a certain bewilderment, among both friends and opponents of socialism and self-management.

Some believe that socialism is a stable and moral system which eliminates exploitation. In as far as injustices occur, it is the Party, they think, that should represent the proletariat and voice complaints on its behalf.

Others take work stoppages as proof that socialism cannot put an end to evil, and that the workers' lot does not, consequently, depend on the social system.

Others, again, ask: if the work stoppage has *de facto* become a right and practice, why not institutionalise it?

A Yugoslav lecturing in Amsterdam in 1971 was asked by a member of his audience to give the reasons for strikes in Yugoslavia. He replied that the most common cause was a tendency to bureaucracy in relations towards workers. Not satisfied with this, the questioner commented: 'I've been a trade union official for thirty years, but I've never yet seen anyone striking because of a tendency!'

His ironic comment is not uninstructive for Yugoslavs, whose style of discussion leans towards generalisation.

Let us here be quite concrete, then.

The most common cause of work stoppages is low personal incomes, which may be the result of poor sales, incompetent executives, or mistakes in general economic policy. By 'mistakes in general economic policy' we mean the whole Yugoslav

---

* The generally-used term 'work stoppage' is not intended as a euphemism for 'strike'. Whichever expression is accepted, this type of manifestation of social conflicts in Yugoslavia is in many respects specific.

situation—the fact that all economic branches do not operate under equal conditions. Economic policy to date has not been fully adequate to cope with the complex conditions of the market and international competition. Income is the tangible form through which all internal and external influences on the enterprise and its work results find expression. The global and internal distribution of income may also be a cause of dissatisfaction, or even technical hitches in this domain (lateness in calculating earnings, certain real or ostensible deductions, 'forgetfulness' in recording certain work performed and the like).

The position of some branches and work organisations depends on decisions taken by the government, assembly, economic bodies or communes (on such matters as the level of taxes, credit conditions, prices, tariffs, etc.).

All such measures, the actual situation, weaknesses and mistakes have an effect on income, and the consequences are borne by workers even when they are not to blame for the poor results of their labour. A strike is a last resort, an effective form of exerting pressure so that certain steps will be undertaken. The myths of the harmony and perfect order of a socialist economy are no help here.

There are likewise many uncertainties and conflicts caused by the market. A worker may give of his best and yet see no results from his efforts. If the professional management lacks business acumen, and if the worker-management bodies have backed up such incompetence, then the workers' anger turns against them as well.

Take, for instance, the situation facing the coal mines. Production is expensive, and new methods need to be introduced. The demand for coal for power production is declining. Is coal or oil more economical for this purpose? The way the discussion runs often depends on the interests of those debating the matter.

Another example is that of large socially-owned farms, on which personal earnings are low despite high productivity. The prices of their products: milk, cereals and meat, are controlled, so that the farm workers' labour is not correctly evaluated. They cannot reconcile themselves for long with low earnings that are not commensurate with work results.

Needless to say, strikes could occur in Yugoslavia only after a certain degree of democratisation had been attained. In a totalitarian or bureaucratic system, strikes usually end in severe repressive measures.

If there are no strikes in a particular country, it does not mean that the working class is completely satisfied with its lot.

Strikes may be a form of demand for some kind of intervention, usually justified, as is the case in Yugoslavia, but they can also take the form of great social and political explosions threatening or paralysing the entire national life and political system. Such dramatic explosions are most common in capitalist countries, but as we know from experience, they can also erupt in socialist societies.

Table 9
Number and Duration of Strikes (12 years to 1972)

Duration	No. of strikes	% of total
Up to 3 hours	166	31·3
From 3 to 7 hours	118	22·3
One day	122	23·0
Two working days	50	9·4
Three working days	16	3·0
Four working days	7	1·3
More than four working days	18	3·5
Unknown	33	6·2
Total:	530	100·0

As can be seen, the majority of stoppages (53·6 per cent) lasted less than one working day, while a further 23 per cent were one-day strikes.

Table 10
Number of Workers Involved per Strike (12 years to 1972)

No. of workers on strike	No. of strikes	% of total
Up to 50	190	35·8
From 51 to 100	120	22·6
From 101 to 200	82	15·6
From 201 to 300	31	5·8
Over 300	52	9·8
Unknown	55	10·4
Total:	530	100·0

Table 11
Strikes by Branches of Activity (12 years to 1972)

Branch of activity	No. of strikes	% of total
Metalworking	142	26·8
Textile industry	53	10·0
Woodworking	66	12·5
Building materials industry	22	4·2
Non-metallic minerals industry	12	2·3
Food processing	11	2·1
Chemical industry	3	0·5
Leather and footwear industry	9	1·7
Rubber industry	8	1·5
Electrical goods industry	29	5·5
Printing industry	3	0·5
Mining	30	5·7
Building industry	42	7·9
Transport	26	4·9
Agriculture	19	3·6
Trade, hotel and catering industry	5	0·9
Iron and steel industry	9	1·7
Craft and service trades	12	2·3
Public utilities	3	0·5
Education	10	1·9
Health service	4	0·8
Civil service	1	0·2
Others	3	0·5

The data in Tables 9, 10 and 11 show the number and duration of strikes in Yugoslavia in the past twelve years, in which branches they occurred, and the number of workers involved.

The largest number of strikes was in industry and mining, with metalworking, woodworking and textile manufacturing most often affected. A relatively large number of strikes occurred in the building materials and building construction industries.

As the survey shows, the majority of strikes (58·4 per cent) involved under 100 workers, while strikes with between 100 and 200 workers formed 15·6 per cent.

o

Thus, strikes were not infrequent, but few workers came out: in some countries, more take part in a single strike than in all the 530 Yugoslav strikes over 12 years put together—a total of 74,000.

So far, strikes have occurred in the main in those economic branches most exposed to market fluctuations, risk and changes in the technology of production.

Two 'case histories' will perhaps be illustrative.

The *Split* Shipyard in Split—5,000 employed.

Annual production: 165,000 GRT—one third of the entire output of Yugoslavia, which ranks ninth among the shipbuilding nations of Europe and tenth in the world. Annual turnover: 800 million dinars.

Split exports almost its whole output.

Over 1,000 of its workers are members of the League of Communists. In the department where the strike started, one worker in six was a member.

The strike began at 12 pm on April 30, 1970, when workers in one department downed tools because of dissatisfaction with their earnings. In protest, they refused to pick up their April earnings, which were being paid out that day. The work stoppage was repeated on May 4 and 5 in the same department, with five other departments joining in on May 5.

The ostensible reasons: failure to pay out a holiday bonus, high prices in the shipyard's canteen, and low earnings in April. But the causes lay deeper: greater financial demands by the community had reduced the enterprise's income. Split is a city with a low employment level. About 1,600 workers in the shipyard are 'commuters',[1] a large proportion of them in the department where it all started. In most cases there is only one bread-winner in the family (the children of manual workers make up the majority of those seeking employment).

The workers raised the question of the high earnings of the expert staff, boosted by payment for supplementary work under contract. The enterprise's system of remuneration is such that, provided productivity is normal, every worker can count on taking home 50 per cent above his basic earnings. This additional money is known as the 'variable part' of his

1. Working in the city but living in surrounding villages.

income or 'surplus'. However, in some departments a piece-work system was introduced and—the norms being set too low —the workers in these managed to chalk up abnormally high earnings. In consequence, those who were on piece-work 'gobbled up' the 'surplus' of the others, who received only 15 to 20 per cent of their variable pay.

Another sore point was the shipyard's average personal income. Though the striking workers were for the most part semi-skilled or skilled, their earnings were below this average (86 per cent of the strikers). They had the feeling that those with low earnings were subsidising those with high earnings, since the expert staff had priority when flats were distributed, though the enterprise's regulations, in fact, made provision for this. Over a two-year period, 700 of the *Split* yard's workers, mostly electrical welders and skilled assembly men, had gone abroad. In Gotheborg in Sweden they receive two and a half times as much as at home.

The officials in the socio-political organisations (the League of Communists, trade union) did not intervene; the whole of the affected departments came out, without exception. At a workers' meeting, the director replied to the strikers' demands. He did not accept them all (for instance, the demand for a 40 per cent increase in earnings), but he was well received by the men. The trade union representative, however, was greeted with loud disapproval.[2]

Another example, this time involving two smaller factories, where the problem was of a different nature:

Lifam of Stara Pazova and *Slavonski partizan* of Slavonska Pozega manufacture butane gas containers and employ a total of 920.

Cause of stoppage: the federal government's approval of the import of 180,000 butane gas containers from Czecho-slovakia. These two factories, producing gas containers from Yugoslav raw materials, can meet the requirements of the home market. The approval of imports in 1970 led to stock-piling and made the factories insolvent in that year. It was clear that renewal of import permission for 1971 would make the situation even worse.

The home producers (these two factories) complained that

2. All data taken from the magazine *Pregledi* (*Views*), no. 3, 1970, Split.

the importation declaration for the containers was inaccurate, and that in any case imports should not have been allowed without consulting them. A warning was sent to the National Bank and federal government. Despite this, imports continued in 1971.

The collectives decided to stop work. The socio-political organisations in their communes were informed, and telegrams sent to political authorities in the province, republic and Federation. During their normal working hours, the strikers strolled around the streets, joined by retired workers. The League of Communist and trade union organisations supported the action.

When their demands were met, the workers decided at a meeting to resume production, and to make up for lost time by working on their next free Saturday and Sunday.[3]

Needless to say, not all demands can be met, nor can this form of expressing dissatisfaction be suppressed.

Many interests come together in a factory, each of which has its justification and some principle on which it is based— the importance of the work being undertaken, inalienable self-management rights, solidarity and social position; some base their claims on the reform, some on the requirements of underdeveloped areas, some on efficiency, some on democracy, while some put rights before duties. Such a complex state of affairs cannot be 'disciplined' by laws, but the atmosphere and practice are sufficiently democratic so that legal prescriptions are not essential.

Strikes may have a variety of causes, but as a rule the workers on strike are not fighting against socialism as a social system. Most commonly, they are protesting over inconsistencies in the implementation of their rights. In any case, energetic reaction by the workers against injustices and short-comings in the system and in economic affairs may be interpreted as a sign of the growing awareness among the working class of their own role. In short, the society and system are not threatened by strikes, but these should not be underestimated, since they are usually a warning signal on the state of affairs in a particular environment.

3. Information of the Confederation of Trade Unions of Yugoslavia, July 1971.

Chapter 18

Self-Management – Its Theoretical Roots

It is not enough to say of an idea that it contributes to humane human relations. At times, more humane relations have been established by inhuman methods. In Marx's view, the fundamental vision of communism would be achieved by the abolition of government authorities that had become alienated from man, of the political hierarchy and bureaucracy, the nucleus of all this being 'self-management of the producers'.

Marx saw history as man's work. History was only what man had created by productive work, and by changing nature, art and culture. 'Man is the highest being for man,' Marx said, in fact making a plea for new social relations in a new society. The founders of socialism: Marx, Engels, Lenin, and before them Saint-Simon, Fourier, Robert Owen, Louis Blanc, in one way or another declared war on all institutions that governed in man's name, and which were alienated from him —above all, the State. Marx and Lenin, in particular, considered that even in a socialist system, a large concentration of authority and power can become a governing force above the working class itself.

In the early decades of the history of socialism, it is true, these fundamental Marxist tenets tended to be overlooked. A mystical State, Party and directives from above were imposed on the workers' movement.

Lenin was opposed to state-run trade unions. Stalin was for the maximum strengthening of the State:

'The State will not be replaced by anything; it gradually withers away. Consequently, the necessity for political authorities also declines. This will be possible when the socialist state fulfils its historical tasks. But for the execution of these tasks it is necessary to strengthen the people's authority. For this reason, the efforts to strengthen the socialist State should not be seen as contrary to the prospects of its withering away. These are two sides of the same medal.'[1]

The stronger it grows, the more the State withers away! This is essentially contradictory. There is no dialectic that can accommodate this thesis of Stalin's.

Yugoslavs are not for the weakening of the state community under the slogan of the withering away of the State. The gradual transfer of economic and political powers from the State to the working class does not mean the weakening of the state community. For no State can replace the activity of the masses, millions strong. No State, with the best administration and police, can be a substitute for the enthusiasm of the individual who knows that the future of his community is in his hands.

Until the Paris Commune, Marx had no solution to this problem either, but this historic event gave him the basic elements of the idea of the supersession of the state organisation in society:

'The Paris Commune was intended, of course, to serve as the model for all large industrial centres in France. As soon as Paris and other centres adopted a communal system, the old centralised government in the regions as well would have had to give way to self-management of the producers.'[2]

Socialist practice in recent decades and Yugoslavia's experience in searching for its own road to socialism have led to the questioning of a whole well-established system of thought and opinion: about a single road to socialism, and about the State and Party as the fundamental driving force of historical development and arbiter on all questions—from the arts to politics.

1. *The Foundations of Marxist Philosophy*, Moscow.
2. Karl Marx: *Civil War in France*.

They have undermined the ideology of such taboo subjects as dialectical criticism of political practice, etc.

From the historical standpoint, the goal of self-management is to ensure that the working class gains the upper hand over all institutions which have thought and governed instead of it, and gradually to create a society in which government will cease to exist as management of people and will become management of things.

But matters do not follow the course laid down by programmes and theses.

What kind of socialism?—Socialism is ever present in the thoughts and actions of all those who are seeking a way out of the difficulties confronting contemporary society. Although it was compromised by Stalinism, the aspirations of the masses have survived the inhumanity of that period. Socialism is returning to its human sources, inspired by new experiences and the ideas of its founders. Today it is not a question of: *Socialism or no?* but: *What kind of socialism?* Revolution in the Marxist sense does not end with the simple assumption of power, or with nationalisation, or with the system of laws that is adopted. Yugoslavia takes part in this debate, drawing on its experience.

Seeking a new path, we have endeavoured, on the basis of social ownership of the means of production, to unite the working man and the fruits of his labour, and make such social relations the driving force of social progress. The practical aim is to ensure that the individual in his place of work, in the enterprise, in the commune, in the whole society, increasingly controls and manages his work, the distribution of the surplus product and its circulation. On this basis, we are trying to develop self-management in political, cultural and all other fields of public life, to pave the way for a new, integrated system of self-management democracy which is essentially direct, but which should also operate in the political system as a whole.

Self-management is a way of solving problems related to the social position and interests of every individual. Government or management in a socialist society cannot be the privilege of politicians and the intelligentsia. Self-management is an effort to eliminate coercion as far as possible from social rela-

tions, to replace simple execution of orders by direct participation in decision-making, conflicts by discussions, political and
other fights by reasoned argument, domination and force by
elections.

Conclusions

Yugoslav self-management is certainly not based on some kind of universal experience, since it grew up under conditions of social ownership of the means of production, in a country with a moderate standard of development. Its practices may be made public without fear that they will rouse passions. It is not for us to judge the degree of interest abroad in this experience. In any case, it is not intended for export. However, the great French Revolution of 1789 was in every respect French, yet it gave rise to far-reaching upheavals since it carried a universal message in its triptych: liberty, equality, fraternity.

If we examine direct social practice in Yugoslavia, self-management may be favourably assessed, from both the human and material standpoints. On the material level, Yugoslavia alone among the underdeveloped countries has managed to narrow the gap between the industrially advanced regions and the backward. Seen from the human aspect, self-management appears more and more as an alternative to the powerful trend towards technocracy and bureaucracy apparent in the more developed industrial societies, both capitalist and socialist.

Self-management, it would appear, can supply an answer to one of the most difficult questions confronting contemporary socialism: is it capable of stimulating the most important source of future strength—human creative ability, and to what extent can it establish its 'superiority' to capitalism in this respect?

Under Yugoslav conditions, self-management has shown itself a suitable system for co-ordinating diverse national and social interests, smoothing out conflicts, and developing a homogeneous Yugoslav community.

Self-management can be an answer to political monopoly by dominant groups or political organisations. It leads away from the professionalisation of politics in general, and towards democratisation of cadre policy, in particular, at all levels. The participation of millions of people in the passing of decisions may diminish people's leisure time, but it makes up for this by ensuring a greater degree of self-discipline, political activity, commitment and incentive in production and work.

The feeling of lack of coercion and of human freedom is perhaps the only sure defence of a small community in the present-day world of terrifying military and economic might.

Democratic self-management of public affairs releases creative energy and powers in the arts, culture and sciences.

Has self-management in Yugoslavia fulfilled its role? It has certainly established and justified itself as a system, but it displays numerous weaknesses and contradictions which there is no attempt to hide.

Despite the big conflicts of individual and group interests, not uncommon examples of human irresponsibility, and different levels of social awareness—some very low—no one wishes to turn back.

In practice, self-management has suffered countless deformations and left many questions unanswered.

Planning, for example, should serve, more than it does today, as a market corrective, programming long-term development, linked with the direct production process. The market will tyrannise economic affairs less if its requirements are planned for.

There are many subjective obstacles hampering the association and merging of enterprises, the more rational division of labour according to economic and technological criteria, interdependence of plants, and the concentration of know-how and resources. Decentralisation does not run contrary to the increased demands for the integration of economic systems. Small nations, in particular, must discover the best ways of developing technologically highly advanced industrial branches, for they are obliged to consider, at the same time, their economic independence.

We cannot be satisfied with the form of income distribution we have at present. Not because collectives would like to waste money or spend wildly and so jeopardise capital formation and reserves, or because we have had second thoughts about distribution according to work results, but because people with the same qualifications, and doing the same or similar work, into which they put the same amount of effort, have different earnings, depending on the type of equipment they have at their disposal, on the position on the market of the enterprise and of a particular economic branch, and on current economic policy.

There is a strong feeling among small and weak economic organisations, and among the unskilled section of the labour force, in favour of the levelling of incomes, regardless of labour input. This may be a vestige of egalitarian sentiment left over from the period of centralised administrative socialism, and perhaps the influence of certain ideological dogma on the minds of a number of people. Whatever the explanation, a levelling campaign would mean a social and economic step backwards.

However, a developed society should be particularly sensitive to wide, unjustified differences in economic position, especially those which are not the result of personal labour.

The human factor, including here the high birth rate and large labour reserves, will in future constitute one of the great advantages of our society. For the time being, although the problem of full employment cannot be solved artificially, the departure of workers abroad, their return, and the creation of jobs in the country are not matters that can be left to chance, without guidance or control.

In self-management, too, there is a danger of the representatives setting themselves apart from those they represent. Management through representatives is not an adequate form of self-management. It must be based on a variety of forms of direct democracy.

The more favourable position of the expert personnel, their growing role and number both in enterprises and in society as a whole, their monopoly of information and know-how, wide powers in taking executive decisions on professional matters—all this, if not checked by the collectives and citizens, would in time lead to the creation of various circles of power in society which would paralyse self-management. It would be absurd to delude oneself that the system will develop spontaneously, according to its own logic. Political organisation and activity therefore have a natural and essential role to play here.

A large section of the population—many farmers, for instance—as yet play no part in self-management. The encouragement of individual initiative, and incentives for the linking-up of the private and socialist sectors, will lead to the socialisation of the private sector rather than to the capitalisation of the socialist sector, giving rise to new forms of self-management in this domain. So far, little has been accomplished in this direction.

The idea of self-management, and even its practice, to a certain extent, is not confined to Yugoslavia. The dissatisfaction and helplessness of modern man when confronted by the gigantic bureaucratic, state and industrial set-ups, turn him towards self-management as the path of 'deliverance'.

The socialist countries, too, are faced by a dilemma: who, on the basis of the nationalisation of the means of production, will hold the huge economic and political power derived therefrom—the State and Party bureaucracy, or the individual engaged in socialised labour?

Considered as a whole, in the world of today self-management is more a vision in which repose some of the most progressive aspirations of contemporary mankind than a present reality.

In Yugoslavia, self-management is not some Utopian idea—the establishment of a society without conflicts—but a process that will gradually develop relations in which labour, as Marx says, is truly free; where management will become to an increasing extent management of things, not people. Progress can be achieved not by any form of external coercion, but by the vested interest of labour itself. Self-management does not eliminate bureaucracy and certain social differences, but it is a proven way of restricting bureaucratic tendencies. The individual exercises his freedom not only through his work in society but also in his local community, in the commune and republic—everywhere that he appears as a consumer and as a participant in cultural activities.

The Yugoslav revolution is not completely satisfied with its achievements to date and is constantly correcting its own faults. Only the dogmatic soul fears to throw open questions for discussion. No dynamic social movement can occur without conflicts, differences in views, dilemmas.

We do not believe in the supernatural power of the self-management system, but we do think it has virtues. We do not consider it some kind of social magic, but we are convinced that it has provided extremely valuable experience.

The fundamental advantage of self-management is that the individual—as citizen and producer—is in the forefront of attention. And man, in socialism, should not be a mere cog but the hub of the universe, the goal to which everything is directed.

All the institutions of society serve their purpose fully only when they create conditions for the individual to give himself rights, and not ask for them.

Afterword

The fact that Yugoslav self-management is continually changing is apt to confuse the foreign observer. This confusion is compounded by the Yugoslavs' habit of discussing their problems and differences of view in public.

The last few years, in particular, have brought numerous changes, including the promulgation of a new Constitution, which has some revolutionary features.

Weak Points

People, as a rule, like stories with a happy ending. Self-management is a story without an end, and certain chapters of this historic tale do not conclude on a very optimistic note.

Our development has been marked by no small number of weak points.

There have been various weaknesses in production relations, for instance, the most dangerous being the tendency towards a technocratic monopoly. Capital accumulation came to assume independent power in the hands of the top administrators in the economy and elsewhere. Though this was not a dominant feature of self-management relations, if it had continued unchecked it would inevitably have led to various conflicts, to the distortion of self-management.

Another weak spot in our system was planning. We abandoned centralised planning before we had established new forms of planning based on the self-management system. The process of capital concentration is essential and cannot be achieved without social guidance. The question was how to do this without violating the spirit of self-management.

What was fundamental in the new Constitution, however, was the position of the working class, its place in the process of social production. It was essential to take further steps forward so that the worker might exercise full control over his surplus labour without restrictions and usurpation of his rights, to guarantee the worker's inalienable right to decision-making in this sphere, thereby ensuring each individual, and the class as a whole, a dominant influence over all aspects of life in the society. Decision-making on surplus labour means control over that part of income which is set aside for strengthening the material basis of labour, for raising productivity, improving the workers' living standard and enriching the society as a whole.

The Constitution ensures this by formulating the rights of the basic organisation of associated labour and its powers of decision-making with regard to social reproduction, i.e. expansion of the productive forces of society. The basic organisation of associated labour is not a closed, self-sufficient entity. The worker could not exercise this right as an isolated individual within such an organisation; he can only do so in conjunction with other workers in other organisations of associated labour.

Experience gained in self-management over the past 25 years has shown that self-management cannot and should not be confined to the domain of direct production. To be successful at the base, it must be present everywhere: in education, health, culture, the arts, science, social insurance, banking, the judicial system and administration. Even the organisation of the system of general national defence in Yugoslavia has a self-management character.

Direct ties were not at first established between material production and social services in the domains of education, science, culture and health. It was therefore the state, as a rule, which served as an intermediary, determining the economy's obligations towards the financing of these services.

Trade enjoyed a more favourable position than production. Large foreign-trade enterprises could, and frequently did, assume a monopolistic stance vis-à-vis production enterprises.

To make Yugoslav federalism more effective, the Constitution increased the responsibilities of the republics and autonomous provinces, basing the federal community on the principle of consensus i.e. negotiated agreement. The aim is to ensure more harmonious and balanced economic development, thereby making the union of the Yugoslav peoples stronger and more natural.

In its state and national structure, Yugoslavia contains, in miniature, almost everything that goes to make up Europe, its culture and historical traditions. Painful traces have remained of the national inequality of the pre-revolutionary period and the nightmare of the past. Nationalist and separatist tendencies have presented no small problem even in the postwar period. At the same time, centralistic and unitarist tendencies—justified, allegedly, on the grounds that they strengthened the country and its monolithic unity—themselves constituted a danger and inflamed nationalist passions.

Such tendencies were the subject of public debate and a fierce struggle in Yugoslavia. Our enemies took advantage of these difficulties, while our friends had reason for concern. The Yugoslavs, for their part, brought this whole question out into the open, since there was no doubt about the mood of the nation and their awareness of the necessity for unity.

The final outcome was the new Constitution, which extends the responsibilities of the republics and autonomous provinces, basing the unity of the federation on the awareness of common interests and the principle of consensus.

The right idea or a new illusion?

There is much in our system of self-management that is not perfect, but we have not seen around us any better, more humane model that we would choose. We have been developing and progressing from the outset.

Each of the existing societies promises continual progress. However, the old world is giving way to the new. The quest for new paths, the choice that is made and the extent to which these paths bring human and economic advancement depends in large measure on the speed at which the old world of exploitation, inequalities and lack of freedom disappears.

Scientific, technical and cultural achievements, and the experience acquired to date, offer us a much better starting basis.

Friends of Yugoslavia and observers of the Yugoslav scene abroad often understand self-management in different ways.

For some it is simply participation in the passing of certain decisions—co-decision-making; for others it is the end to exploitation. In fact, it is neither one nor the other. We see self-management above all as giving the working people control over society's production forces and the results of their labour on all levels, from the base to the top, from the production unit to the federation.

To some this may seem to be commercialising and vulgarising a noble idea.

We are under no illusions that self-management is a magic wand that puts an immediate end to all inequalities, class conflicts, conflicting group interests, and the appetite for power and monopoly. Neither socialisation of the means of production nor the mere introduction of self-management at this level of development can automatically effect a radical transformation of relations in the process of work, nor can it guarantee against vestiges of the old class relations and arbitrariness.

Strengthening the sovereignty of the republics

A term often heard in Yugoslavia is 'social compact'. This is a strategy for voluntarily reaching agreement on various matters, mostly in the domain of economic policy and development. Such agreement is of particular importance in relations between the republics and provinces, and their relations with the federation. The new Constitution increases the responsibilities and rights of the republics and autonomous provinces, founding its unity and development policy on the principle of consensus. Only in this way can Yugoslav federalism be effective, and the Yugoslav community a strong and natural one. The Constitution consistently adheres to the principle of the equality of the peoples and nationalities living in Yugoslavia.

This is a very complex community, but closely bound together by shared interests—historical, economic, moral, national, cultural, developmental, and security. For this reason, our federalism lays primary stress on the equality of republics and provinces, peoples and nationalities.

Under the new Constitution, the republican assemblies have three chambers instead of the previous five: the chamber of associated labour, the chamber of communes and the socio-

P

political chamber. These are made up of delegates of the corresponding self-management chambers at communal level.

The new Federal Assembly has two chambers instead of five (the Federal Chamber and Chamber of Republics and Provinces).

These are, however, largely changes of an organisational nature. The essential changes are those introducing delegational representation, direct representation from the base (economic organisations, local communities, communes) in the assemblies of the republics and Federal Assembly. What the Constitution wished to achieve was to make the Assembly above all a self-management body. Article 282 states: 'The Assembly of the Socialist Federal Republic of Yugoslavia is a body of social self-management and the highest organ of authority in the federation'.

The highest collective state organ—the Presidency of the Socialist Federal Republic of Yugoslavia—retained its place, since the previous four years had shown this solution to be in keeping with the spirit of a multi-national, socialist, self-management-based community. An innovation, though, is that each republic and province now supplies one member of the Presidency instead of two. The President of the League of Communists of Yugoslavia is a member and the President of the Presidency by virtue of his office. The members of the Presidency are elected for a five-year term. Its members cannot have any other self-management or social function (though they may hold office in a socio-political organisation), and cannot be elected to the Presidency for more than two terms of office.

*   *   *

The Yugoslav Constitution of February 1974, reflects three fundamental goals:

—that as many economic and political decisions as possible should be taken at the base, which is the source of all authority, by way of the newly-established delegational system;

—that the workers should participate in decision-making and the improvement of their life and living standard in their local communities and communes, in agreement with those directly concerned, so that self-management becomes an integral part of the entire life and society;

—that social planning should not be a means of limiting the rights of organisations of associated labour, local communities, communes, republics and provinces. The earlier hierarchy of plans, described elsewhere in this book, would now restrict the Constitutionally-guaranteed equality of the nations, republics and provinces.

Endeavouring to put the new Constitutional provisions into practice, self-management faces a further and very important test. These three goals therefore deserve separate treatment.

The Delegational System

One of the problems that long confronted Yugoslavia was how to put self-management into practice at all levels, from the enterprise to the federation, from the local community to the Federal Assembly. It was clearly not enough to have decision-making and direct participation only at the base, since there was a risk that vital decisions would be strongly influenced by the technocracy, bureaucracy, banks and giant economic organisations. This proved, in fact, to be more than a risk.

'Parliament' of millions

The 1974 Constitution changed the old representational electoral system, replacing it by a new, delegational system. The purpose was to eliminate some of the traditional weaknesses of the representational system which had been present even under self-management. The delegations, numbering over 90,000, with over a million members, constitute a unique kind of parliament. It is composed 56 per cent of direct producers, 22 per cent of women, and almost one fifth of young people (18–25 years of age).

The right of electing and forming delegations is given to the basic organisations of associated labour and not to the enterprise (i.e. large, complex economic organisations), so as to eliminate the possibility of the enterprise's techno-bureaucracy deciding in the workers' name and over their heads.

All forms of government and management are based on the principle of direct involvement of the basic cells of society —the basic organisations of associated labour and the local communities. The delegations, elected for a term of four years, form the bodies of government and management in the commune, republic, province and federation.[1] This parliamentary practice is new in essence not only in form.

Self-management has greatly changed the attitude and awareness of the working class in Yugoslavia, whose traditions and experience are of armed revolution rather than political and trade union struggles, as is the case with the West European proletariat. Previously, the advantage of the self-management organisations was simply that it gave the workers and other citizens a chance to keep a check on those they elected. The self-managing worker has now reached a level of awareness when this is not enough. With the economy growing more and more complex, and the system of state planning abandoned, there was a real danger (in some places it became a fact) of decision-taking shifting to the executives and technocrats in banks, large enterprises and republics. The Constitution is intended to prevent this by means of the system of delegations.

The basic units—the basic organisations of associated labour (work organisations), local communities and socio-political organisations—elect their delegations by direct, secret ballot for the commune assemblies, and the latter send their delegates to the supreme state organs (of the province, republic and federation).

In view of the present level of awareness among the workers and Yugoslavs as a whole, self-management now means much more than simply electing and controlling representatives. Some early experience has already been gained. But regardless of the shortcomings which will surely accompany this new and revolutionary undertaking, the election of representatives in the old, traditional parliamentary sense had to be changed to the election of direct representatives— delegates.

1. Of the total number of delegations, 81 per cent are delegations of basic and other organisations of associated labour, 16 per cent of local communities, and 3 per cent socio-political delegations.

Diagram VI
THE DELEGATIONAL SYSTEM IN YUGOSLAVIA

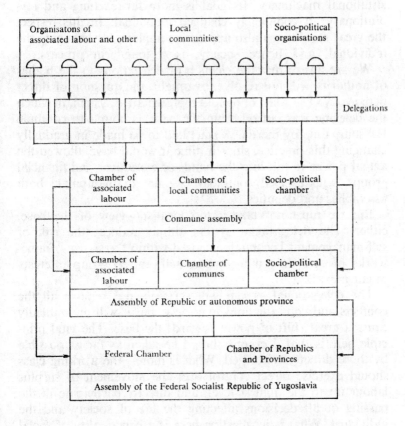

The individual and institutional machinery

Certain friends, supporters of self-management abroad, regard the results of the Yugoslav experience as rather 'pale'. They set the highest standards, considering complete self-management a matter of perfect machinery, norms and great national debates. But it is not just a matter of norms and institutional machinery. Its goal is more far-reaching and revolutionary: a completely changed individual. In this respect the great revolutions also appear incomplete, for changing the individual, and hence society, is a long-term process.

We are aware that the election of delegations to the bodies of authority will not resolve, overnight, the question of direct democracy. The spirit of the old representative system, in which the delegate was cut off from the base, is bound to continue for some time by inertia. A start had to be made in gradually changing this practice, since in time it would have allowed the actual power to fall into the hands of executives and financial groups, who exerted continual pressure to manipulate both assemblies and deputies.

But we must not take a too idealistic view of the base, either. The delegational system simply reduces the risk of self-management becoming enclosed within the narrow frameworks of economic units, where self-centred group interests might prevail.

The delegational system will certainly not remove all the conflicts and contradictions in society, but it will undoubtedly cause a great shift of power towards the base. The vital principle here is that decisions should be taken as far as possible by those directly concerned. What is more—the working class should exercise direct control over the movement of surplus labour up to the highest level, and directly participate in the passing of all decisions affecting the life of society and the individual. What is in question here is a new quality of social relations. We are not guided by formalism. What we aim to achieve is the fullest degree of decision-making by the workers themselves and their authorised delegates, instead of decision-making in the name of the workers.

The delegates have the Constitutional obligation to adopt stands on all questions on the agenda. Self-management requires all decisions to be taken on the basis of consensus.

Consequently, the delegates, who have the mandate and suggestions of the base on what stand to take, do not simply represent the interests of one group of workers, since the decision will not reflect group interests but a synthesis of interests. From the outset, group interests come up against others, until those that concern the entire community are reached.

The delegates are authorised and bound by the instructions of those who elected them, and are obliged to report on their work. They are not, however, simply transmitters of group interests. The delegates are independent and act on their own responsibility, since decisions must constitute a synthesis of individual and general interests.

How the delegational system functions

The Chamber of Republics and Provinces, which represents national and regional interests, is made up of delegations of 12 members each from each of the republics, and eight-member delegations from the provinces and regions all have their economic interests which must be brought into line. Most of the questions decided by the Chamber are from the domains of the economy, foreign trade, the monetary system and social control of prices.

The notable innovation here is that this Chamber must previously consult all the republican and provincial assemblies, which means that the republics and provinces are directly involved in federal matters.

The delegates and delegations concern themselves with the passing of laws and decisions—from their proposal to their final adoption.

The debate on Yugoslavia's economic and social development up to 1980 and up to 1985, i.e. the passing of medium and long-term development plans, is now evolving for the first time in accordance with this self-management procedure. The Yugoslav government and social planning agency first presented the Assembly delegates and public with basic ideas which contained various alternatives. This phase is followed by the drafting of the plan, which is the topic of very lively debate. Many enterprises have submitted objections that this or that economic branch is not given an adequate place or sufficient attention, and put forward their suggestions.

The delegations have already introduced greater liveliness into the work of commune assemblies. The commune in Yugoslavia, as stated elsewhere, has considerably greater powers than the communes or local government units in West European countries.

The delegation system is linked up with work and decision-making in the basic work organisations, and in society as a whole. In this way the most direct ties are established between the working class and working people as a whole at all levels, from the basic organisation of associated labour to the Federal Assembly.

The composition of the workers' councils and delegations must correspond to the social structure of the basic organisation of associated labour. According to the Constitution, they must allow proportionate representation of direct producers, who make up three-quarters of the employed.[2]

But the worker's interest does not end with the basic organisation of associated labour. It also extends to other spheres in the place where he lives (schooling, the health service, housing, public utilities, shops, transport, etc.). The Constitution therefore makes provision for the organisation of the working people on a self-management basis in the local communities where they reside.[3]

The new assembly system also means a step towards taking politics out of the hands of professionals. The elected delegates are not professional politicians, except for a small number of delegates of socio-political organisations, where a very limited number of professionals are employed (as mentioned elsewhere). The delegates remain in their jobs and continue to do their work normally, getting paid for it as before. This fact serves as a very important defence against bureaucratisation.

2. Of the total number of delegation members, the largest group are miners, industrial and allied workers—21 per cent, followed by those employed in commerce and service trades—17 per cent, and agriculture —19 per cent. Of the remaining 43 per cent, clerical and allied workers from 15 per cent, experts, scientists and artists 8 per cent, and executive personnel 3 per cent.
3. Since the majority of local communities are in rural areas, agricultural workers are the largest group in the delegations—41 per cent, while workers in industry and service trades make up 26 per cent.

Early models

In view of Yugoslavia's multi-national structure, it is extremely important that there should be no imposition of opinions by means of outvoting.

In the basic organisation of associated labour, too, all major questions are decided by all the employed. Although this system takes a lot of effort and time to make it work, the Yugoslav Constitution was designed to ensure consistent, democratic, self-management procedure.

The idea is not, of course, new: representatives of the shires and municipalities entered the English House of Commons, while during the French Revolution this idea was advocated by Robespierre and Saint-Just. The Paris Commune of 1871 revived the idea of delegation. Drawing on this experience, Marx in his 'Civil War in France' conceived of a 'communal system' of political organisation in which the basic cells of political power—the communes—elected delegates which made up the assemblies of the departments, while these assemblies chose from among their ranks delegates for the national parliament.

The Paris Commune is the first example of revolutionary political power being exercised by way of delegations. This system replaced the traditional system of political representation for the first time in revolutionary Paris. Marx laid particular stress on the delegational rather than representational character of the assembly, stressing the direct link between the delegate and voters, who could recall him at any time.

In Lenin's Constitution of 1922, the representative bodies of the young Soviet state—the Congresses of Soviets for larger territorial units—were composed of delegates of local soviets. This was changed in the Constitution of 1936.

Of one thing we may be sure: the delegational mandate allows the base to play a more active role, and increases the initiative and responsibility of delegates.

The previous, traditional representative system made it difficult to ensure the dominating role of the working class. The general political representatives were intermediaries between the working class and the state. The classics of Marxist literature considered that the main purpose of direct representation was that all functions of management and government should derive from the function of labour, and that it should ensure the participation and dominance of the working class and working people as a whole.

Communities of interest[4]

The worker-manager is not, of course, simply a producer, he is also a consumer, tenant, user of the health and education services, public transport and the electricity supply, a parent . . . It follows that production and the individual producer must be closely linked with schooling, culture, health, science, the environment, housing . . . But in what way? In a self-management-based system, this is conceived as voluntary organisation of those who provide and those who use various types of services, on the basis of mutuality and solidarity.

Unusual 'taxation system'

From the very early days of self-management it was clear that the right of citizens and working people to manage and govern their affairs would not be realised unless participation were made possible from the bottom to the top, and horizontally as well, in all spheres of activity, including public services and service trades.

In the Constitutional provision for voluntary agreements between production enterprises and organisations providing services (science, culture, education, health, social welfare), the foreign observer may see an unusual form of 'taxation', based on the principle of voluntariness. Instead of taxes to finance these services being paid to a state institution, where all trace is lost of the way they are used, communities of interest are

4. The Constitutions of the Federation, republics and provinces provide for the formation of several types of self-managing communities of interest:
  —in the fields of education, culture, health and social security, where it is obligatory to form such interest communities,
  —in the fields of pension and disability insurance and other forms of social insurance,
  —in the sphere of housing (agreements on building, quality, terms, concentration),
  —in the domains of public utilities, power supply, transport and so on.
  Such communities may be established for other spheres, when the initiative is forthcoming. They are now being set up for youth work drives, environmental protection, and certain cultural and scientific programmes.

formed in which all those involved, from both sides, participate. In the community, they discuss, for instance, what level
of funds is needed for particular activities, and what quality
of service is required.

At first sight, this resembles a complicated game of norms
and forms of organisation and institutions, but this is not so.
The political and self-management motives for this type of
organisation are most important.

In the majority of societies today, the areas of education,
science, and culture are increasingly being taken over by the
state. Formerly independent and self-supporting, these activities have become socialised, their relations based on an administrative hierarchy. Their separation from the influence of
the producers and citizens leads to bureaucratic management
and dehumanisation of these public services.

Self-management wishes to promote an opposite process:

The principle of 'free exchange of labour'[5] between the
working people engaged in production and in the domain of
service activities calls for new social relations in which both
sides gain in importance. The producers decide on the resources
available and are able to put forward demands regarding the
quality of services, while the providers of services (scientists,
teachers, physicians and others) achieve a socio-economic
position similar to that of workers in other, 'productive' work
organisations.

The revolutionary significance of this principle is that for
the first time in history the division between wage-earning
workers and salaried employees is abolished. This also promotes the gradual abolition of the division between physical
and intellectual labour, and of the civil service bureaucratic
psychology we inherited from capitalism and from the so-
called administrative, state centralised socialism. An extremely
important section of society, essential to every system, is being
included in the basic production relationship and thereby becoming part of the working class.

5. This means that persons engaged in the non-productive spheres of activity extend their services to those engaged in production and in return
receive an income commensurate with their contribution to the value
created in material production, to the overall increase of productivity,
and the development of society as a whole.

The Constitution gives workers in the sector of social services (health, science, culture, education), the same status as workers engaged in direct material production, and the same or similar conditions of acquiring income. But in view of the nature of their work, relations with the productive sector are regulated in a specific fashion. The relationship between the workers engaged in material and non-material production is vital. The association and voluntary agreements of the working people in communities of interest should at the same time prevent the unchecked appropriation of the production workers' income on the simple excuse that the money is to be used to satisfy other needs.

Enriching human relationships

Local communities and communes are naturally not the only logical frameworks for forming communities of interest: in keeping with the society's needs, they are established on the republican and even federal level.

The Constitution starts from the supposition that the working people will find it in their interest and wish to co-operate, 'to exchange labour', with the so-called non-productive sector. However, this is not left entirely up to them. In essential fields such as education, culture, public utilities, the pension system, and so on, the formation of communities of interest can be required by law.

The delegational system forms the basis of decision-making in the self-managing communities of interest, as it does elsewhere. It is most encouraging that workers in direct production make up the majority in the interest communities. In the Socialist Republic of Serbia at the end of 1974, about 60 per cent of the delegates in all assemblies are persons directly engaged in production either in industry or in agriculture. This is expected to enrich the personality and promote the emancipation and humanisation not only of the delegates but also of the entire environment and each individual.

The individual's aspirations are suppressed under capitalism not only by his position in the work process, but also by the creation of an ever wider gulf between productive and non-productive work. They are deadened by the publicity, aggressiveness and commercialism of the consumer society. In a capitalist society, virtually everything turns on consumption and the market, which dominate all spheres of life—from housing to the cinema and sex. This is undoubtedly accompanied by the impoverishment of human relations.

A self-managing socialist system aims to keep the plague of consumerism out of society. It does everything possible to make relations humane, to give everyone an opportunity to have his say in shaping conditions for a higher living standard, and a richer life for the individual in the community where he works and resides. Science, technology and production should serve man and better the society's living conditions. Machines can liberate, but they can also enslave, depending on the class and system they serve.

SELF-MANAGEMENT PLANNING UNDER THE NEW CONSTITUTION

Dilemmas

Experience to date has confronted us with many questions relating to self-management planning:

—how to achieve social planning without curtailing the independence of enterprises, of the basic organisations of associated labour;

—how to express and defend one's own interests;

—how to ensure, at the same time, responsibility and efficiency;

—how to implement, through planning, the idea that collectives decide on investments, that workers decide on the nature and extent of expansion in the enterprise and control the movement of surplus labour at all levels.

We were quite certain what role we did not wish the state to play, but we have not always known precisely what role society, the state and work organisations should fulfil in the domain of planning. In the meantime, the technocratic structures gained strength in this sphere, so that it was the banks and not the workers who began to have an ever greater control over investments.

The new Constitution adopts stands on self-management from the work organisation to the federation. The dilemma was not whether to have planning or not, but what kind of planning would be most appropriate, since social planning can be a means of limiting self-management rights. On the other hand, limitation of rights in the sphere of planning as a rule leads to conflicts, particularly in inter-republican and inter-nationality relations. The hierarchy of plans that previously existed would today be an obstacle to the equality of nations, republics and provinces.

Most polemics centred on the question of whether state intervention was necessary and when. Some considered it essential, whereas others thought it should be extremely slight.

The new Constitution provides for an original system of planning in which, it is true, the interests of the state have their place, but a limited and precisely defined one. The aim of the Constitution was to give much greater importance in planning to the basic organisations of associated labour, communes and republics.

It is normal that the state should occupy a significant role in the planning system. What is crucial here, though, is the procedure the state uses and the circumstances in which its role comes to the fore.

The Constitution makes planning compulsory at all levels (the basic organisation of associated labour, the enterprise, association of producers, local community, commune, region, province, republic, federation). Every institution is free to establish with others the type of relationship which best serves its interests, and to voluntarily undertake obligations but it is also obliged to account for its actions to society, even before a self-management court if it does not fulfil its obligations.

Self-management planning—the right to differ

Unless adopted democratically, a plan cannot truly reflect the political will. Self-management is a system in which the units at the base (the basic organisation of associated labour, local community, commune) enjoy a high degree of autonomy in decision-making. Planning, as conceived in the Constitution, should be a creative procedure serving to encourage initiative and innovation. The significance of this type of planning is not simply political; it helps the correct economic choice to be made and stimulates the implementation of the plan. The actual process of drawing up and adopting plans involves a continual dialogue between the centre and the base.

On the grounds of planning needs and efficiency, a centrally-determined plan can lead to the subordination of the workers' interests for the sake of 'higher goals'. All material relations and processes must serve to strengthen self-management as a whole. In answer to the question: which takes precedence, economics or politics? we would reply that the plan is simultaneously both an instrument of social relations and a factor in the struggle for higher productivity, forecasting and guiding future development.

The Constitution makes it possible for the community to provide organised guidance for economic behaviour, for instance, to promote integration of labour, to forestall primitive concepts of a market economy and competition, to prevent so-called economic liberalism (uneconomical duplication of industrial capacities, technocratic and bureaucratic power), to exert a decisive influence on the behaviour of amalgamated industrial concerns and large and powerful enterprises, particularly from the base. Great importance is also attached to the programming of development, expert management and specialised personnel in general.

From the bottom upwards

Plans are adopted in the first place by:

—basic organisations of associated labour, enterprises, complex work organisations, and financial and credit associations;

—work organisations providing social services (science, education, health), which earn their income on the basis of free exchange of labour, though their plans must take into account the wishes of workers engaged in production;

—local communities, communes, provinces, republics and the federation, whose plans provide the framework within which the working people realise their common social interests.

Plans must first be drawn up at the lowest level, and then co-ordinated, or rather, these processes must run parallel.

The basic organisations of associated labour independently prepare their draft plans, consulting with all other basic organisations with which they are linked, with other enterprises, with the communities of interest, in fact, with all organisations with which they have common interests.

The plan of the whole collective is the first important step for each separate organisation of associated labour. It is here that the first disputes occur, for instance, over the setting aside of funds for future joint projects.

The plan of the local community in fact constitutes a kind of territorial association for the satisfaction of common needs (culture, social welfare, public utilities, housing, and so on). These communities co-ordinate their plans through consultations and these then enter into the plan of the commune.

Planning within the framework of the individual branches is likewise an economic requirement. However, there is a danger here of monopoly and of one branch overstressing its own needs at the expense of others. The various branches may have common interests, but also conflicting ones. When these cannot be eliminated, they must be harmonised and reconciled.

When planning at federal level, inter-republic relations, in their regional and national aspect, come to the fore. The economic and general social interests of the workers cannot be separated from their national and regional, and class interests. In this case, class interests cannot be placed above the national, that is, one subordinated to the other.

Under the Constitution, the federation is responsible for co-ordinating economic development and the plans, and ensuring a balanced economy and stable market. The federal plan is in fact a means of regulating inter-republican relations of the basis of negotiated agreement. It has a high degree of independence in the domains in which the republics and provinces have previously reached agreement.

All who are involved in planning are obliged to co-operate with one another while drawing up the plans and to keep one another fully informed. While everyone is obliged to participate in planning, no one is compelled to accept the consensus, except in a few cases laid down in the Constitution and by law. Free decision-making is the rule, and coercion the exception, applicable only when it is a question of the rights of the state, which must be precisely formulated by law. State intervention is allowed to forestall possible self-centred, but short-sighted, attitudes that would harm the common interests. The socio-political community ensures the implementation of plans passed on the basis of consensus.

Free association and adjustment of interests, starting from the base, is the only method that accords with self-management. But since joint determination and co-ordination of require-ments is one of the premises of self-management, then the planning process cannot be confined to the narrow framework of the enterprise and commune.

Self-management consensus

A very wide spectrum of social relations is co-ordinated by way of consensus, i.e. negotiated agreement. Self-management in a multi-national community cannot evolve into an inte-grated system unless the relations between the nations are also based on self-management principles.

Since the revolution, Yugoslavia has never been a unitarist state. But while the economy was still centrally controlled, the scope for self-management relations within the federation was limited. The development of self-management has created a new, more favourable situation.

The realisation of the principle of equality of peoples and nationalities is a condition for the further growth of self-man-agement relations. Under the new Constitution, all matters relating to economic policy which affect the creation and dis-tribution of income can be settled only by consensus of the republics and provinces. The federation cannot be a 'supra-national' power.

As is the case with every contract, the consensus is signed by the parties concerned. The signatories are those with a material interest in or social obligation towards the matter to be agreed upon, and who are mutually dependent upon the fulfilment of the agreement.

Naturally, the technocrats also have their say in the adop-tion of plans, assuming responsibility for their preparation and implementation.

If the workers meet their obligations, but the planned results are still not achieved, then someone is clearly responsible. In such cases, the workers demand an explanation and hold the technical services accountable.

Q

A plan cannot contain anything that has not been previously agreed upon by all concerned. But when it is passed, it must be adhered to by all, like a kind of contract.

The procedure for adopting plans is similar to an agreement between local communities and a commune, the communes and a republic, the republics and the federation.

While all this may appear very complicated, it is less so than the kind of planning which does not make those who conceive the plans directly responsible for their implementation. If a plan is adopted on the basis of general consensus, then all who had a hand in it are obliged to see that it is carried out.

Test of self-management planning

Every modern society is confronted by the problem of how to secure concentration and centralisation of resources for expanded reproduction. i.e. capital investment. Every society solves this problem in its own way, with the concomitant social and economic consequences.

Discussions are now in progress on medium and long-term development plans, up to 1985. This involves a great many social compacts and self-management agreements covering the fields of agriculture, transport and communications, ferrous and non-ferrous metallurgy, the basic chemical industry, oil, petroleum, non-metallic mineral and cement production, and tourism. Social compacts will also be reached in the domains of general and joint consumption, use of international credits and loans, the accelerated growth of the insufficiently developed republics and Kosovo province, and the financing of the federation's functions.

By 1985, the national per capita income is expected to rise to 2,000 US dollars, which would mean a GNP growth rate of around seven per cent annually.

VITALITY OF THE SYSTEM AT TIMES OF CRISIS

The world situation today does not favour the Yugoslav economy. The gravity of the current world economic crisis, unprecedented in the postwar period, exerts a certain pressure on Yugoslavia as it does on other states.

The present inflation and stagnation is not the classical type of crisis caused by hyperproduction, which resulted only in large-scale unemployment. On the contrary, it threatens general social stability in many countries, and undermines the international economic order, with grave consequences in particular for the underdeveloped states.

In view of the openness of Yugoslavia's economy and the fact that its main trading partners have been hard hit by inflation, it was impossible for our economy to go unscathed. This is undoubtedly a test of the vitality of the Yugoslav self-management-based economy and its ability to undertake effective measures against inflation.

The Yugoslav situation, however, cannot be compared with the 'stagflation' in the most developed countries. The results for 1974 were more favourable than the average for the foregoing five-year period. (The GNP rose by 7 per cent, the number of employed by 5 per cent, and labour productivity also by 5 per cent).

The present level of growth and efficiency can be maintained provided we further improve social and economic organisation. This was taken fully into account in the new Constitution.

Further discussions on medium and long-term development will not be simple and straight-forward because of the differences in economic structure and interests of the individual regions, which also coincide with the national aspect. Considerable efforts will be needed to co-ordinate and adjust these interests, but the agreed adoption of joint programmes is the best guarantee of social discipline in their implementation.

The current crisis in the advanced capitalist states is not of the classical type and cannot be regarded simply from the economic standpoint. The social consequences of this crisis are the most critical component, and can be removed only by socio-economic and not by purely economic measures.

The broad masses of the workers are becoming aware that the existing system is outdated and the time has come for new, more radical solutions, not simply adjustments. More and more people see a way out of this situation in a form of self-management, worker participation and co-decision-making.

Q*

This is receiving consideration even in circles that have no connection with Marxism, who know nothing about Yugoslav self-management, and are maybe not even inclined to socialism in any form.

In short, there is a growing belief that the deep economic crisis of the contemporary world, with all its social and political consequences, cannot be resolved without the direct participation of the working class and other working people in the affairs of the state.

In some socialist countries with a centralised economy, in which the state maintains complete control and can enforce disciplined behaviour, inflation is absent, or very slight. However, this system fails to provide adequate economic stimulus to achieve high productivity. Yugoslavia abandoned the system of centralised state administration not only for socio-political reasons, but also because it considered the system inefficient from the economic standpoint. Closed economic systems are less affected by the current economic crisis, but the growth rate is maintained by high investments, and technological progress does not keep pace with these.

The economic crisis has affected us much less than many other countries, whether advanced or developing. But it has given us a timely warning against laying too much stress on manufacturing and consumption, at the expense of power, raw materials and food production, for which Yugoslavia has favourable conditions. The world food shortage does not threaten Yugoslavia, since its agriculture can produce a surplus for export, if well organised. In this domain, not all our measures have proved to be correct.

The world economic crisis did not, however, give rise to either stagnation or a recession, nor did it increase unemployment. The inflationary pressure that has been felt results from the openness of our system, and the fact that the major part of our foreign trade is with the advanced countries affected by inflation.

The self-management system in Yugoslavia has shown itself to be rational, efficient and quick to react to world trends.

Time will show whether future events confirm this, as the author unreservedly believes.

'The Workers' Constitution'
(Law on Associated Labour)

Yugoslavs wish to achieve a unification of self-management prospects and the revolutionary process of social development in practice as well as in theory.

Self-management involves not only the basic production organisations and local communities, but the society as a whole. It should mobilise the creative initiative of both individuals and nations, and utilise this to promote the closer interlinking of production forces and the progressive aspirations of society. In this process, the creative freedom of the individual producer, the freedom of man and his labour, comes to the fore, as does that of the society and all its parts.

In November 1976, the Yugoslav Assembly passed the Law on Associated Labour. To a certain extent this may be regarded as an historic document since it codifies the main experiences gained in self-management over a twenty-five-year period, while charting its future development. This was the first time that relations in a society based on the rule of the working class and worker self-management were regulated in a comprehensive manner. The 1974 Constitution and its implementation provided the basic starting point of the Law.

More than two years were spent preparing the Law on Associated Labour. Public discussion of its draft, in which every worker had a chance to participate, resulted in the addition of 32 new articles, and the amendment of 207 others of the total 646 articles. In the course of this debate, over three million copies of the draft law were sold, a fact indicating that employed people recognised its importance; they saw the need to study its contents and actively participate in the law-making process.

During these discussions, the Law came to be called the Workers' Constitution.

Together with the Constitution of 1974, the Law on Associated Labour was to provide the basis for some two dozen other laws: on planning, the prices policy and regime, foreign trade, the monetary system, joint investment (and the division of income following investment), the banking system, the law on business relations with foreign partners, on foreign currency dealings and so on.

This was not a new course in the development of self-management, but a question of adaptation and more radical attainment of goals on the basis of experience.

The changes were primarily directed towards two aims:

—first, to enable the working man to exert even greater direct influence than previously on the means, conditions and results of his work, starting from the economic policy in his own enterprise, up to the socio-economic development of the country as a whole;

—second, to provide, by means of the law and other measures which would follow it, further impetus for Yugoslavia's social and material progress, bearing in mind the fact that the present age calls for a high degree of concentration of the means of production, for the integration of labour across national boundaries and close interdependence of nations.

These changes were undoubtedly introduced as a result of Yugoslavia's experiences, both good and bad.

The latter included the alienation of financial resources, placing them out of reach of the producers' influence and decision-making. The state agencies, banks, foreign trade organisations, and the technocrats and executives in enterprises had assumed an unjustifiably large say in the distribution of resources and particularly of investments.

The positive experiences resulted in the political action, started several years earlier, aimed against bureaucratic and technocratic usurpation of self-management rights, which inspired, among other things, the new Constitution (1974). The closer one got to the grassroots, to the factories, the louder was the criticism against anti-self-management tendencies. The resistance to the technocratic-bureaucratic upsurge which restricted the power of the worker-managers was most strongly apparent at the base. This was no accident. The Yugoslav working class is a permanent and vital element in the social structure, as can be seen from the fact that it now produces four-fifths of the country's social product (GNP).

Experience to date has shown that bureaucratic tendencies can be effectively countered only when the great mass of producers is mobilised.

The Law stresses the fact that the worker-managers should be the prime movers of economic life and social progress, and not only at the base but in the highest forums (through their delegates). At the same time, the long-term interests of the society and the individual make it necessary to look beyond the narrow interests of the enterprise or group and the immediate effects of the market. These interests call for carefully planned development, both in the basic organisation of associated labour,[6] and in the local, regional and Yugoslav state community.

Much more than previously, the producers now decide on production trends, investments, pooling of resources and labour, joint investments, prices, exports, and the division of income between personal earnings and the satisfaction of other needs.

The workers have thus attained the right to replace decisions made only in their name by deciding for themselves.

Innovations in income distribution

No one has the right to alienate from the workers the resources they create by their work, or to relieve them of the obligations entailed by this. More precisely: the Law endeavours to prevent appropriation through a monopoly position on the market or by economic or political force.

Income is not the group property of those workers who created it on the market, but is socially-owned, like the means of production used by the workers. A part in the creation of income is also played by the workers who manufacture the equipment, by those who produce raw materials, those who work in the fields of education, science, health, culture, and so on.

A critical analysis was made of previous methods of evaluating the results of labour and distributing income which did not always take sufficient account of the above-mentioned fac-

6. The 1974 Constitution provides for the establishment of so-called basic organisations of associated labour. Every department in a factory or other work organisation which can operate as an independent economic unit can become a basic organisation of associated labour with its own workers' council, deciding independently on its income distribution, earnings, production and employment matters. The basic organisations have their own workers' councils, elect representatives to the central workers' council, and choose representatives (delegates) for local government bodies (communal assemblies), and republican and federal assemblies.

tors. There was, and remains, the problem of low efficiency and lack of economy in the use of socially-owned resources. The new Law tried to establish conditions in which the worker feels that his personal earnings, and all other social and living conditions, are related to the rational investment of 'social capital', and not only to the current productivity of individual labour. This means that the basic organisations of associated labour will in future be more concerned to ensure that the joint income is as large as possible, so that individual earnings will likewise be larger.

According to the new concept, income is of two types.

First, there is total income—this is the amount left after the deduction of material production costs (including depreciation) from the gross amount realised by the sale of goods or services. This sum, the new value which an organisation has created or appropriated on the market, includes everything— resources for general social requirements and resources for the working collective's joint needs, resources for reserves, for solidarity funds, for meeting contractual obligations, for personal incomes and for capital accumulation.

To ensure a completely responsible relationship between work organisations and the other sectors of society, a part of the income is controlled by the worker-managers indirectly: through their delegates (in assemblies and interest communities) while the other part of the income remains at the disposal of the individual work organisation. This latter part is known as clear or net income. After social and contractual obligations have been met, it is this clear or net income which is left for the basic organisation of associated labour to dispose of as it sees fit.

The clear or net income is divided into four parts:

—the fund for personal incomes of the employed, distributed in accordance with work and the results of work;

—the joint consumption fund (resources for meals at work, housing, education, social assistance, workers' transport, recreation, etc.);

—investment resources for capital accumulation, which are used in two ways: one part directly invested in the actual work organisation in question, and the other pooled with other organisations linked to the former technologically and economically, the method of pooling, priorities, economic criteria, and obligations being fixed by self-management agreements;[7]

—reserve funds, for use when an organisation encounters economic difficulties (losses and so on), under conditions stipulated by the self-management agreement.

The same type of agreement likewise applies to distribution of personal incomes, criteria being set for evaluation of the labour performed, norms, incentives and other common measures, taking into account economic and social criteria, solidarity and mutuality.

Before the system of social compacts began to be applied in 1972, differences in earnings between persons with the same qualifications and working in the same branch amounted to 1:3·82, as against a range of 1:1·65 in 1975.

Self-management agreements bear no resemblance to tariff agreements in a capitalist society, since they are not made either with the state or with a capitalist, but among the producers themselves in the common interest. There must, how-

---

7. The differences between a self-management agreement and a social compact should be noted to avoid confusion.

The participants in an *agreement* are the organs of self-management of basic organisations of associated labour which have an interest in the matter in question. There are two types of agreement: those of a general nature which form the basis for the Statute (i.e. internal regulations) of a work organisation, and separate agreements which precisely and directly solve individual questions (internal prices, participation in joint investments, shares in joint income, and so on, these having more the character of a contract). *Social compacts* are drawn up by representatives of socio-political communities, communes, trade unions, chambers of the economy and others in order to establish common criteria and incomes policies, thereby avoiding wide disparities and a chaotic situation on the one hand, and government, i.e. administrative regulation of these matters on the other. At the present time for instance, the questions of energy development, ferrous and non-ferrous metallurgy, agriculture, and the food industry, mining and basic chemical industry are under discussion. The various republics have both shared and divergent interests: shared, since the problems of development are closely interconnected; and divergent, since there are disparities in level of development and differences in the economic structure of the individual republics, provinces and regions. Social compacts are not implemented directly, i.e. by administrative means, but serve as the basis for pursuing economic organisations of associated labour, nor to regional criteria. The compact provides a guideline for economic policy, while concrete decisions, in accordance with this guideline, are passed by the organisations of associated labour.

ever, be some general social criteria and norms governing the
drawing up and signing of such agreements.

The law provides for the participation of the trade unions
also, primarily when questions of income distribution are being
settled:

—concerning the distribution of clear income,

—concerning the distribution of personal incomes,

—when decisions are being made on joint consumption,

—when self-management agreements are drawn up to regulate working relations, i.e. the rights, duties and responsibilities of workers.

The rights belonging to the basic organisations of associated
labour cannot be transferred to an enterprise (amalgamated
organisation, business association), since these rights are inalienable. If this were not the case, it would again become possible for the income to be taken out of the control of those who
created it. The risk of the micro-community becoming self-
centred and selfish is avoided by the establishment of general
criteria, self-management agreements and social compacts.

The clear or net income is thus that part of their organisation's income which the workers really do dispose of as they
see fit. The other part is in fact already 'spoken for' since it
must go to meet various fiscal obligations set by law or by
contracts and agreements that the organisation has entered
into. The clear income is therefore of great importance when
it comes to planning. Let us take the example of investment.
Previously, proposals were prepared and submitted to the
workers' councils by teams of experts. Naturally, the latter still
play their part in preparing proposals, but now no investment
decision can be taken unless approved by a workers' referendum. When investment decisions are taken in the commune,
republic, community of interest or federation, the workers
express their views and vote through their delegates in the
relevant decision-making bodies at every level. *Carte blanche*
powers are given neither to the state bureaucracy nor to the
technocrats. Everything goes from the worker-managers
through the delegate assemblies, where decisions are passed,
and then back to the base as information or action, giving it a
further chance to intervene.

The aim is to ensure that the worker is also the manager

of surplus labour, unlike in a capitalist system, where the worker sells his labour and the surplus labour (profit) is managed by the capitalist. In a centralised state-managed economy, the producer is remote from decision-making on the use and movement of the income he has created. Regardless of the fact that the state may be said to represent, to a greater or lesser extent, the common interest, the worker is alienated from the results of his labour.

The social and cultural superstructure

The new Law has also brought some interesting innovations in the relations between the economy and what are known as non-economic activities (science, education, culture, etc).

The traditional budgetary method of financing these activities usually provided only funds for salaries and wages. Those employed in these fields of public activity exerted no influence on development and investment policies. The process of 'emancipation' in these spheres, that is, their equal treatment with regard to self-management rights, began, though slowly, several years ago.

Now greater stress is laid on the society's concern for these activities, the need for a higher degree of solidarity between the economy and non-economic activities, the necessity for creating, on a long-term basis, conditions which allow the worker and his family to live a more cultured life.

It is emphasised that these activities likewise play a role in overall labour productivity and contribute to the creation of social income, and that they therefore have the right to share in its distribution. The importance of education, both vocational and general, is even more enhanced in a self-management-based society, since self-management cannot be effective unless the working people are fully conscious of their responsibilities and capable of coping with them. The producer is concerned not only about his personal income, but about the entire movement of 'social capital', the rationale of its investment whether in industry or in education, health and other public services. In this way the producer plays an intellectually creative role.

Another aim is to achieve a higher degree of solidarity and 'equality' in the sphere of income distribution between the economic and non-economic activities. A serious moral and political problem had arisen because of the neglect of non-economic activities and lower personal incomes in these spheres.

At the same time, the new conditions allow the workers in production to exert greater control over the rational investment and expenditure of that part of the total income set aside for social (non-economic) activities. Income from material production cannot be siphoned off into social activities without the consent of the producers.

Hidden centres of economic power

In the period prior to the adoption of the new Constitution, large resources had been accumulated in the domain of trade, thanks to its privileged position in the production-marketing process. Banks and foreign trade enterprises became powerful centres of social and economic might, while production gradually assumed a subordinate position in relation to trade organisations.

Three or four years ago, measures were undertaken to regulate the position of organisations engaged in trading activities, particularly wholesale trade and import-export trade, on self-management lines, efforts have been made to place production and trade on an equal economic footing and establish closer business and development ties between them.

In the discussions on the Law, much was said about the need for wholesale trade, import-export organisations and banks to share the fate of the producers. Trade organisations for the most part previously operated on the principle of the profit margin, i.e. the difference between the factory and sales prices. Now they are obliged to share with their producer partners not only the profit but the risk, to take part in investment, planning and the forecasting of market requirements.

In a well-developed market economy, trade is an essential economic activity. The process of reproduction does not stop with the manufacture of goods, but with their sale, as Marx stated. The Law endeavours to find a solution within the framework of associated labour, by linking up production and sales organisations through the pooling and association of their resources and labour. They are required to jointly adapt themselves to the needs of the home and foreign markets, engage in joint planning and evolve joint business policies.

Major social deformations had occurred in the domain of banking and other financial services. Banks had enormous resources at their disposal and had become powerful centres of economic and social might. The political gravity of the situation was all the greater since banks were so located, from the territorial standpoint, as to exert a very detrimental effect on relations between the nations in Yugoslavia, thereby creating serious problems between the republics and provinces.

Following the latest self-management changes, banks no longer exist as independent centres of power and decision-making. Instead, they are, or rather should be, organisations in which associated labour, i.e. the founder-members of the banks, has the main say. All the same, there is still a danger of monopoly and interference of the banking apparatus, or other bureaucratic elements outside associated labour through banks.

The bank members distribute the income created in the bank on the basis of a self-management agreement. This is intended, among other things, to achieve greater mobility of resources and labour on the entire territory of the integral Yugoslav market.

The idea is to stimulate as far as possible the pooling and association of resources and labour whenever production and technological considerations call for this. The result should be higher labour productivity and accelerated growth.

Safeguards for Self-Management
Other matters have also been regulated in greater detail. These include: socialist solidarity of basic and other organisations of associated labour in overcoming business difficulties; self-management responsibility of workers and managing bodies, depending on the work post and degree of responsibility; the rights and responsibilities of socio-political communities; the protection of self-management rights, etc.

Self-management, the result of social and political revolution in our country, must be protected by the organised representative forces of the working class and by the proletarian state itself. The emphasis, however, is not placed on a repressive mechanism for safeguarding the self-management system, but on internal social self-production. No state agency can protect self-management as well as the workers themselves can do.

Full availability of information is an important measure in safeguarding self-management rights. A whole chapter in the Law on Associated Labour is devoted to this matter. The Law treats failure to perform the duty of keeping workers informed as a violation of work obligations for which an executive or executive body can be fined. The right to be informed is one of the vital self-management rights of the workers.

The trade union's role

Nowhere in all this does the trade union appear as a wielder of power or authority. It does not share self-management authority with the producers. It serves to give political guidance; puts up candidates during elections for self-management bodies and delegation assemblies; takes part in the appointment of directors (to prevent narrow circles from pushing through their choice); strives for democratic relations and protects the general social interests; fosters class consciousness and defends class interests; prepares the workers for self-management by way of social actions or organising courses and seminars. Over two million people are simultaneously active in all the self-management bodies throughout Yugoslavia. It is the trade union's task to see that they are fully qualified to carry out their responsibilities.

The role of the trade union has grown, and not declined, with the development of self-management, and increasingly reflects the purposes for which workers originally began to organise themselves in unions: to be capable of using their power, to take decisions, to be a decisive factor in society and not merely performers of tasks set by others.

The regulations give the trade union no fixed tasks, but stipulate the obligations of state agencies, executive bodies in enterprises and the administration with regard to initiatives and actions undertaken by the trade unions.

These complex social goals can only be achieved through a long process of development in Yugoslav society and the people living in it. Our vision of a socialist self-managing society is

based on Marx's ideal of a society of freely associated producers in which freedom of the individual is the condition for
freedom for all.

* * *

Yugoslavs long ago made the choice of the type of society
they wished to build. But while keeping the model, or as
some say, myth, in mind, we have to construct an actual society. As a rule, of course, the real thing never looks as good
as the model.

Some foreign observers have claimed that in recent years
Yugoslav self-management has been a failure, that it is not
self-management but co-decision-making, since it does not fit
the clear-cut model they have in mind.

While admitting that Yugoslav self-management is not perfect, we cannot see any better model of a society around us
that we would choose instead. Consequently, we have directed
our efforts towards improving our self-management-based democracy on all levels and in all domains, thereby giving self-
management greater scope and prospects. We can see no
alternative for us but the further improvement of this system
and boldness in seeking fresh solutions.

Self-management leads to social equality, but to achieve
this we need a long period of continual struggle to reduce
the inherited inequalities of the transitional period, which
derive ultimately from the former capitalist society.

If it is Yugoslavia's misfortune that it has no example to
follow (since we might thereby avoid many mistakes, and even
skip stages of development that were not essential for us),
this circumstance does have its favourable side, for it makes
for an open and enquiring state of mind, ready for innovation.

In an underdeveloped society, state centralism might be
considered supportable, even essential, but in a more advanced
socialist society it can lead the country astray, away from its
true goals.

We live in an age of extremely advanced technology and
complex systems. It is a much more complex task, however, to
build a new social system than to construct any type of technological system.

We know that what we are striving to achieve is not impossible, but we are striving to build it alone, without any models to copy. A developed system of self-management relations cannot be introduced directly, but only created through the organised and guided practical efforts and work of millions of working people, supported by the contribution of scientific thought.

Index